Berlitz HANDBOOK

INDIA

Contents

FAMILY FRIENDLY SYMBOL

This symbol is used throughout the Handbook to indicate a sight, hotel, restaurant or activity that is suitable for families with children.

Top **25** Attractions

1 **Taj Mahal, Agra** The epitome of Mughal finesse and, in spite of all the brouhaha surrounding it, a sight still guaranteed to take your breath away (see p.87)

2 **Rice boat cruising on backwaters, Kerala** Explore the winding rivers, canals and glassy lagoons of Kerala's Kuttanad region (see p.237)

3 **Ghats, Varanasi** Pujas at the 'City of Light's' ghats reveal the intense devotion with which Hindus worship the sacred River Ganges (see p.93)

4 **Ajanta caves, Maharashtra** Incredible murals adorn these ancient rock-cut cave temples *(see p.151)*

5 **Snorkelling, Andaman Islands** Swim with turtles, fish and elephants off the beaches of Havelock *(see p.228)*

6 **Gokarna** Hindu religious intensity and the beach at this Konkan coast pilgrimage town *(see p.211)*

7 **Tiger spotting, Bandhavgarh, Madhya Pradesh** India's tiger hotspot is this wildlife sanctuary *(see p.158)*

8 **Watch a Bollywood film** See the latest hit at a Mumbai Art Deco cinema *(see p.148)*

9 **Ayurveda massage, Kerala** Soak up rejuvenating herbal oils in Kerala's ayurveda spas *(see p.58)*

10 **Sun Temple, Konark** This opulently carved shrine was medieval India's architectural peak *(see p.190)*

12 **Udaipur** Rajasthan at its most romantic: a fairy-tale vision rising from Lake Pichola *(see p.127)*

11 **Toy-Train to Darjeeling** Enjoy the view of Kanchenjunga from this Himalayan hill station *(see p.184)*

13 **Holi festival, Mathura** Expect to be plastered in coloured powders during the Holi festival *(see p.25)*

15 **Golden Temple, Amritsar** The Sikhs' holiest shrine rivals the Taj for its serene beauty *(see p.85)*

14 **Palolem Beach, Goa** Far from a secret these days, but still a gem of a tropical beach, fringed by palm trees and forested hills *(see p.172)*

16 **The Blue City, Jodhpur** Lose yourself in the bazaars of Jodhpur's cuboid labyrinth *(see p.123)*

17 **Camel trekking, Jaisalmer** Experience the unique atmosphere of the Thar Desert on the ultimate low-impact vehicle *(see p.125)*

18 **Gangotri: trek to the source of the Ganges** Soak up the rarefied atmosphere of the Inner Himalaya with this two- to three-day trek to the source of the sacred Ganges, flanked by dramatic ice peaks (see p.111)

19 **Hampi, Karnataka** Evocative ruins, scattered over giant boulder hills and banana groves on the Deccan Plateau (see p.208)

20 **Shree Meenakshi temple, Madurai** A giant, ornately decorated gateway introduces Tamil Nadu's most revered shrine (see p.225)

21 Erotic sculpture, Khajuraho Eyebrow-raising erotica encrusts these famous temples (see p.155)

22 Tikse, Ladakh One of the most striking Buddhist monasteries that line the Indus Valley (see p.107)

23 Elephant safaris, Western Ghats Spot wild elephant in south India's wildlife sanctuaries (see p.40)

24 Delhi The capital's many monuments span the full spectrum of Indian history (see p.64)

25 Pushkar camel fair A week-long livestock market and festival held on the desert edge (see p.126)

India Fact File

India encompasses virtually every landscape present on the planet, from lush tropical rainforest and coral atolls to permanently frozen ice peaks and parched deserts. Its five largest cities – Delhi, Mumbai (Bombay), Chennai (Madras), Kolkata (Calcutta) and Hyderabad – are expanding at a staggering pace, yet just under three-quarters of the population still reside in rural areas where farming provides the main livelihood.

BASICS

Population: 1.2 billion (2nd largest in world)
Area: 3,287,263 sq km (1,269,219 sq miles)
Official language: Hindi
State religion: Secular
Capital city: New Delhi
President: Smt. Pratibha Devisingh Patil
National anthem: Jana Gana Mana
National symbol: Lion Capitol of Ashoka
National sport: Cricket
National airline: Air India

TIME ZONE

GMT + 5hrs 30min

In January:

New York: 1.30am
London: 6.30am
New Delhi: noon
Sydney: 5.30pm
Auckland: 7.30pm

In July:

New York: 2.30am
London: 7.30am
New Delhi: noon
Sydney: 4.30pm
Auckland: 6.30pm

CURRENCY
Rupee (Rs)

The following figures are approximate:

£1 = Rs68
€1 = Rs56
$1 = Rs46

KEY TELEPHONE NUMBERS
Country code: +91
International calls: 00 + 91
Police: 108
Ambulance: 108
Fire: 108

AGE RESTRICTION
Driving: 18
Drinking: 18
Age of Consent: 18

Smoking is banned in public places.

ELECTRICITY
240 volts, 50 Hertz
2-pin plug, European-style

OPENING HOURS
Banks: Mon–Fri 10am–2/4pm, Sat 10am–noon
Shops: approximately Mon–Sat 9.30am–6.30pm
Museums: are mostly closed on Mondays

POSTAL SERVICE: INDIA POST
Post offices:
Mon–Fri 10am–5pm,
Sat 10am–noon
Postboxes:
red, but don't use them as collections are sporadic and unreliable
Standard Post: Rs5
Airmail: Rs20

Trip Planner

WHEN TO GO

Climate

India's climate ranges from the permanent snows of the Himalaya to the tropical conditions along the coasts and the continental climate of inland areas. There are also many regional and seasonal variations. In general, the best time to visit is after the southwest monsoon.

October to March is the cool season and the best time of year in peninsular India. The weather is beautifully predictable in winter, with blue skies and bright sunshine in most areas. Parts of the south and east see a brief spell of rain from the northeast monsoon in October and November, while snow and sleet make the extreme north very cold and often inaccessible.

Summer, from April to June, is very hot and dry for most of the country, and humid along the coasts. The hills are particularly lovely at this time of the year.

Public Holidays	
26 January	Republic Day
15 August	Independence Day
2 October	Mahatma Gandhi's Birthday
25 December	Christmas Day

Due to the many religions in India, public holidays are plentiful and confusing. Other holidays vary according to region. A list of official holidays can be obtained from tourist offices.

The southwest monsoon begins to set in along the western coast towards the end of May, bringing varying amounts of rain as it moves across the rest of the country through June and July, and withdraws by late September. Northeastern India has heavy rain during this season, making it one of the wettest regions in the world. The southeast coast also receives a sharp monsoon season from October to early December.

Cloud descending on Tonglu, near Darjeeling; the Himalaya region is best visited in summer

Another glorious day on Palolem beach in Goa

High and Low Season

The main tourist season in India lasts from November until mid-March, peaking over Christmas and the New Year period, when the cost of accommodation in major visitor resorts can double or triple. Goa, in particular, is best avoided at this time. Elsewhere seasonal fluctuations are less marked, with the exception of the Himalayan hill stations, whose peak season is during high summer, in May and June.

Out of season, it is not recommended to travel to the coastal resorts of the south, where most hotels close during the monsoons. The same is true of the hill stations during the depths of winter, when snowy conditions make travel difficult.

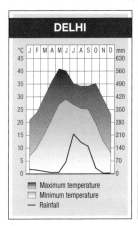

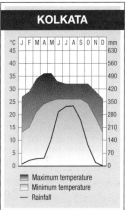

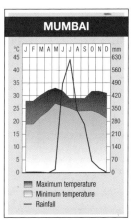

ESSENTIAL EVENTS

Durga Puja is a major and colourful festival

Festivals are a part of daily life in India, perhaps an inevitability given the thousands of deities, saints, prophets and gurus who must be worshipped, propitiated and remembered. Numerous local, and regional, events are marked, but the most important are celebrated nation-wide. Note that dates fluctuate year-on-year.

January–February

Vasant
Honouring Saraswati, goddess of scholars and artists; everyone dresses in bright yellow and flies kites.

February–March

Shivaratri
Cannabis, in the potent form of bhang, is consumed and offered in massive quantities to Lord Shiva.

Holi
This famed full-moon festival welcomes the arrival of spring. Indians typically celebrate by throwing dyed water and paint over one another, creating a surreal spectacle. Not for the faint-hearted.

April–May

Baisakhi
The Hindus' solar New Year. Sikhs celebrate the anniversary of Guru Gobind Singh's exhortation to form the Khalsa ('Army of the Pure').
Buddha Jayanti
Celebrates the birth of the Buddha and also his reaching of enlightenment. Jains commemorate a similar event at Dip Divali, marking the liberation of the tirthankara Mahavira from the wheel of life.

August–September

Janmastami

Plays recounting light-hearted episodes from the life of Lord Krishna are performed to mark the god's birthday.

Ganesh Chaturthi

Huge effigies of the elephant-headed god Ganesh (or 'Ganapati') are led through the streets and immersed in the sea or rivers.

Ramadan

The start of a month during which Muslims must fast between sunrise and sunset, abstaining from food, drink, sex and smoking.

Id ul-Fitr

Muslims feast to celebrate the end of Ramadan.

September–October

Navaratri

Major puja for the goddess Devi or Shakti in her more fearsome aspects, Kali and Durga. The first of the pan-Hindu festivals to occur after the monsoon when planting in the fields begins again after a period of relative rest.

October–November

Diwali

Celebrating both Rama's return from exile, and Lakshmi, the goddess of wealth. Also known as the 'Festival of Lights'.

November–December

Dusshera

The celebration of Durga's victory over Mahisasura, the buffalo-demon, marked most fervently in eastern India, especially Bengal, Orissa and some hill states, where it is known as Durga Puja *(see p.23)*.

Dusshera is celebrated all over India in various forms

ITINERARIES

It would take a lifetime of travelling to see all of India. In practice, most visitors settle on the north or the south, and then devise an itinerary based around the region's highlights. First trips tend to focus on the 'Golden Triangle', with extensions deeper into Rajasthan, or over to Varanasi, if time permits. With three weeks or more, you can cross the country widthways, taking in one or two tiger sanctuaries along the way, and experience the unique atmosphere of the country's interior. The south of India tends to occupy visitors on their second trips, or on longer itineraries. You can, of course, fly there from most hubs in the north.

Two Weeks in the Golden Triangle and Rajasthan

Days 1–2: **Delhi**. Acclimatise with tours of the Red Fort and Old Delhi, and the tomb gardens and Raj-era capital of New Delhi.

Days 3–4: **Agra**. Between repeat visits to the Taj Mahal, explore Agra Fort and Akbar's tomb at Sikandra.

Day 5: **Keoladeo National Park.** Cycle and birdwatch in the country.

Days 6–7: **Jaipur**. After a tour of the Pink City's palaces and bazaars, ride an elephant up to Amber Fort.

Days 8–9: **Ajmer and Pushkar.** Visit the Muslim dargah in Ajmer while based at Pushkar; take lakeside ambles around the ghats and hilltop walks for amazing desert views.

Day 10: **Jodhpur.** Walking tour of the Blue City and Meherangharh Fort.

Day 11: **Jaisalmer.** Camel safari from Rajasthan's desert citadel.

Days 12–13: **Udaipur.** Have a candlelit dinner by the lakeside and visit the Sisodia's sumptuous palaces.

Day 14: **Mt Abu.** See the intricately carved Jain temples and superb mountain views over the plains.

Three Weeks through India's Heart

Days 1–2: **Delhi**. *(See left.)*

Days 3–4: **Agra**. *(See left.)*

Day 5: **Gwalior.** Visit the Maharajah's palace and hilltop fort.

Day 6: **Orchha.** Explore riverside shrines and ruined palaces.

Days 7–8: **Khajuraho.** Take a tour of Chandelas' erotic temples.

Days 9–12: **Bandhavgarh and Kanha National Parks.** Tiger spotting in India's best sanctuaries.

Days 13–14: **Bhopal.** Visits to the ancient Buddhist site of Sanchi.

Day 15: **Mandu.** A night amid the ruined Afghan tombs and palaces.

Day 16: **Maheshwar.** Bathing ghats on the banks of the Narmada River.

Days 17–19: **Ajanta.** Trips to the cave sites of Ellora and Ajanta.

Days 20–21: **Mumbai.** Take in a Bollywood flick, get lost in the markets and eat superb regional food.

Four Weeks of Temples and Tea

Day 1: **Chennai.** Acclimatise with sightseeing in Fort St George.

Day 2: **Kanchipuram.** Tour of the town's ancient temples.

Days 3–4: **Mamallapuram.** Visit the famous Shore Temple and stone-carved monuments.

Day 5: **Puducherry.** Relax in the pretty backstreets of the former French colony.

Day 6: **Thanjavur.** Gawp at the Brihadeshwar temple and Royal Palace.

Day 7: **Trichy and Srirangam.** Tour of the rock fort at the mighty Sri Ranganathaswami temple.

Days 8–9: **Madurai.** Repeat visits to the mother of all Tamil shrines.

Day 10: **Coimbatore.** A night in transit to catch the early-morning toy train.

Days 11–12: **Ooty.** Trips to tea plantations and view points in the Nilgiris.

Days 13–14: **Periyar.** Raft safari to see wild elephant by the lakeside.

Days 15–16: **Munnar.** Stay in cosy Raj-era bungalows on tea plantations.

Days 17–19: **Kochi.** Explore the colonial monuments and atmospheric backstreets of Fort Cochin, with evening performances of Kathakali.

Days 20–22: **Alappuzha.** Rice boat cruising on Kuttanad backwaters.

Days 23–26: **Varkala.** Chill on Kerala's loveliest beach.

Day 27: **Kovalam.** Ayurveda massages and city sightseeing.

Day 28: **Kanniyakumari.** Call at the Padmanambhapuram Palace en route to India's sacred southern tip.

Five Weeks of Himalayan Highs

Days 1–2: **Delhi.** *(See opposite.)*

Day 3: **Chandigarh.** Visit Le Corbusier's concrete capital and Nek Chand's surreal Rock Garden.

Days 4–5: **Shimla.** Admire the Himalayan views and quirky British vibe of the Raj's former summer hub.

Days 6–9: **Kullu Valley.** Trips to forest temples, side valleys and Himachali villages, based at Manali.

Days 10–11: **Manali–Leh.** The world's ultimate road trip across the Himalayan Range.

Days 12–28: **Indus Valley.** Jeep trips and day treks around the monasteries, and over the region's highest passes into Nubra and Zanskar.

Days 29–31: **Leh–Srinagar.** Hairpin bends and stupendous views.

Days 32–35: **Srinagar.** Relax on a houseboat on Dal Lake, with day trips to the Mughal pleasure gardens.

Trip Planner

Temples and palaces line the banks of the Ganges at Varanasi

BEFORE YOU LEAVE

Visas and Entry Requirements

Tourist visas are issued for six months from the date of issue (not entry); single- and multiple-entry visas cost the same, so you may as well opt for the latter. To get a visa you'll need to apply either in person, online or (much slower) by post to your nearest embassy or consulate. Some firms will also arrange visas for you – in the UK, try **India Visa Office** (tel: 0844-800 4018; www.indiavisaheadoffice.co.uk), **India Visa Company** (tel: 020-8582 1117; www.indiavisacompany.com) or **India Visa 24** (tel: 0800/084 5037; www.indiavisa24.co.uk); in the US, try **Travisa** (indiavisa.travisaoutsourcing.com) or **Travel Document Systems** (www.traveldocs.com).

Tourist visas cannot be extended; you must leave the country and re-enter on a new one – very difficult to do from neighbouring countries. Note too that following the terror attacks on Mumbai in 2008, a minimum of two months has to elapse from the expiry of your old visa before you are permitted to apply for a new one. In addition, special permits are required for certain areas, while other areas are out of bounds to foreigners altogether.

Vaccinations

No inoculations are legally required for entry into India, but diphtheria, typhoid and hepatitis A jabs are recommended for travellers to many parts of the country, and it's worth ensuring that you are up to date with tetanus, polio and other boosters.

Nationality	Visa Required
UK	✓
US	✓
Canada	✓
Australia	✓
New Zealand	✓
Ireland	✓
South Africa	✓

Vaccinations for hepatitis B, rabies, meningitis, Japanese encephalitis and TB are also advised if you're travelling to remote areas, or working in environments with an increased exposure to infectious diseases. Malaria prophylaxis may also be required *(see p.258)*.

Booking in Advance

It's a good idea to pre-book onward travel tickets as far in advance as possible before your arrival in India. In the case of trains and planes, this can easily be done online through the portal www.cleartrip.com.

Tourist Information

The main tourist website for India Tourism is www.incredibleindia.org.
Australia: Glasshouse Shopping Complex, 135 King St, Sydney NSW 2000; tel: 02-9555; email: info@indiatourism.com.au.
Canada: 60 Bloor St (West), Suite 1003, Toronto, ON M4W 3B8; tel: 1-416/962-3787 or 8; email: info@indiatourismcanada.ca.
South Africa: PO Box 412542, Craighall 2024, Hyde Lane, Lancaster Gate, Johannesburg 2000; tel: 011-325 0880; email: goito@global.co.za.

Come prepared for whatever you plan to do in India, whether trekking or sunbathing

UK: 7 Cork St, London W1S 3LH; tel: 020-7437 3677; email: london5@indiatouristoffice.org. **US:** 1270 Ave of Americas, Suite 1808 (18th floor), New York, NY 10020; tel: 1-212-586-4901; email: ny@itonyc.com

Packing List

- mosquito net
- plug adaptors
- spare mobile phone recharger
- head torch
- earplugs
- high-factor sunblock (Indian products are less effective)
- pocket alarm
- universal sink plug
- various-sized combination locks
- gaffer tape or Sellotape (for plugging holes in mosquito net mesh)
- Prit-stick glue (for affixing postage stamps)
- re-hydration powders (also available cheaply in India)
- water purification tablets

Maps

The government forbids the sale of detailed maps in border areas, including the entire coastline, for security reasons; those which can be bought may not be exported. Some good maps to bring with you include: Bartholomew's or Lascelles 1:4,000,000 map of South Asia, Nelles Verlag maps, the Eicher series of detailed city maps and their India Road Atlas.

Tourist offices can supply visitors with larger-scale city maps. The most detailed are held by the Survey of India, Janpath Barracks A, New Delhi.

Many of these maps are available from www.indiamapstore.com.

Books

City of Djinns, William Dalrymple. Exploration of Delhi's layered history. *Nine Lives*, William Dalrymple. Nine life stories revealing contrasting forms of Indian religious devotion. *India: A History*, John Keay. Readable, definitive modern national history. *Maximum City*, Suketu Mehta. A compelling portrait of Mumbai. *The God of Small Things*, Arundhati Roy. Haunting Booker-prize novel set in the Keralan backwaters.

Websites

www.bollywoodworld.com
www.eventsinindia.com
www.guardian.co.uk/world/india
http://india.gov.in
www.indiamike.com
http://indiatoday.digitaltoday.in
www.mapsofindia.com
www.neemrana.com
http://timesofindia.indiatimes.com
http://weather.nic.in

Trip Planner

UNIQUE EXPERIENCES

The Gods at Play

Indians devote an exceptional amount of time, energy and resources to religious festivals. You're bound to stumble upon plenty of them by chance, but there exists a category of much larger, more fervently celebrated festivals which it's definitely worth knowing about in advance, and going out of your way to attend.

India's religious festivals include some of the most extravagant spectacles and extreme outpourings of collective emotion on earth. Nowhere else will you find 17 million bathers gathered on a single river bank for one auspicious moment in time, nor an ancient ritual at which an 18m (60ft) -tall colossus is showered with gold coins, precious stones and flower petals from a helicopter. Which other nation but India would mark the arrival of spring with mass paint- and powder-ball fights, or celebrate the harvest by painting cows in riotously colourful patterns?

Far from eroding the country's passion for religious festivities, the technologies of the digital era seem only to have intensified the way they're celebrated. Elaborately sequenced, flashing lights, lasers, chest-thumping PAs and all manner of digital audio trickery are deployed at temples and churches these days – and you'll find snippets of even the most obscure celebrations posted on YouTube.

Any reputable tour operator can tie the festivals mentioned below into a tailor-made tour; a few of them also feature on set group itineraries. Try: **Audley Travel** (tel: 01993-838 300; www.audleytravel.com), **Cox & Kings** (tel: 020-7873 5000; www.coxand kings.co.uk), or **Bales UK** (tel: 0845-057 1819; www.balesworldwide.com).

Water Festivals

In a land where the climate alternates between drought and downpour, and where the survival of literally tens of millions depends on the annual rains, it's hardly surprising that water forms the focus of many of India's religious festivals. Rivers are revered throughout the subcontinent for their purifying and life-giving powers, but 'Ma Ganga' – 'Mother Ganges' – is the most adored of all, worshipped as a living Goddess by more than 800 million Hindus. Her confluence with the Jamuna and mythical Saraswati

A vividly painted cow joins in the festivities

Crowds gather for the Maha Kumbh Mela

effigies of the elephant-headed God Ganesh receive the same honour at the height of the monsoon in Mumbai for the festival of **Ganesh Chaturthi**, only here, in the midst of India's largest metropolis, they're pitched headfirst into the sea, cheered on by huge crowds.

Fire Festivals

The return of the God-Prince Rama to his palace at Ayodhya after defeating the demon Ravana is the mythological inspiration for **Diwali**, one of many Indian religious festivals in which fire and light form the primary focus. The five-day celebration is marked all across the country in October–November, by Hindus, Jains and Sikhs alike. Oil lamps, towers and lanterns are lit in homes, and fairy lights strung across streets .

Rama's victory is also the subject of **Dusshera**, another popular pan-Indian festival, the culmination of which is the burning of huge statues of Ravana, his brother Kumbhakaran and son Meghanath at open public spaces.

One especially beautiful fire-related celebration you can witness year-round is evening **Aarthi** at Har-ki-Parui Ghat in Haridwar, where prayers are offered at dusk to the Goddess Ganga, at the place the river gushes on to the great north Indian plain. Thousands gather each evening to commemorate deceased relatives by placing *diyas* – tiny floral floats illuminated with oil wicks – on the surface of the water and watching them float away – an enchanting spectacle, accompanied by music and song.

Rivers at Prayag, Allahabad, in the state of Uttar Pradesh, is the venue for the biggest gatherings of human beings on the planet – the **Maha Kumbh Mela**. Armies of naked, trident-wielding sadhus, their bodies smeared with ash, spearhead the rush for the water in a festival which alternates every four years between three different sites.

At the opposite end of the Ganges, where the river becomes the Hoogly, larger-than-life statues of the many-limbed Goddess Durga, garlanded by strings of severed heads and with blood oozing from her protruding tongue, are ritually immersed each year at harvest time, at the end of **Durga Puja** (see p.15). Gigantic

Colourful masks and costumes mark the festival of Hemis, in Ladakh

Mountain Festivals

Some Indian mountains are revered by Hindus as sacred. A few – notably Nanda Devi in the Garhwal area of Uttarkhand – are worshipped as actual abodes of deities. In those beautiful regions overshadowed by the shining white giants of the Himalaya, the principal religious celebrations are processions of gold-faced temple deities, or *devtas*, carried amid considerable pomp and noise on the shoulders of devotees to join a mass procession of gods through the main market towns. The biggest and most colourful of all such parades is the one held at Kullu in Himachal Pradesh to mark the festival of **Dusshera**. Between 250 and 300 resplendently attired temple gods descend on the town to pay their respects to Kullu's Lord Raghunatha, watched by members of the local royal family and huge, animated crowds.

In the Buddhist regions further north, **monastery festivals** are the main events of the annual religious calendar. They tend to revolve around the unfurling of giant *thangkas* – iconographic pictures rendered in wonderful swirling colours – which the locals believe hold special powers. As troupes of monks perform masked dances in the courtyard below, accompanied by blasts from huge brass trumpets and deafening cymbal clashes, the paintings are unrolled down crumbling, red- and white-washed walls. Winter, when the high Himalayan valleys are snowbound, is when the majority of monastery festivals are held, but there's a notable exception: **Hemis**, in Ladakh, which switched its date to summer so that foreign tourists could attend.

A mountain backdrop that couldn't be more different from the snow-streaked peaks of Ladakh is the setting for India's largest pilgrimage, conducted each winter in the southern state of Kerala. Between 40 and 50 million male devotees, dressed in regulation black *lunghis* with strings of *rudraksha* beads over their bare chests, make their way on foot through the sweltering jungles of the Western Ghats to worship at the forest shrine of **Lord Ayappan**, open only from November–January. The festival of **Makara Sankranti** is the height of the pilgrimage *(see p.239)*. Women are not allowed to participate (until they're of post-menopausal age), although everyone watches the main rituals on television.

Colour Festivals

Vibrant colours are central to most Indian festivals, but on the occasion of **Holi**, held in late winter or early spring, the colours aren't limited to the participants' costumes. To mark the onset of spring, brightly dyed powders – both dry, and mixed with water to form runny paint – are flung liberally over family members, neighbours and, as the day progresses and mania intensifies, over complete strangers in the street. The result is truly surreal, with whole towns full of people covered head to toe in pink, red, purple and yellow pigments. Holi is celebrated with particular gusto at locations connected with the God Krishna, especially Mathura in the Braj region of Uttar Pradesh.

Coloured powders are put to more creative uses across India during Diwali *(see p.15)*, when they're used to draw striking floor patterns, or *rangoli*. Images from nature, notably peacocks, swans, fruit and flowers, provide the principal motifs for the designs, which are generally produced by female members of the family.

Keralan women have their own characteristically flamboyant twist on *rangoli* called *pookalam*, where the

Holi is celebrated by people throwing coloured powders at each other

Sacred Records

- **The largest gathering of people ever recorded in a single day:** the Maha Kumbh Mela at Prayag, Allahabad, in January 2007 drew an estimated 17 million worshippers
- **The world's biggest pilgrimage:** between 40 and 50 million Hindus visit the Lord Ayappan temple at Sabarimala, Kerala, each year

- **The world's worst stampede:** 800 people were crushed to death during the Maha Kumbh Mela of 1954
- **The world's oldest continuously celebrated festival:** Rath Yatra in Puri, Orissa, in which colossal wooden chariots bearing the temple deities are hauled down the town's main street – a tradition thought to date back 3,000 years or more

patterns are made not with powders but with brightly coloured flower petals. Spread before the entrances to houses or over verandas, the elaborate designs are created for the harvest festival of **Onam**, and are changed every morning throughout the 10-day celebration. Patterns for them were traditionally handed down from mother to daughter, but these days they're just as often downloaded off the internet.

Animal Festivals

Festivals associated with animals are a facet of Indian life and especially popular with foreign visitors. A temporary city of tent camps springs up in the Thar desert around Pushkar, in Rajasthan, for the annual **Pushkar Camel Fair**, or *Mela*. Villages from across this arid region turn up to buy and sell livestock, dressed in their finest traditional garb: the men in bulky, Day-Glo turbans, the women in voluminous pleated skirts and bodices spangled with mirrorwork.

A similar market, the **Sonepur Fair** *(Mela)*, is held near the town of Sonepur, in the northern state of Bihar, only here elephants rather than camels are the chief stock in trade. A lot of them are sold to temples in Kerala, where lines of sumptuously decorated tuskers feature prominently in Hindu festivals. The most intense of these is **Puram**, held in the heat of late April in the town of Thrissur, where two long lines of tuskers perform an epic stand-off, regaled by massed drum orchestras and extravagant firework displays.

The same streets are thronged again from late August to early-September for the annual **Pulikali Tiger Dance**, in which troupes of masked men with intricately painted tiger designs daubed on their bodies dance, strut and wiggle their way around the town's central intersection.

Saints and Gurus

For India's Muslims and Christians, Saints' Days provide the principal

A cheeky face at the annual Pushkar camel fair

A worshipper lights a candle at the Saint Francis Xavier Day celebrations in Goa

- **Aarthi Haridwar:** Brahmakund, Hari-ki-Pauri Ghat
  Daily: evenings at dusk
- **Kumbh Mela:** Prayag (UP), Nasik (Maharashtra), Ujjain (MP)
  Every 4 years: the next Kumbh Mela will be at Prayag on 25–27 Jan, 2013
- **Puram:** Thrissur, Kerala
  Annual: April–May
- **Hemis Festival:** Hemis, Ladakh
  Annual: July
- **Ganesh Chathurthi:** Maharashtra, especially Mumbai
  Annual: late Aug–early Sept
- **Onam:** Kerala
  Annual: late Aug–early Sept
- **Pulikali:** Thrissur, Kerala
  Annual: 4th day of Onam, late Aug–early Sept
- **Durga Puja:** India-wide, but especially Kolkata (Calcutta) and West Bengal
  Annual: six days in late Sept
- **Dusshera:** India-wide
  Annual: late Sept–early Oct
- **Kullu Dusshera:** Kullu, Himachal Pradesh
  Annual: early Oct
- **Diwali:** India-wide
  Annual: mid-Oct–mid-Nov
- **Pushkar Camel Fair (Mela):** Pushkar, Rajasthan
  Annual: late Oct–early Nov
- **Sonepur Fair (Mela):** Sonepur, Bihar
  Annual: early Nov

excuses for religious celebrations. All-night *qawwali* music serenades pilgrims filing through the shrine, or Dargah, of the mystic Sufi holy man **Khwaja Muin-ud-din Chishti**, on the occasion of the annual **Urs** at Ajmer, in Rajasthan. To keep the pilgrims going, huge cauldrons called *degs*, installed on raised platforms, are used to prepare special *kheer*, a deliciously creamy, spicy rice pudding regarded as *tabarruk*, or 'blessed', by Indian Muslims – when it's ready, a decidedly unholy scramble begins as the devout dive headfirst into the *degs* to grab a helping.

No such haste attends worship at the tomb of **Saint Francis Xavier** in Goa, whose annual Saint's Day on 3 December attracts Catholics from across the subcontinent and beyond. The object of their devotion, interred here for over four centuries, is the wizened corpse of the Basque Jesuit missionary-priest who first evangelised the southwest coast of India. Until recently, his remains were regarded as miraculously incorrupt. The cadaver is less intact these days, but remains the object of a mass pilgrimage every 10 years, when it is placed in a glass case before the altar of the Sé Cathedral in Old Goa for a month-long Exposition.

Riding the Rails

Rail travel is the quintessentially Indian form of transport. Whether in the air-conditioned comfort of a first-class carriage, or the heat and crush of a general compartment, travelling by train will give you a vivid taste of India's 'functioning anarchy' – its contradictions, complexities and, above all, its daily life, both on the train and through its windows.

Like Bollywood and cricket, India's vast railway network is one of the common denominators unifying the modern nation-state. Its tentacles extend to some of the most remote corners of the subcontinent – even Himalayan hilltops in a few notable instances – providing an affordable means for ordinary Indians to get around: for families to meet up, for workers to return home on leave, and for pilgrims to visit distant sacred sites. Every day around 20 million passengers ride the rails across the country, along with 20 million tonnes of freight.

Much criticism is directed at the Indian government for the generally dilapidated, overloaded, dirty and unstable state of the train system, but the fact it functions at all given the bewildering scale of the operation is a miracle. With more than 1.6 million staff on its payroll, **Indian Railways** (IR) is officially the largest employer on the planet. Around 7,000 stations punctuate a total network of 63,327km (39,316 miles). Some 8,000 locomotives may be trundling around the lines at any given time, hauling 50,000 carriages – all but the first-class, air-conditioned of them seemingly on the brink of collapse.

Carriage Comforts

For the foreign traveller accustomed to the neat and orderly railways of more developed parts of the world, the IR experience can come as a shock at first. Once you've got used to its manifold eccentricities, however, you'll soon find yourself falling in love with Indian train travel.

The first thing to get to grips with is the intricate system of classes, which at times can seem as arcane as the country's caste system. IR lists 10 of them in all, defined by the

Mumbai commuter trains are regularly so packed, their status is defined as a 'super-dense-crushload'

Morning mist hangs over Darjeeling station

number and quality of the berths or seats, and how many people the carriage accommodates.

Top of the pile are the carpeted first-class a/c coaches, which have recliners as spacious as dentists' chairs and liveried staff serving delicious meals. At the middle of the range are a/c carriages with swing-down berths. The hoi polloi are kept at bay by stern-faced TCs (Ticket Controllers) in blue peaked caps, assisted by 'bearers' who hand out freshly laundered cotton sheets to sleep under. For the vast majority of train travellers in India, however, cheaper, crowded 'general' carriages will be the only affordable option. Passengers are squeezed into them like sardines, the toilets are the stuff of nightmares and the only respite from the sweaty heat inside is blasts of hot, diesel-filled air.

Watching the World Go By

In the cheaper carriages of Indian trains, however, boredom is one problem you'll definitely not have to contend with. Settled in your seat, with a sustaining cup of sweet, milky *chai* in hand, you can sit back and enjoy a never-ending parade of buskers (many of them traditional folk musicians with fantastic voices), shoe polish-wallahs, beggars, mendicant holy men, trinket hawkers and – most welcome of all – vendors of hot snacks and drinks, each of whom announces their presence with their own unique, attention-grabbing call.

Views out of the window change as constantly as the scene inside the carriage. Impressions of India are all too often dominated by urban landscapes, but long train journeys, in particular, underline how predominantly rural the country remains – and how little everyday life in its villages has really altered over time compared with that in the country's cities.

Every now and then, the endless sea of fields, interrupted by oases of mango trees and hamlets moulded from mud and red bricks, will give way to rivers which the train crosses via rattly iron bridges erected a century and a half ago by British engineers. Far below, clumps of soapy children wave at the passing locomotives, while their mothers lay out washing to dry on the sun-baked rocks lining the river bank, watched by buffaloes lazing in silty pools.

Fleeting scenes like these, sliding hypnotically past as the train sways along, are what really make rail travel so rewarding in India. And rest assured that, with most journeys lasting several hours, or even days, there'll be plenty of them to keep you entertained.

Slow Travel Fast Food

Whichever class you're travelling in, eating and drinking are among the great pleasures of riding the rails in India. Vendors carrying urns of hot *chai* and trays of freshly fried samosas or *vada* (savoury doughnuts made from lentil flour) squeeze through the general carriages at regular intervals, while in the a/c coaches, passengers tuck into delicious and inexpensive set meals, prepared in attached 'pantry cars' and served in neat little foil parcels with freshly made *puris* and chutney.

A general (non a/c) carriage on a cross-country Indian train

Preparing food in the 'pantry car'

Even in the dead of night, when an express pulls into a station, the platforms erupt into life as food sellers frantically ladle spicy hot chickpea stew or tangy, tamarind-flavoured *sambar* into little dried-leaf bowls, which assistants deliver to hands stretched through barred windows.

Every station has its own speciality, and sampling these can be a hugely entertaining diversion on longer journeys, particularly if the train crosses from north to south India, when as if by some mysterious pre-arranged signal, wheat flour chapatis give way to rice and *idlys* (steamed rice cakes). Mysore does a brisk trade in its trademark *dosas* (pancakes made from a batter of part-fermented rice and lentil flour), Agra stations are famous for their *pethi* (candied pumpkin) and New Delhi for its *aloo tikki* (potato patties), served up with a blob of firey mango pickle. In Hyderabad, you can tuck into delicious local biriyanis, baked in old terracotta pots, and in Lonavala, Maharashtra, passengers stock up on cashew *chikki* – a sticky, dentally challenging toffee filled with nuts.

Expect, too, to have seasonal fruit thrust at you through the windows whenever the train stops. At Nerul, just outside Mumbai, commuters feast on *jambhool* plums, while in May, travellers heading south on the Konkan Railway can buy bags full of legendary Alphonso mango for next to nothing.

Waiting for the Toy Train at Darjeeling station

End of the Line

When the train does eventually arrive, foreigners often find themselves ill-prepared for the chaos of the average Indian station. Even before it stops, passengers trying to 'de-train' (disembark) jostle with those attempting to 'en-train' (embark), while red-shirted coolies barge their way through the melee, heads piled high with suitcases. As the British writer William Dalrymple once remarked: '(anarchy) is to to the porters … what order is to the clerks of the Crédit Suisse in Geneva: without it they would be lost.'

32

Unique Experiences

Indian Railways Trivia

- The first scheduled train in India departed from Bombay in 1853
- India boasts the oldest functioning locomotive in the world – the *Fairy Queen*, originally built in 1855, but still in occasional use hauling luxury tourist trains around Rajasthan
- Four to five major crashes occur annually in India, causing 700–800 fatalities, making this the most dangerous network in the world. Most deaths are directly attributable to human error.
- The Guwahati–Trivandrum Express is reputed to be the most unreliable train on the IR network, with delays typically running to 10 or 12 hours. It often shows up more than a whole day late, and has not arrived on time once in the past decade.
- The longest station name in India is Srivenkatanarasimharajuvariipeta, in Andhra Pradesh

The mayhem subsides only slightly once you're in the main concourse, where literally hundreds of families may be camped out at any one time, sprawled on the floors beneath giant departure boards, waiting for connections that have been delayed for hours, or days. All the while, a barrage of station announcements, *chai* wallahs, and film clips broadcast from ranks of overhead screens bombard the weary travellers. If you are leaving the station, then you've the barrage of auto-rickshaw drivers to contend with, who in tourist towns actually fight over customers (because of the hefty commission they could pocket for taking you to a hotel). To sidestep the melee, look for the prepaid auto stand, usually found just outside the exit; or better still arrange in advance for your hotel to send a driver to pick you up.

Palaces on Wheels

The rough and tumble of modern Indian rail travel is a world away from the high style in which the country's

India has five surviving narrow-gauge hill railways. Built by the British, they're used mainly to transport tourists these days, but remain hugely popular branch lines, winding through rugged scenery, often at record-breaking gradients. The only one that routinely still runs steam locomotives is the Nilgiri Blue Mountain.

- **The Darjeeling Himalayan Railway,** West Bengal *(see p.184)*
- **The Nilgiri Blue Mountain Railway,** Tamil Nadu
- **The Kalka–Shimla Railway,** Himachal Pradesh *(see p.105)*
- **The Matheran Hill Railway,** Maharashtra *(see p.150)*
- **The Kangra Valley Railway,** Himachal Pradesh *(see p.105)*

ruling Maharajahs and their retinues moved around in former times. Special trains were commissioned for royal tours or pilgrimages, fitted with the latest European luxuries. After the dissolution of the princely privileges at Independence in 1947, however, such opulence was frowned upon and the trains were confiscated by the government, which in recent times has converted several of them for use as luxurious tourist trains.

Inspired by the Orient Express, services such as the **Palace on Wheels** and **Royal Rajasthan on Wheels** (both: www.royalpalaceonwheels.net) in north India, and the **Deccan Queen** (www.deccan-odyssey-india.com) and **Golden Chariot** (www.deccan-odyssey-india.com) in the south, whisk passengers around their regions' prime sights, with evenings of pampering and culture shows of music and dance back at the richly appointed carriages.

33

Riding the Rails

Luxurious accommodation on the Palace on Wheels

Into the Wild

Animals and birds are never far away in India, but for a glimpse of the country's most exotic creatures, you'll have to travel well away from major population centres to pockets of heavily protected habitats on the country's margins – which are the home of the richest biodiversity on the planet.

Indians have a rather ambivalent attitude to their country's wildlife. Respect for nature may be enshrined in the mythology and ritual of the nation's main faiths, particularly Hinduism and Jainism. But as the subcontinent's population explodes and pressure on land becomes more intense, poaching – even of the rarest species – has become rife.

It was primarily to shield endangered animals such as tiger and rhino from illegal hunters that the government first drafted the Indian Wildlife Protection Act in 1972. **Project Tiger** was set up the same year, followed soon after by a raft of other environmental laws paving the way for the creation of fully fledged sanctuaries and reserves.

Today, some 560 protected areas exist across the country, among them 80 national parks, sheltering habitats that range from mangrove swamps to deserts, and Himalayan glaciers to evergreen rainforest and coral reefs.

The Last Tigers

Some 65,000 species of fauna have been identified in India, including 1,200 birds and 340 different mammals. The one that tops most visitors' 'must-see' list, however, is the **Bengal tiger** – and with good

The Bengal tiger is highly endangered

reason. Sighting India's iconic big cat in the wild can be an unforgettable experience, especially if you're fortunate enough to be on elephant back, padding silently through a tunnel of undergrowth in dense forest. Unfortunately, it's also one that's increasingly rare. A census carried out in 2008 showed that tiger numbers had plummetted to 1,411 (down from 3,642 in 2002); some experts claim the actual figure may be as low as 800, and that the animal will be extinct in the wild by 2015 (it already is in 17 of India's 37 tiger reserves).

Poaching has been the main cause of the decline. With dealers paying $5,000 or more for a carcass, the temptations for poor villagers living on the margins of sanctuaries are irresistible. Recently, however, tourism too has been cited as a contributing factor. Fears that tigers are about to disappear altogether have spawned a rush to India's national parks, resulting in erosion of the tigers' habitat and constant disturbance of the herds of deer they prey on. In May 2010, the Indian government threatened to close all tiger reserves to the public in a last-ditch attempt to revive numbers – an announcement that caused uproar in the tourism sector.

Open grassland, fringed by mixed deciduous forest, is the tiger's favourite terrain. But the animal has also adapted to the wetter landscape of the Sunderbans on the Ganges Delta, in the northeast of India. Here, tigers take to the water and swim between islands in the mighty river – though the only sign of their presence in this flat, grassy landscape is usually the telltale pug marks they leave in mud along the river banks.

Rhinos and Elephants

To the north of the Sunderbans, the **Kaziranga National Park** and **Manas Wildlife Sanctuary**, both in Assam close to the foothills of the Himalayas, are the only places in India you can spot a large mammal even rarer than the tiger: the **one-horned rhinoceros**.

The rhino is one of the rarest species in India

Armour-plated like a tank, the Indian rhino is perennially under threat from poachers too, for the perceived aphrodisiacal properties of its horn and magical powers of its flesh. The giant herbivore shares its habitat with various omnivorous **crocodiles**, including the ominously named **mugger**, and long-nosed **gharial**; both can be

Tiger Numbers

- 40,000: the estimated tiger population a century ago
- 1,411: India's wild tiger population in 2008
- 832: tigers killed in India between 1994 and 2007
- $5,000: the price paid by middlemen direct to poachers for a dead tiger
- $50,000: the price paid for a complete tiger on the black market

spotted lurking in the shallows waiting for unwary **sambar deer** or bite-sized **pygmy hogs** to wander to the water's edge.

Wild **elephant** are the other heavyweight survivors in the deltas of the northeast, where they're also domesticated and ridden for a variety of reasons – not least wildlife viewing. Watching herds of wild elephant while astride a tame one is an amazing experience. Apart from allowing you to get much closer to wild animals than you could in a vehicle, elephants are also good at sniffing out tigers, often coming to a restless halt with trunk raised to warn of the big cat's invisible presence nearby.

You stand your best chance of sighting wild elephant amid the dense, moist forests of the Tamil Nadu, Kerala and Karnataka borders, in the far southwest. At Tholpetty, in the Wayanad district of Kerala, close encounters with large herds, grazing noisily among the teak trees and stands of giant bamboo, are virtually guaranteed, along with glimpses of rarer lion-tailed macaques, Nilgiri langur and Malabar squirrels.

The Wild West

At the opposite climatic extreme to the jungles of the deep south are the salt flats of the Rann of Kutch, Gujarat, in the far west of India. Bone-dry, sun-bleached and treeless, this most inhospitable of terrain shelters India's last surviving herds of wild ass, or **khur**. With their sandy-coloured coats and dark manes, this elusive creature grazes scant, saline-resistant vegetation. It's said to be among the

The snow leopard is highly elusive

fastest animals in the world, clocking up speeds of 80km/hr (50 miles/hr). Numbers dipped below 1,000 in the 1960s after a spate of diseases, but have since rallied to sustainable levels.

The southern shores of Gujarat, on the far side of the Saurashtra peninsula from Kutch, host another of India's rarest mammals. Having once roamed from the shores of the Mediterranean to the far northeast of India, the **Asiatic lion** is now confined to less than 1,500 sq km (580 sq miles) of grass and woodland in the **Sasan Gir Forest**

National Park, where a breeding population of only 359 survives. Considering the fact that the lions kill local livestock each year, they're treated with great tolerance by local herders.

Ghost of the High Mountains

India's other, and most enigmatic, big cat inhabits the more sparsely populated, remote and beautiful terrain of the high Himalaya. So elusive is the **snow leopard**, and so difficult to spot as it moves over the scree slopes and boulder fields, masked by its pale grey coat speckled with rosettes and spots, that the animal is attributed with ghost-like powers by local people. Only 3,000–5,000 survive in the wild, spread over a vast area of mountains, where their preferred prey is Himalayan blue sheep (**bharal**), **ibex**, wild **goats** and **marmot**. In winter, when hunting is tougher, they also descend to the valley floors and take domestic **yaks** and goats – a habit which has brought them into conflict with mountain dwellers.

Both in retribution for livestock theft, and for the price of their thick coats, killing of these magnificent creatures is not uncommon, although the Dalai Lama recently called for an end to all poaching.

Know Your Monkey

India is home to dozens of species of primates, but there are two you'll encounter regularly – and it's worth knowing the differences between them.

The first, and most in-your-face, is the ubiquitous, cheeky little **rhesus macaque**. Distinguished by its red,dimply bottom, this is the monkey that has best adapted to town life. You'll see troupes of them scampering over temple towers in the south, across Mughal ramparts in the north, and thundering over corrugated-iron roofs in Himalayan bazaars. There's even a dedicated monkey shrine on the outskirts of Jaipur in Rajasthan where literally hundreds of macaques subsist on bananas and peanuts offered by Hindu pilgrims.

Here, and at most places where they congregate in numbers, male macaques, in particular, can be aggressive, snarling at passers-by if they don't give food, and growling at each other when scraps are in short supply. Rabies being an ever-present threat, it's worth keeping well clear of these bad-tempered primates, which will also steal from any bags left open. Priests at a hilltop temple in Hampi, Karnataka, make a decent living from tips given by tourists for retrieving camera bags and other belongings pilfered by the resident macaques.

No such problems are likely to mar meetings with India's other most common monkey, the **Hanuman langur**. Named after the beloved monkey general who helped the Hindu God-Prince Rama retrieve his bride, Sita, from the clutches of the evil demon Ravana, the langur is a much more reticent and peaceable creature, preferring to retreat to the safety of treetops than growl or scratch. Out in the wild, langurs are also the alarm sirens of the forest. One of the surest signs a tiger may be on the prowl is the distinctive whoop of a langur sentry stationed high in the canopy while his or her troupe is feeding.

Hornbills are just some of the exotic birds you might spot in India

Unless you've months to spare, and are prepared to trek to some of the most remote corners of the Himalayas, you're unlikely to spot a snow leopard. But, like all of India's rarest mammals, it's reassuring to know they're still out there somewhere.

Birds

Many rare birds stop over in India on migration, joining the spectacular array of year-round residents. Heavy-headed **hornbills** fly in pairs over northeastern and southern jungles. Apart from the ubiquitous crows and kites, raucous flocks of rose-ringed **parakeets** wheel over the trees in city parks, while in rural areas look out for the bright blue flash of exotic **kingfisher**. Other water birds to be found in India include the gigantic **Saras crane** – whose size and conjugal fidelity have earned it a place in local folklore across the subcontinent.

A good place to spot them is the **Keoladeo Ghana Sanctuary** at Bharatpur, near Agra. Until recently, this was also the winter nesting ground for rare Siberian cranes, but in recent years they have failed to show up. Scientists blame fighting in Afghanistan, which lies beneath their migratory flight path, for the disruption of their journey.

Another major problem is the near extinction of the once widespread **vulture**, whose numbers have declined by 98 percent in the last 10 years or so. At first it was thought that an unknown virus was to blame, but researchers have now found a link between the drug diclofenac (widely used as a veterinary painkiller in South Asia) and kidney failure in vultures. Vultures perform the vital function of scavenging rotting carcasses (from which they absorb the diclofenac). This helps prevent the spread of disease and keeps down the population of feral dogs. The Parsis of Mumbai are also facing problems because it is the vultures that dispose of corpses from their Towers of Silence.

Viewing Wildlife

In order to minimise impact (and maximise receipts for the government), access to Indian wildlife sanctuaries is strictly controlled. Only vehicles run, or approved by, the park in question are permitted to enter them. They're generally noisy diesel Jeeps, though in some parts you've also the option of quieter petrol 4WDs. In reality, the difference between these in terms of wildlife sightings is negligible as the animals have become well accustomed to both.

Each vehicle carries a maximum number of passengers (normally three or four), accompanied by a warden who also acts as a guide. Obviously you'll get a lot more out of your drive if he or she speaks English, but this can never be guaranteed, which is why most upscale lodges provide their own resident expert to accompany guests.

Parks are divided between Core Zones (areas which only Forest Department rangers are allowed to enter) and, encircling these, Buffer Zones (less heavily protected areas often open to local villagers). The latter is where all the wildlife drives take place, following clearly

Into the Wild

India's Wildlife Highs

- **Bar-headed goose**, Indian Himalayas. This exquisite bird migrates between Central Asia and the Indian plains, overflying the Himalayas en route – sometimes at altitudes in excess of 10,000m (33,000ft). See them on solid ground at Keoladeo National Park, near Bharatpur, on the UP-Rajasthan border.
- **Red panda**, Assam. Resembling a ginger racoon, the endangered red panda has to be the cuddliest-looking bear in India. Spot them in the temperate forests lining the Himalayan foothills of Sikkim and Assam.
- **Golden Langur**, Assam. Found only in a tiny enclave near the Brahmaputra River in Assam, this golden monkey is one of India's rarest and most unusual-looking creatures, with lustrous, cream-coloured fur burnished with reddish-gold, chestnut eyes and a fine-featured black face.

- **Elephants**, Andaman Islands. Elephants were introduced to the Andamans to help with timber extraction, but since a ban on logging they now roam free and take to the waves. Swim with one each morning at Radhnagar Beach, Havelock Island.
- **Olive Ridley Turtles**, Orissa. Each year in late February, around 200,000 female turtles swim ashore to lay their eggs on the beaches of the Ghitarkanika Sanctuary in Orissa. About 50 days later, the eggs hatch and a flotilla of millions of baby turtles heads for the surf.
- **Asiatic lions**, Gujarat. Only on the Saurashtra peninsula's south coast do these great beasts roam wild on the beach.
- **Tigers**, Rajasthan. Wild tigers and exotic Rajasthani architecture make for an irresistible combination. See them in glorious juxtaposition at the Ranthambore Wildlife Sanctuary.

demarcated routes, although in some parks these may run quite close to the Core areas.

Despite limitations on numbers, overcrowding of the routes is a major drawback of the more popular national parks in India, such as **Ranthambore** (tel: 0120 405 2615; www.ranthamborenationalpark.com; Oct–June), **Corbett** (www.corbett-national-park.com; Nov–June), **Kanha** (tel: 07642-250 760; www.kanhanationalpark.com; Oct–June) and **Bandhavgarh** (www.bandhavgarhnationalpark.com; Nov–June). Once word gets around that a tiger has been spotted, literally dozens of Jeeps may descend on a given site, which does little to enhance the wilderness experience – there's nothing likely to spoil you enjoying of a wild tiger sighting more than the presence of up to a hundred other visitors, all clicking away with their cameras .

Travelling on the back of an elephant is the best way to get close to other wildlife

Elephant Safaris

The best way to avoid such a rush is to opt for an elephant safari, if it's offered. Quite apart from being a novel experience in itself, riding 3m (10ft) off the ground gives you a great vantage point. Moreover, animals such as tigers and rhinos tend to be much less wary of elephants than of humans in cars, which means you can often get much closer to them; and of course it's a lot quieter, too, allowing you to appreciate the calls of birds and monkeys ▥.

In the **Periyar Wildlife Sanctuary** (tel: 4869-224 571; www.periyartigerreserve.org; all year) of central Kerala – famous as a site for spotting herds of wild elephants, which graze the shore of a large reservoir high in the Cardamom Hills – the Forest Department runs popular boat safaris. Once again, engine noise often scares off the wildlife, but here you also have the option of taking to the water on punted rafts, which the animals are less disconcerted by, stopping at remote, otherwise inaccessible locations en route.

Recommended Wildlife Tour Operators

A number of specialist operators run wildlife tours to India. Aside from sparing you the hassle of booking flights and hotels, these outfits also know the best places to sight the species you'll want to see, and invariably have arrangements with park authorities ensuring prioritised access to the best game drives at busy times. Established companies worth consulting include: **Steppes Discovery** (tel: 01285-643333; www.steppesdiscovery.co.uk); **Peregrine Tours** (tel: 0844-736 0170; www.peregrineadventures.com); **Trans Indus Travel** (tel: 020-8566 3739; www.transindus.co.uk); and **Western & Oriental Travel** (tel: 0845-277 3355; www.westernoriental.com).

Lodges, Camps and Trekking

The other factor that will significantly influence your experience of wildlife viewing will be your accommodation. There's a lot of it on offer at the major parks these days, especially at the high end of the scale. Luxury lodges and tent camps offer first-world comforts, but although many enjoy idyllic locations on the edges of the sanctuaries, they won't yield as intense an experience of the natural environment as you get by sleeping actually inside the park – in treehouses, forest lodges or on viewing platforms. **Parambiku-lam** in Kerala is a ground-breaker in this respect, offering a range of huts and tents for visitors to stay in that are deep inside the park's forest, as well as an isolated cottage on an islet.

Best of all from the point of view of wildlife sighting – though not necessarily for the nerves – are walking safaris. Many Indian parks offer options for trekking these days – usually with an armed ranger as an escort in case of encounters with angry young elephant bulls. Only by getting into the forest this way – on foot – will you appreciate the elemental power of the animals and their habitat. Coming face to face with a primeval gaur bison, wild boar, cobra or tiger at ground level will leave a longer-lasting impression than seeing such beautiful creatures from the relative safety of a Jeep.

India's Top Ten Wildlife Sanctuaries
• **Bandhavgarh**, Madhya Pradesh Tiger, leopard, nilgai antelope When to visit: Nov–Mar
• **Corbett Tiger Reserve**, Uttarkhand Tiger, mugger and gharial crocodile When to visit: Nov–Mar
• **Kahna National Park**, Madhya Pradesh Tigers, leopards, chital, block buck, wild dogs, gaur bison, pythons When to visit: Nov–Mar
• **Kaziranga**, Assam Rhinoceros, tiger, wild boar, elephants When to visit: Nov–Mar
• **Keoladeo National Park**, Rajasthan 375 bird species When to visit: July–Aug and Nov–Feb
• **Mudumalai**, Tamil Nadu Elephant, tiger and leopard When to visit: Dec–Mar
• **Parambikulam**, Kerala Elephant, gaur, Nilgiri langur, lion-tailed macaque When to visit: Dec–Mar
• **Ranthambore National Park**, Rajasthan Tigers, nilgai and jackals When to visit: Nov–Mar
• **Sasan Gir National Forest**, Gujarat Asiatic lion When to visit: Oct–Mar
• **Sunderbans Tiger Reserve**, West Bengal Tiger, spotted deer, turtles, mugger and gharial crocodiles When to visit: Nov–Mar

Into the Wild

Mountain Highs

The Himalayan regions of India encompass some of the highest peaks, and most inviting and varied scenery, on the planet. The mighty snow summits serrating the great watershed itself hypnotise anyone lucky enough to set eyes on them, but they're only a part of the picture.

There can be few experiences in life more enthralling than ascending the flank of an isolated Himalayan valley, days from the nearest road, towards a phalanx of shining white ice peaks, with everything you need to keep you warm, dry and fed for weeks strapped to a train of ponies. This is India as the nomadic shepherds, wool traders and itinerant monks of past centuries would have seen it – a wild, vast, awe-inspiring tract of mountains miraculously sheltered from the teeming plains below, where Buddhist monasteries cling to the vertical sides of canyons like swallows' nests, and the boulder fields resound to the clatter of stones dislodged by invisible ibex and snow leopard.

The price of glimpsing this rarefied world, however, can be high – in time and energy, if not necessarily in money. Many days or weeks of walking may be required to reach the highest, most beautiful pastures. Dangerous stream crossings, slopes of loose scree or mud, and perilous paths over melting glaciers often have to be negotiated even before you tackle the high passes, framed by strings of fluttering prayer flags, where for much of the year the threat of a snow storm is never far away.

Buddhist prayer flags at Annapurna Sanctuary in the Himalayan mountains

Wherever you go trekking in the Indian Himalaya, therefore, you'll find yourself heavily reliant on local knowledge to keep you safe. In the absence of dependable maps, guides who know the region, and its weather, are indispensable. They'll not only be able to ensure you keep to the right path, but will also be able to arrange accommodation along the route, and will be best placed to recruit porters, ponies and horsemen before you set off.

Heading for the Hills – Choosing a Route

Each of India's Himalayan regions has its own unique character. Choosing the best one for you will depend on your own personal limitations, how much time you have, and which kind of scenery you find most inspiring.

The defining topographical feature of the **northwest Himalaya** is the watershed of the Great Himalayan range itself. By blocking the flow of annual monsoon clouds, this tract of mighty saw-toothed summits has created a climatic transition as abrupt as any on earth. To the south and west of it, where rainfall is high between June and September, lush valleys wrapped in *deodar* cedar woods culminate in Alpine meadows carpeted with wild flowers during spring and early summer. Up here, the people are mostly fair-skinned Hindu and Muslim herders, shepherds and farmers of Aryan ancestry. Some even have fair hair and pale green or blue eyes, claiming descent from the exiled Macedonian army of Alexander the Great.

On the far side of the dividing ridge, by contrast, begins an immense

Kanchenjunga is the world's third-highest mountain peak

high-altitude desert of arid brown, grey and ochre scree, streaked with splashes of coloured minerals, where the only greenery is fields of barley fed by carefully channelled snowmelt. Technically on the Tibetan Plateau, the so-called **trans-Himalaya** region is predominantly Buddhist, its inhabitants central Asian in appearance.

The same is true of people living in the far eastern arm of the Himalaya, squeezed between Nepal and Bhutan, where the prime trekking destination is Sikkim, home of mighty **Kanchenjunga**, India's highest peak. Further east, the hill state of Arunchal Pradesh also holds some awesome mountain scenery, with the added attraction of unique indigenous cultures in its valleys.

Ladakh and Zanskar

Whitewashed monasteries, set against spellbinding backdrops of snow-capped mountains, rise above every village in **Ladakh** – 'the Land of High Passes' – and neighbouring **Zanskar** – the two corners of the far northwest most favoured by trekkers. Routes in these sparsely populated, starkly beautiful regions tend to be long, taking upwards of three weeks to complete, and arduous, with lung-stretching climbs over passes of 5,000m (16,600ft) the norm.

The classic trekkers' path into Zanskar starts at Darcha, on the Manali–Leh highway, and winds over the famous Shingo La pass (5,091m/16,970ft), notorious for its freak blizzards, to the district capital, Padum (Trek grade: hard; duration:

10–12 days; season: late-June–mid-Oct). One of the many cultural highlights seen along the way is the amazing monastery of Phuktal, hollowed from a vertical cliff. Plans are afoot to render this ancient artery motorable, so enjoy it while it's still car-free.

In winter, when snow blocks the high passes into Zanskar, the only way for its inhabitants to reach the outside world is via the frozen surface of a river flowing through the world's deepest gorge – a route the locals call **Chaddar** (Trek grade: hard; duration: 4–7 days each way; season: Jan–Feb). With overnight halts in caves or tents pitched on ice, it's a full-blown expedition requiring specialist cold-weather kit, but a handful of operators these days offer the route as a package, including **The Mountain Company** and **Himalayan Frontiers** *(for both, see box, opposite)*.

Himachal Pradesh

Since the onset of the troubles in Kashmir, middle-class Indians looking for an escape from the heat of summer have favoured the well-watered mountains of **Himachal Pradesh**. Only a day's journey from the plains, Himachal's trekking hub, and starting point for the staggering bus ride to Ladakh, is **Manali**, at the head of the Kullu Valley – itself a springboard for numerous superb treks into scenery reminiscent of the Alps.

A challenging but superbly scenic trek here is the route leading up the beautiful Parvati Valley and over the snowbound **Pin–Parvati Pass** (5,319m/17,730ft) at its head to the

The remote Zanskar is the end point of a well-trodden trek route from Darcha

The extreme and beautiful Pin-Parvati pass in Himachal Pradesh

remote region of **Spiti** (Trek grade: hard; duration: 11–12 days; season: July–Sept). Few routes in the world involve such dramatically contrasting landscapes, as you walk from the verdant roof of Himachal to the lunar-like, Buddhist trans-Himalaya. You'll need the best part of a fortnight, an expert guide and a couple of porters for this strenuous expedition. **Mountain Kingdoms** (*see box, right*) offer it as an off-the-peg trip.

The same firm can also tailor-make treks along the wonderful **Kinner Kailash Parikrama**, in Kinnaur district (Trek grade: hard; duration: 5–7 days; season: July–Oct). An exquisite, needle-topped massif deep in the remote eastern corner of HP, **Kinner Kailash** (6,050m/20,166ft) is a mountain held sacred by both Hindus and Buddhists, and each summer pilgrims file around its spectacular lower flanks by means of a zigzagging path, starting at the village of Morang. Independent walkers will have to arrange the necessary permits in advance at the district headquarters, Shimla.

Kashmir

In spite of its long history of political instability, **Kashmir**, to the west of Ladakh, has always been regarded as the Jewel in the Crown of Himalayan kingdoms. The Mughal emperor Jahangir, who used to spend his summers here, famously said of the region 'if there be a Paradise on earth, this is it,

---

Recommended Trekking Outfits

For those who can afford the luxury, trekking agencies and tour companies – both at home, and on the ground in India – are on hand to handle such logistics for you if time is short. The following five firms rank among the leaders in their field, operating the routes mentioned:

- **The Mountain Company** tel: 0207-498 0953; www.themountaincompany.co.uk
- **Himlayan Frontiers** tel: 01902-250 130; www.himalayanfrontiers.com
- **Indus Tours** tel: 0208-901 7320; www.industours.co.uk
- **Mountain Kingdoms** tel: 01453-844 400; www.mountainkingdoms.co.uk
- **Wild Frontiers** tel: 0207-736 39 68; www.wildfrontiers.co.uk

this is it, this is it...' The ongoing insurgency has stifled tourism for decades, but trekkers are starting to take advantage of a lull in the conflict, drawn by the picture-postcard glacial valleys around Sonmarg and Pahalgam. One great route tracking the Himalayan watershed is the four-day trek from **Aru to Sonomus**, taking you through old-growth cedar forest and over high passes, with a relaxing spell on one of Srinagar's famous houseboats at the end. **Wild Frontiers** (*see box, p.45*) are among the few adventure companies that offer trekking itineraries in this region, and can arrange the necessary insurance for trekking in a zone which many governments still advise their nationals to avoid.

Pastures near Jammu, Kashmir

Uttarakhand

To see the most spectacular of all the mountains in the northwest, however, you'll have to follow the streams of pilgrims who pour during the summer through the region sandwiched between Himachal Pradesh and Nepal, in the state of **Uttarakhand**. Revered as the home of four of India's most sacred temples, **Garwhal**'s landscape is one of truly mythic splendour, culminating in the majesty of **Nanda Devi** (7,816m/25,643ft) – the 'Bliss-Giving Goddess'. To service the temples, roads penetrate higher up the valleys here than any other corner of the Himalaya, though you still have to climb high and hard to witness the mighty white giants at close quarters.

Skirting the fringe of the **Nanda Devi National Park** (www.india wildliferesorts.com/national-parks/ nandadevi-national-park.html), the benchmark trek in this region is the **Curzon Trail** (Trek grade: moderate; duration: 10–11 days; season: Apr–Oct) – an extremely varied path leading through a series of roadless

---

Trekking Tips

- Ensure your porters or pony men are adequately equipped and provisioned for your chosen trek before you set off
- Bear in mind the potential dangers of Acute Mountain Sickness (AMS), which can strike at altitudes above 2,000m (6,600ft) – and how to avoid it
- When it comes to keeping warm, think 'lots of thin layers' rather than 'a few thick ones'
- Dispose of non-degradable waste responsibly
- Never drink stream water unless it's well boiled or chemically purified

valleys punctuated by Garwhali villages, cedar forest and high passes. It was originally named after the British viceroy, Lord Curzon, but was re-christened 'the Nehru Trail' after Independence. From its highpoint, the Kuari Pass (4,258m/14,193ft), you get an astonishing view of the region's Hiamalayan colossi, including Trisul (7,120m/23,733ft) and Changabang (6,804m/22,680ft), as well as the 'bliss-Giving Goddess' herself.

Indus Tours *(see p.45)* are India trekking specialists who can arrange escorted expeditions along the Curzon Trail, as well as the most famous route of all in the Garwhal, the 2–3-day hike from Gangotri up the head of the Bhagirathi Valley to **Gaumukh** – source of the River Ganges (Trek grade: easy; duration: 2–3 days; season: mid-Apr–Oct). Trekkers usually camp at Bhojabasa, in the shadow of Shivaling (6,543m/21,810ft), to arrive at the source at dawn, when naked sadhus bathe in its freezing water as it gushes from the snout of a spectacular glacier.

The Eastern Himalaya

India's highest peak lies at the opposite, eastern, end of the Himalaya from Uttarakhand, in the state of **Sikkim**. Seen from distant Darjeeling, **Kanchenjunga** (8,586m/28,169ft) appears no less aloof than Nanda Devi, but its skirt-tails are rather more easily accessible to trekkers, reachable in a fortnight's round-route that takes you through a bucolic landscape of terraced rice villages and rhododendron forests (Trek grade: moderate; duration: 14 days; season: May–Sept).

Further east still, **Arunachal Pradesh**, known as 'the Hidden Land', ranks among India's least-visited hill states, requiring special permission to enter, though it's also correspondingly less spoilt, with a unique traditional culture. Both destinations are well served by Mountain Kingdoms *(see p.45)*, whose week-long Arunachal route traverses the homelands of the Monpa and Sherdukpen people, whose cultural highlight is the ancient Buddhist monastery of Tawang.

The stunning peaks of Garwhal are now being developed for sport as well as pilgrimage

The Perfect Beach

India's immense coastline and island archipelagos hold plenty of scope for getting away from it all. Whether you want to wild camp on a sand spit in the middle of nowhere, snorkel in clear blue waters, or be pampered in a luxurious lagoon-side spa, the perfect beach is never too far away.

Red silt swept from the interior mountains into the Arabian Sea and Bay of Bengal has blended with shell sand to form beaches of breathtaking beauty along the Indian shoreline. Dense groves of coconut palms back most of them, shading red-tiled or thatched fishing villages whose inhabitants still depend to a large extent on what they can haul from the waves, and grow in patches of seasonal rice paddy.

Couple this with a climate that's blissfully hot and sunny for at least five to six months of the year, and it's hard to imagine a more idyllic backdrop for a beach holiday. Precisely what kind of experience you can expect, however, varies hugely from place to place, depending on the level of development.

At one extreme are the kind of empty, endless stretches of sand you find lining most of the country's shores, where the only sounds you're likely to hear are the pounding surf, the occasional thwack of a machete harvesting coconuts and jangling of bells from a nearby temple. At the other are beaches backed by massive luxury hotels, complete with their own helipads, infinity pools and ayurveda spas. The truly amazing thing about India, however, is that you can still find the full gamut of

beach types, from remote coves frequented only by the odd dreadlocked backpacker, to neatly swept sands lined with Punjabi honeymooners and sunburnt Russian millionaires – all in the space of a few kilometres.

When to Go

When it comes to planning a beach break in India, timing is crucial. For half of the year, violent monsoon storms render the country's beaches

Fishermen on Benaulim beach, Goa

Boats resting on the sands in Vizhinjam harbour, Kerala

off-limits to all but adrenalin junkies. Only when the annual deluge subsides in late November can you be assured of calm seas and blue skies. Average surface water temperatures at this time hover around a blissful 27°C (81°F) – warm enough to jump in without the least shock to the system, but cool enough to still be refreshing. Conditions are ideal from late December until early February, when the heat and humidity start to build again. By April the weather can be oppressive, and by May totally unbearable, with periodic downpours interrupting blasts of intense tropical heat. The big cyclones arrive in spectacular fashion around the beginning of June, when an intimidating wall of black cloud sweeps landwards from the Arabian Sea, unleashing huge waves and winds that bend the palm trees sideways.

Best Beaches

Looking at a map of India, you might expect the subcontinent to be ringed with resorts. In reality, however, only a handful of coastal locations offer the kind of experience foreign travellers expect of a beach holiday. Local attitudes to nudity are the main reason for that – which is why sun worshippers tend to congregate only in those places where communities, and visiting day-trippers, have become accustomed to the bathing habits of Western tourists.

The most laid-back and tolerant of all India's beach regions is the former Portuguese enclave of **Goa**, on the southwest coast. This is where sun-and-sand tourism got started back in the 1970s. The charter boom of ensuing decades, followed in recent years by a surge in the numbers of Russian holiday-makers, has transformed the complexion of the main resorts, but it's easy enough to sidestep the crowds by venturing to quieter villages in the far north and south of the state.

Kerala, in the tropical far southwest of India, has become the country's other most developed beach destination. The big plus here is that you can alternate spells in smart hotels on the coast with trips on converted rice barges through the atmospheric backwater regions, as well as forays into the hills inland, draped with lush coffee and tea plantations. A couple of small planes also leave the capital, Kochi, each week for the remote coral atoll of **Lakshadweep**, where a solitary eco-lodge provides access to some of the clearest, most brilliant turquoise seas in Asia.

The east coast of India holds comparatively few bona fide resorts (**Mamallapuram** being the main exception), though its shoreline is prime territory for nesting Olive Ridley sea turtles. Chennai (Madras), capital of Tamil Nadu, is the springboard for trips further east across the Bay of Bengal to the remote **Andaman Islands**, where the possibilities for exploring wild shell-sand beaches and snorkelling off coral reefs are innumerable.

The Perfect Beach For...

...a hippy holiday:

Arambol, Goa

Arambol's sweeping arc of gold sand, lined by slender palms and ranks of old wooden fishing boats, is the last bastion of hippy-dom in Goa . Yoga, chakra balancing and fire juggling routinely accompany the sunsets here, but there's also a more hedonistic edge to the place, with succulent seafood on offer in the beachfront cafés and a lively music scene. Jump in the deep end with a course of Kundalini yoga at **Organic Karma** (www.organickarma. co.uk), Viriam Kaur's rooftop studio.

On Goa's Palolem beach

...a sunset stroll:

Palolem, Goa

Cradled by an amphitheatre of jungle-covered hills, this superbly scenic bay is the centre spread of Indian beaches – though also one of the most jam-packed in peak season. Wander around the headland to the south for a more relaxed vibe at neighbouring **Colom** and **Patnem**, where you can brush up on your yoga poses and Bollywood dance grooves at the **Harmonic Healing & Eco Retreat Centre** (tel: 9822-512 814; www.harmonicingoa. com). **Dreamz Diving** (tel: 9326-113 466; www.dreamzdiving.com) are the people to contact if you're in search of a scuba adventure in this area, while **Goa Sailing** (tel: 9850-458 865; www. goasailing.com) rent out catamarans for explorations of desert coves

- **Tandoori pomfret**, Goa.
  Flounder stuffed with firey, sour chilli paste and baked in a hot tandoor oven – a favourite of Goan beach shacks. Try it at **Joencon's** in Benaulim.
- **Prawn gassi**, Mangalore.
  This pungeant, flavour-packed curry, soured with kokum seeds, is the tastiest staple of the Konkan Coast. Mop it up with soft *appam* – steamed rice cakes made with fermented rice flour. **Apoorva** in Mumbai serves a legendary *gassi* with deliciously light *appam (see p.161).*
- **Malabari mussels**, Kozhikode.
  Calicut's Muslim population are mad for

mussels, fried in a spicy coat of millet. Taste them at their crunchiest in the city's **Paragon** restaurant *(see p.246).*
- **Karimeen pollichathu**, Kerala. Pearlspot marinated in fragrant Malabari spices and steamed in a banana leaf is the quintessential dish of Kerala's Kuttanad backwaters. It's also a speciality of the **Grand Hotel** in Ernakulam.
- **Lobster in butter-garlic sauce**, Mamallapuram.
  All of the beach shacks in this old-style Tamil seaside town serve sumptuous fresh lobster, straight off the boats and grilled to perfection in front of you.

...a scenic dip:
Om beach, Gokarna, Karnataka
Gokarna receives Hindu pilgrims and backpacking beach bums in roughly equal numbers, and both mingle happily on the breathtakingly picturesque twin coves of Om Beach – so named because their shape replicates that of the auspicious 'Om' symbol. The bay takes an hour of rough hiking over a shade-less laterite headland to reach; fishing boats can whisk you there more quickly – and beyond to remote coves only accessible by water. Check into the ethno-chic **SwaSwara** (tel: 0484-301 1711; www.cghearth.com) for a stay in high Indian style.

...snorkelling in crystalline water:
Bangaram, Lakshadweep
The Lakshadweep Islands form a necklace of jade and turquoise islets scattered across the Arabian Sea, 400km (250 miles) east of the mainland. Ringed by coral reefs, Bangaram is the

only one open to visitors, and its sole accommodation option is the **Bangaram Island Resort** (tel: 0484-301 1711; www.cghearth.com), a campus of thatched eco-cottages a stone's throw from the water's edge. Snorkelling, volleyball games with staff and beach badminton are the only distractions.

The Perfect Beach

The distinctive shape of Om beach

...recovering from an all-night Theyyem ritual:

Kannur, Kerala

The stretch of coast running south from this hectic market town in north Kerala is indented with a string of refreshingly undeveloped beaches, from tiny cliff-backed coves to sprawling bays of soft yellow sand. Plans to build a new international airport nearby look set to spoil them forever, so enjoy the serenity while you can at any one of around half a dozen local guesthouses. Trips inland to experience elaborately costumed spirit possession rituals known as *theyyem* are an additional incentive to stay here. Find out what's on at www.theyyam calendar.com, or through owners of local guesthouses, such as the **Kannur Beach House** (tel: 9847 186 330; www.kannurbeachhouse.com).

...walking on empty sands:

Nileshwar, Kerala

The owners of the ultra-chic **Nileshwar Hermitage** (tel: 0467-228 7510; www.neeleshwarhermitage.com) couldn't have picked a more serene spot on the Indian coast to site a stylish beachside retreat. Many kilometres of empty white sand yawn in either direction, and there isn't another building in sight. Accommodation comes in thatched, Keralan-style gable-roofed cottages with their own pillared verandas and exclusive sea views. Yoga, ayurveda therapy and local seafood provide diversions from the serious business of swimming and sun lounging.

...watching Hindu rituals:

Varkala, Kerala

Papanasam Beach, in the southern Keralan village of Varkala, has long been an important pilgrimage destination for Hindus, who come here to immerse the ashes of recently deceased relatives in the waves. Enfolded by spectacular red laterite escarpments, its peripheries have more recently been colonised by Western backpackers, serviced by a line of clifftop cafés and guesthouses affording mesmerising sea vistas. Between bouts in the crashing surf, you can hire a motorbike to reach deserted beaches further north – try **Mahindra2Wheelers** (tel: 9846-701 975) or **Wheels of South India** (tel: 9847-080 412) – a local elephant camp or any number of wild temple festivals. **Kerala Connections** (www.kerala

The pristine sands of Lakshadweep

A glowing red sunset at Varkala beach

connections.co.uk) can put together a package for you, with stays in one of four luxury hotels in the village **M**.

...body surfing and ancient ruins:
Mamallapuram, Tamil Nadu
Its intricately carved surfaces blurred by centuries of salt winds, the elegant Shore Temple at Mamallapuram, an hour and a half's drive south of Chennai (Madras), presides over this low-key beach resort **M**. After a day clambering over giant boulders, visiting deity sculptors' workshops and marvelling at ancient Pallava rock-cut shrines, you can while away the evenings over grilled local lobster and Tamil sangria at one of the beach shacks. A handful of **Trans Indus Travel's** tours (tel: 0208-566 3739; www.transindus. co.uk) stop for a night here.

...swimming with elephants:
Radhnagar Beach, Havelock, Andaman Islands
A two-kilometre (1¼-mile) curve of fine white sand and transluscent turquoise water, backed by giant *mowhar* trees, makes Radhnagar the most photogenic beach in this isolated archipelago, a three-hour flight from Chennai, which includes islands still occupied by tribes of hunter-gatherers. Snorkelling in pristine water where dugong and giant rays are regular visitors keeps most tourists busy here for weeks on end, and accommodation is plentiful **M**. You can even swim with an elephant at the gorgeous **Barefoot** eco-retreat (tel: 044 -2434 1001; www. barefootindia.com).

The Perfect Beach

Top 5 Beach Hideaways

If privacy, luxury and superb sea views are your top holiday priorities, give the following exquisite Indian beach hideaways a browse.

- **Elsewhere**, Aswem beach, Goa (tel: 022-2373 8757 or 9820-037 387; www.aseascape.com). *See p.173*
- **Dwarka Eco Beach Resort**, Khola beach, Goa (tel: 9823-377 025; www. dwarkagoa.com)
- **A Beach Symphony**, Marari beach, Kerala (tel: 477-224 3535 or 9744 297123; www.abeachsymphony.com)
- **Karrikathi Beach House**, Nellinkudu beach, Kerala (tel: 0471-240 0956; www.karikkathibeachhouse.com). *See p.244*
- **Bungalow on the Beach**, Tranquebar, Tamil Nadu (tel: 011-4666 1666; www.neemranahotels.com)

Yoga and Ayurveda

India was where the ancient practices of yoga originated and remains the home of its most illustrious gurus. Ayurveda has equally antique roots in the subcontinent's system of herbal medicine but has recently been reborn as a spa therapy. Both thrive in the beach resorts of the south and Himalayan foothills of the north.

Ever since yoga was first introduced to the West in the 1950s and 1960s, foreigners have travelled to India to imbibe its ancient wisdom at source. Institutes run by its most famous exponents are regarded as the wellspring of traditional yoga, which evolved over many centuries in remote Hindu monasteries, perfected by generations of ascetics, philosophers and Sanskrit scholars.

However, for the less committed, India also holds plenty of places where you can learn the basics of yoga from scratch, brush up on poses you've already mastered or acquire new ones – often in fabulously exotic settings by the banks of the Ganges, amid medieval ruins or on sun-drenched beaches.

Ayurveda treatments of various kinds are often offered alongside yoga tuition, and on the face of it the two seem perfect partners. What better way could there be to ease those stretched limbs than a massage with exotic herbal oils, followed by a cleansing steam bath?

However, as any qualified ayurveda doctor will remind you, there exists an important distinction in Indian medicine between genuine ayurveda

treatments (which may be less than pleasant, last for months and only be available in hospitals) and 'rejuvenation', where diluted forms of ayurveda are deployed as revitalising therapies. While the latter may fit comfortably

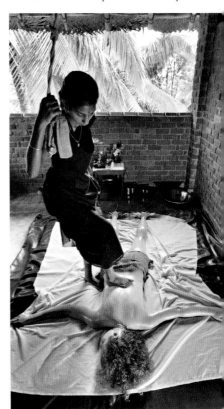

A traditional back massage at Somatheeram Ayurveda Resort (see p.59)

into a fortnight's beach break, the former is only likely to be really beneficial – and safe – if the patient avoids direct sunlight, and refrains from bathing in the sea – a regime completely at odds with most people's idea of a tropical sun-and-sand holiday.

Yoga in India

No one knows for sure when, or where, yoga first originated, but the discovery of seals in the ruins of ancient Indus Valley cities showing what look like sages in full lotus position suggests its roots may be very

Ten Great Places to Learn Yoga

India has more than its fair share of fake yogis, eager to relieve unwitting tourists of their rupees. The following centres, by contrast, are all the real deal.

- **Ashtanga Yoga Institute**
  Mysore; www.kpjayi.org
  The birthplace of ashtanga vinyasa, taught by the grandson of the great guru himself, Pattabhi Jois
- **Bihar Yoga Bharati**
  Munger, Bihar; www.yogavision.net
  Offshoot of the famous Bihar Bharati Yoga ashram founded in 1964 by the guru Swami Satyandanda Saraswati, offering courses pitched at foreigners
- **Brahmani Centre**
  Anjuna, Goa; www.brahmaniyoga.com
  All-ability, drop-in classes (mostly Ashtanga), at a beautifully set up yoga school a short cycle from the beach
- **Harmonic Healing & Eco Retreat Centre**
  Patnem, Goa; www.harmonicingoa.com
  Sat astride a headland overlooking one of India's loveliest beaches, this is a funky, foreign-run centre where you can also try your hand at Bollywood dance
- **Himalaya Yoga Valley**
  Arambol, Goa, and Dharamsala, Himachal Pradesh; www.yogagoaindia.com
  Goa is the winter home of this reputed Iyengar school, which migrates to the Dharamsala mountains during the summer

- **Krishnamacharya Yoga**
  Mandiram Chennai; www.kym.org
  Famous ashram founded by TKV Desikachar, the son of the man who taught both Iyengar and Pattabhi Jois
- **Parmath Niketan Ashram**
  Rishikesh, Uttarkhand; www.parmath.com
  Ashram of the famous guru Pujya Swami Chidanand Saraswatiji, on the banks of the Ganges, where you can follow short or intensive courses in Iyengar yoga, along with Vedic philosophy. It hosts a popular yoga festival in March.
- **Purple Valley Centre**
  Assagao, Goa; www.yogagoa.com
  Well-established Ashtanga school at a leafy location a drive away from north Goa's busy beaches
- **Ramamani Iyengar Memorial Institute**
  Pune, Maharashtra; www.bksiyengar.com
  Regarded by many as the finest yoga school in the world, the ashram of BKS Iyengar has a two-year waiting list
- **Sivananda Vedanta**
  Rishikesh/Neyyar Dam; www.sivananda.org
  India's two most popular Sivananda ashrams offer identical mixes of yoga, meditation and philosophy – but Neyyar Dam, where students can swim in a lake between classes, wins for location

Yoga and Ayurveda

old indeed, dating back 4,000 years, or more. Elaborate texts expounding yogic philosophy and practice were later set down in writing between the 2nd century BC and 4th century AD, the best known of them the Yoga Sutras of Maharishi Patanjali.

For Patanjali, yoga was in essence a means of 'unifying individual consciousness with the Divine'. This was achieved through a variety of different disciplines – mental, spiritual and physical – but the one which would become most widely known in the modern era was '*asana*' – poses which, along with special breathing techniques, stretch and relax the body as a preparation for meditation.

Regarded, at best, as a religious eccentricity by the British, yoga was confined to Hindu ascetic circles, and a handful of old-style *shalas*, or gymnasia, until it was rediscovered by the Indo-phile 'hippy' generation of the 1960s and 1970s. The two great masters who spearheaded its eventual revival were BKS Iyengar, who still teaches in Pune, Maharashtra, and the late K Pattabhi Jois from Mysore. Both men were regarded as geniuses in their youth, and would go on to develop their own distinctive brands.

Gurus and Ashrams

Iyengar's **Ramamami Memorial Institute** in Pune (www.bksiyengar. com) and Pattabhi Jois' **Ashtanga Yoga Institute** in Mysore (www. kpjayi.org) have become the high altars of yoga for serious students. However, unless you're already a committed practitioner, with several years' experience under your belt, neither is likely to accept your application to attend one of their courses.

Travellers wishing to have a taste of yoga during their trip to India have, broadly speaking, two options. The heavyweight one, for those who want to immerse themselves fully in the discipline, is to sign up for an intensive course in a dedicated ashram. Usually run by a reputed Guru, these places tend to bundle yoga tuition, classes in Hindu philosophy, vegetarian meals and basic accommodation into an all-inclusive fee, which is generally not very high. Their regimes can be strict – sex, drugs, rock 'n' roll are definite no-nos – and you'll have to get up at an ungodly hour of the night to chant and perform poses before breakfast.

Practising yoga poses in Udaipur

Goa is a popular location for yoga-themed holidays

A prime purveyor of this austere, fast-track approach that's extremely popular among Westerners is the famous Sivananda Vedanta ashram. The organisation has branches all over India, but its headquarters are in the country's yoga capital, **Rishikesh** – the town the Beatles travelled to in 1967 to study with Maharishi Yogi.

An ancient Hindu pilgrimage centre in the Himalayan foothills overlooking the Ganges, Rishikesh is chock-full of places to embark on spiritual quests, using every conceivable kind of Indian religious pursuit, from chakra balancing to dynamic meditation, *bhajan* (Sanskrit hymn) singing and Vedic chanting. Telling the fake babas (holy men) from the pukka yogis (genuine yoga experts) isn't always easy to the uninitiated, but that's all part of the fun of this quirky town.

The other option for learning yoga is to hole up for a few weeks in one of the many tourist spots in India where small schools and individual teachers ply their trade. These include **Varanasi**, **Hampi** and numerous beach resorts in the south. Drop-in classes, where you turn up for hour-long sessions, tend to be the norm, but lots of places also offer longer courses. The main difference between this kind of setup and an ashram is that you generally don't have to commit to a regime. The vibe tends to be more laid-back and sociable, and altogether less intense – plus you get to soak up the atmosphere of India more than when you're incarcerated in an ashram.

Preparing bags of herbs for use in ayurvedic compressions

During the winter months, **Goa** offers the widest choice of yoga schools in India, and is fast emerging as a rival to Rishikesh in terms of popularity among travellers. It's easy to understand why. The combination of stretching, swimming and great seafood, all in tropical sunshine, is a powerful antidote to the heat and pollution of life on the road.

The 'Science of Life': Ayurveda

A whole new form of tourism has evolved on the back of ayurveda, the subcontinent's own traditional form of medicine. Visitors from Germany and Scandinavia trailblazed the trend, embracing its herbal treatments with an almost religious enthusiasm in the late 1990s, since when legions of stressed-out Indian execs from the big cities have followed suit. Five-star chains across the country were quick to see the money-spinning potential of ayurveda as a spa therapy. Nowadays every self-respecting resort boasts its own treatment centre, fitted out with sumptuous tropical hardwoods and traditional utensils made of bell metal, where teams of uniformed masseurs will ease away your stresses and strains using exotic Indian oils and steam baths.

The highest concentration of upscale spas is in the far south of **Kerala**, where a necklace of resorts has sprung up behind the coves and beaches to the south of Kovalam, near the capital, **Thiruvananthapuram** (Trivandrum). Having flown direct from northern Europe, guests are whisked away in air-con minibuses to campuses hidden under the palm canopy, where they receive treatments in pillared rooms open to the sea breezes.

Accommodation is in thatched 'eco-cottages' looking through the coconut groves to the beach.

At the core of ayurveda is the belief that disease is caused by imbalances in three elemental *doshas*, or humours: *Pitta* (fire and water); *Kapha* (earth); and *Vata* (air, space, wind). Restore these to their natural equilibrium, the theory goes, and good health will ensue.

Re-balancing is achieved firstly by purging the body of toxins – through a variety of largely unpleasant procedures (including enemas and induced vomiting). Diseases can then be tackled using internal medicines (foul-tasting 'decotions') and by applying oils to the body in rather more pleasant ways: massage, hot compresses of herbs and dribbling over the forehead, to name but a few.

Needless to say, it's the massages and gentle herbal compresses that have proved most popular with Western holiday-makers.

Ayurveda Spas and Centres

Ayurveda packages are offered by specialist India tour operators such as **TransIndus** (tel: 020-8566 2729; www.transindus.co.uk) and **Kerala Connections** (tel: 01892-722440; www.keralaconnect.co.uk). But you'll often save money by booking direct with the spa itself. This is a list of recommended establishments:

- **Ananda**
  Rishikesh, Uttarkand; tel: 011-2656 8888; www.anandaspa.com
  Set on the banks of the Ganges, Ananda occupies a restored Maharajah's palace swathed in sal forest near the sacred town of Rishikesh
- **Ayurveda Mana**
  Preingode, Kerala; tel: 0466-2370660 or 9846 045696; www.aurvedamana.com
  Staunchly traditional treatments in the grounds of an antique mansion, buried deep in the rice fields of central Kerala
- **Coconut Lagoon**
  Kumarkom, Kerala; tel: 0484-301 1711; www.cghearth.com
  You have to jump on a boat to reach this über-luxurious backwater spa, on an island in serene Vembanad Lake

- **Kalari Kovalikom**
  Polengode, Kerala; tel: 0484-301 1711; www.cghearth.com
  The Maharaja of Ayurveda retreats, offering top-drawer therapies in the magnificent confines of a traditional, 18th-century royal palace
- **Somatheeram**
  Kerala; tel: 0471- 226 6501; www.somatheeeram.org
  The original and best of south Kerala's seaside ayurveda resorts, with accommodation in little cottages above a spectacular fishing beach
- **SwaSwara**
  Gokarna, Karnataka; tel: 0484-301 1711; www.cghearth.com
  A five-star spa at a five-star spot behind sublime Om beach
- **Wildflower Hall Resort**
  Shimla, Himachal Pradesh; tel: 0177-264 8585; www.oberoihotels.com
  Set amid cedar forests, with views of the distant snowcapped Himalayas, Wildflower combines ayurveda with aromatherapy in magnificent surroundings

Yoga and Ayurveda

PLACES

Getting Your Bearings

India is a vast, multifaceted nation, with a complex geography. In the far north, the Himalayan mountains tumble into the great river plains of the Ganges, Yamuna and Punjab. To the west, the Thar Desert straddles the border with Pakistan, while further south, the high tableland of the Deccan Plateau forms the core of peninsular India, which tapers as it approaches the country's southernmost tip at Kaniya Kumari (Cape Comorin).

Delhi, the nation's capital, presides over the northern plains, and Mumbai (Bombay), India's second city, sits on the shores of the Arabian Sea in the southwest. The largest population centre in the far south is Chennai (Madras), on the southeast coast, while Kolkata (Calcutta) dominates the country's northeast, at the head of the Ganges Delta and Bay of Bengal.

Distances between regions in India can be great and journeys long, which is why it makes sense to plan your route in detail before setting off. To help with this process, the cities and towns in the guide are featured in the order in which they tend to be visited.

For ease of reference when using this guide, each region is covered by a dedicated chapter, colour-coded for quick navigation. The north of the country is divided into five sections: Delhi; the Northern Plains; the Northwest Himalaya;

THE NORTHWEST HIMALAYA
Pages 102 – 117

DELHI
Pages 64 – 81

RAJASTHAN AND GUJARAT
Pages 118 – 141

MUMBAI AND CENTRAL INDIA
Pages 142 – 163

GOA
Pages 164 – 177

KARNATAKA AND ANDHRA PRADESH
Pages 202 – 217

KERALA AND LAKSHADWEEP
Pages 234 – 247

Rajasthan and Gujarat; and Kolkata and Northeast India. Central India, along with Mumbai, is featured in another chapter, while the south is covered in four parts: Goa; Karnataka and Andhra Pradesh; Tamil Nadu and the Andaman Islands; and, finally, Kerala and Lakshadweep. Detailed regional maps are found at the beginning of each chapter.

NORTHERN PLAINS
Pages 82 – 101

KOLKATA AND NORTHEAST INDIA
Pages 178 – 201

MUMBAI AND CENTRAL INDIA
Pages 142 – 163

Additionally, every chapter provides in-depth information on what to expect in the region it covers. A listing index is located at the end of each section identifying the best hotels, restaurants and activities. The listings cater to all budgets, from shoestring travel to high-end luxury.

TAMIL NADU AND THE ANDAMAN ISLANDS
Pages 218 – 233

Delhi

Appropriately for a county as culturally mixed as India, the nation's capital, Delhi, is a true melting pot, with a population of 15 million drawn from all four corners of the subcontinent. Today's metropolis, sandwiched between a spur of the Aravalli Hills and the Yamuna River, is merely the latest, however, in a succession of cities dating back at least 3,000 years.

Delhi

Population: 15 million (21.5 million in Greater Delhi area)

Local Dialling Code: 011

Local Tourist Office: Government of India Tourist Office: Janpath; tel: 011-2332 0008; www.incredibleindia.org

Hospitals: All India Institute of Medical Sciences: Ansari Nagar East, Gautam Nagar, New Delh; tel: 011-26588500; www.aiims.edu.

24-hour emergency ambulance: East West Medical Centre: B-28 Greater Kailash I; tel: 011-2469 9229; www.eastwestrescue.com

Postal Service: GPO, on intersection of BKS Marg and Ashoka Road

Media: The listings magazine *Time Out* has its own dedicated Delhi edition, available at newsstands across the city, and also published online at www.timeoutdelhi.net

From the Mauryans in the 3rd century BC and the Sultanates of the medieval era to the Moghuls and, finally, the British, each of Delhi's conquerors has left their own impressive remains, and these stand today in often surreal juxtaposition to the modern urban sprawl.

Growth has accelerated at an exponential rate since Independence, with seemingly little or no attention to central planning. This has meant all manner of discomforts for its inhabitants: appalling pollution, water and electricity shortages and illegal construction, to name but a few.

The new millennium, however, has marked a renaissance for the Indian capital, now regarded as one of the most forward-looking and best-run cities in India. Pollution has been reduced (thanks to a ban on diesel for public transport vehicles), illegal slums cleared and a state-of-the-art new metro system built. Mumbai may remain the financial hub, but Delhi is where the country's wealthy elite – its leading industrialists and designers, as well as its writers, artists and musicians – all want to live. The new affluence has spawned a booming retail sector, too, with a swathe of glossy new malls and chic boutiques spreading southwards towards the state boundary in tandem with luxury housing projects.

OLD DELHI

In the 17th century, the Mughal emperor Shah Jahan shifted his capital from Agra to the area now known as 'Old Delhi' – calling it 'Shajanabad.' The British laid waste to much of the old walled city in the wake of the 1857 uprising, and today little remains of the once sophisticated, Indo-Muslim culture that formerly held sway here, but it is still a fascinating district to explore. Labyrinthine, hectic and teeming with traffic, the bazaars of Old Delhi form one of the most densely populated neighbourhoods in India – an inexhaustible storehouse of intense local colour, sounds and smells.

In addition to their historical interest, the grounds of the Red Fort are a pleasant place to spend time

The Red Fort

Dominating Old Delhi, the **Red Fort** Ⓐ (Lal Qila; Tue–Sun 9am–6pm; charge) was built by Shah Jahan as the centrepiece of his new capital. Considerable damage was inflicted on the citadel and its palatial apartments inside by successive invaders (not least the British in 1857), but the surviving monuments still vividly conjour up the splendour of the Mughal court. *(See walking tour of the site on p.70.)*

Raj Ghat

Overlooking the Jamuna River to the southeast of the Red Fort is **Raj Ghat** (daily Apr–Sept 5am–7.30pm, Oct Mar 5.30am–7pm; free), where a simple memorial marks the place Mohandas K Gandhi was cremated. The **Gandhi Memorial Museum** (Gandhi Smarak Sangrahalaya; Tue–Sat and every other Sun; free) houses a display of Gandhi's personal belongings and library of recordings of his speeches.

Further north, Shanti Vana is another important national monument where members of the Nehru dynasty were cremated.

> **Victorian Vandals**
>
> Mongols and Persians were not the only plunderers to vandalise Delhi. Most of the Red Fort's palace apartments were dismantled by the British to build army barracks after recapturing the city from the 'mutineers' in 1857. This officially sanctioned vandalism has to be understood within the context of the vindictive climate that reigned after the mutiny. Some of the more enlightened viceroys did their best to make amends in order to protect and restore India's patrimony. But Lord Curzon and other officials often had to contend with philistine circuit judges, who thought nothing of whitewashing or plastering over frescoes in a Mughal mausoleum while turning it into a rest house.

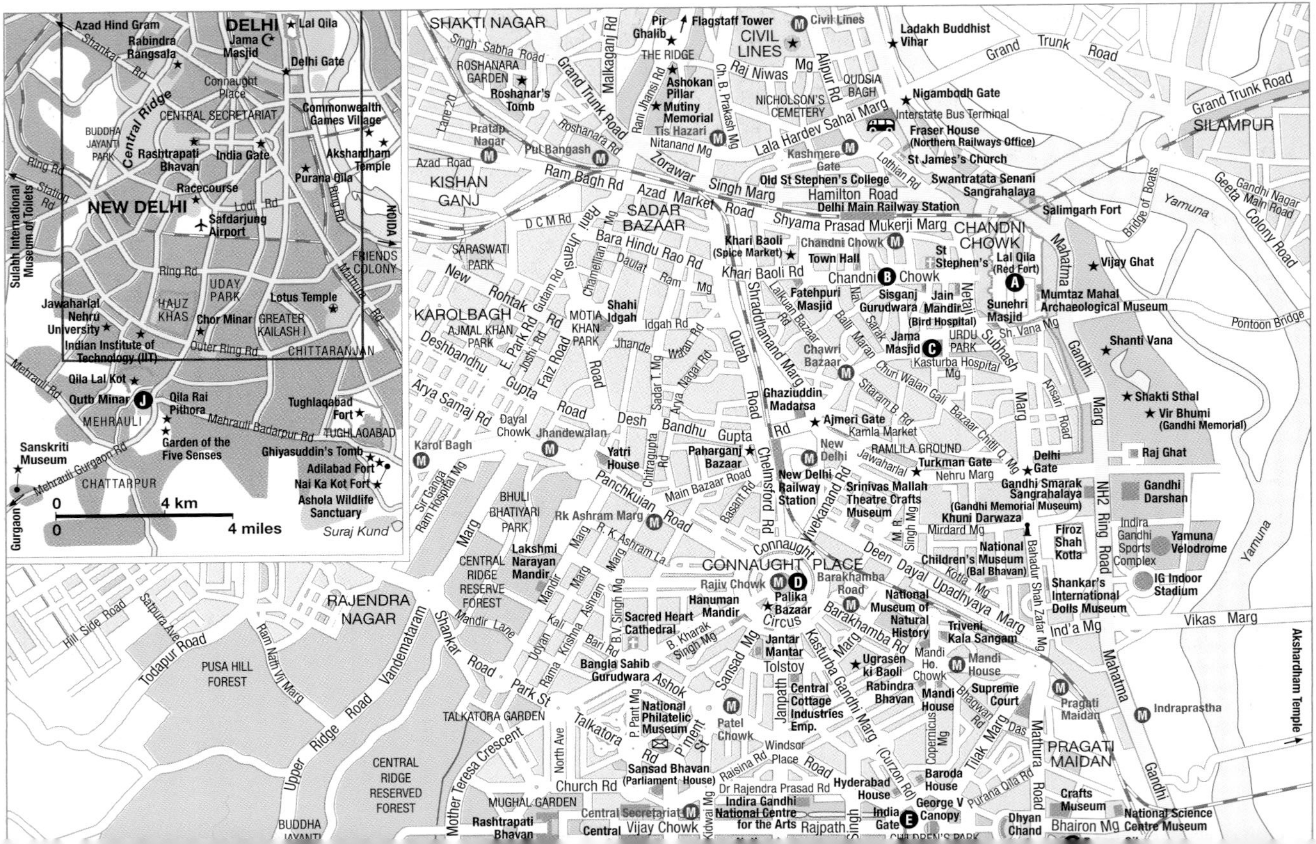

Azad Hind Gram
Rabindra Rangsala
Shankar Rd
DELHI
Jama Masjid
Lal Qila
Delhi Gate
Connaught Place
Central Ridge
CENTRAL SECRETARIAT
Commonwealth Games Village
Akshardham Temple
BUDDHA JAYANTI PARK
Rashtrapati Bhavan
India Gate
Purana Qila
Ring Rd
Station Rd
Racecourse
Lodi Rd
NEW DELHI
Safdarjung Airport
NOIDA
Sulabh International Museum of Toilets
FRIENDS COLONY
Mathura Rd
UDAY PARK
HAUZ KHAS
Lotus Temple
Jawaharlal Nehru University
Chor Minar
GREATER KAILASH I
Indian Institute of Technology (IIT)
Outer Ring Rd
CHITTARANJAN
Mehrauli Rd
Qila Lal Kot
Qutb Minar
Qila Rai Pithora
Tughlaqabad Fort
MEHRAULI
Mehrauli Badarpur Rd
TUGHLAQABAD
Sanskriti Museum
Garden of the Five Senses
Ghiyasuddin's Tomb
Mehrauli Gurgaon Rd
Adilabad Fort
CHATTARPUR
Nai Ka Kot Fort
Ashola Wildlife Sanctuary
Gurgaon
0
4 km
0
4 miles
Suraj Kund
SHAKTI NAGAR
Singh Sabha Road
ROSHANARA GARDEN
Roshanar's Tomb
Grand Trunk Road
Malkaganj Rd
Pir Ghalib
THE RIDGE
Flagstaff Tower
CIVIL LINES
Civil Lines
Ladakh Buddhist Vihar
Grand Trunk Road
Lane 20
Rani Jhansi Rd
Ashokan Pillar
Mutiny Memorial
Ch. B. Prakash Mg
Raj Niwas Mg
Alipur Rd
QUDSIA BAGH
NICHOLSON'S CEMETERY
Nigambodh Gate
Interstate Bus Terminal
SILAMPUR
Pratap Nagar
Roshanara Rd
Tis Hazari
Nitanand Mg
Lala Hardev Sahai Marg
Kashmere Gate
Fraser House (Northern Railways Office)
St James's Church
Azad Road
Pul Bangash
Ram Bagh Rd
Zorawar Singh Marg
Lothian Rd
Swantratata Senani Sangrahalaya
Old St Stephen's College
Hamilton Road
Delhi Main Railway Station
Salimgarh Fort
Bridge of Boats
Yamuna
Geeta Colony Road
Gandhi Nagar Main Road
KISHAN GANJ
Azad Market Road
SADAR BAZAAR
Shyama Prasad Mukerji Marg
CHANDNI CHOWK
D C M Rd
Rani Jhansi Rd
Bara Hindu Rao Rd
Khari Baoli (Spice Market)
Chandni Chowk
Town Hall
St Stephen's
Lal Qila (Red Fort)
Mahatma Gandhi Marg
Vijay Ghat
SARASWATI PARK
New Rohtak Rd
Chamelian Mg
Daulat Ram Mg
Khari Baoli Rd
Chandni Chowk
KAROLBAGH
AJMAL KHAN PARK
Gutam Rd
MOTIA KHAN PARK
Shahi Idgah
Fatehpuri Masjid
Sisganj Gurudwara
Jain Mandir (Bird Hospital)
Netaji Subhash Marg
Sunehri Masjid
Mumtaz Mahal Archaeological Museum
Pontoon Bridge
Deshbandhu Gupta Road
E. Park Rd
Joshi Rd
Faiz Road
Idgah Rd
Jhande Walan Rd
Lalkuan Bazaar Rd
Balli Maran
Sarak
Jama Masjid
URDU PARK
Sh. Vana Mg
Shanti Vana
Arya Samaj Rd
Sadar T. Mg
Arya Nagar Rd
Qutab Road
Shraddhanand Marg
Chawri Bazaar
Kasturba Hospital Mg
Ansari Road
Ghaziuddin Madarsa
Churi Walan Gali
Sitaram B. Rd
Bazaar Chitli Q. Mg
Shakti Sthal
Vir Bhumi (Gandhi Memorial)
Dayal Chowk
Jhandewalan
Desh Bandhu Gupta Rd
Ajmeri Gate
Kamla Market
Karol Bagh
Yatri House
Chitragupta Rd
Paharganj Bazaar
Chelmsford Rd
New Delhi
RAMLILA GROUND
Jawaharlal Nehru Marg
Turkman Gate
Delhi Gate
Raj Ghat
Sir Ganga Ram Hospital Mg
Panchkuian Road
Main Bazaar Road
New Delhi Railway Station
Vivekanand Rd
Srinivas Mallah Theatre Crafts Museum
Gandhi Smarak Sangrahalaya (Gandhi Memorial Museum)
NH2 Ring Road
Gandhi Darshan
BHULI BHATIYARI PARK
Rk Ashram Marg
Basant Rd
M. R. Singh Mg
Khuni Darwaza
Mirdard Mg
Firoz Shah Kotla
Indira Gandhi Sports Complex
Yamuna Velodrome
Lakshmi Narayan Mandir
R. K. Ashram La.
Connaught Circus
Deen Dayal Upadhyaya Marg
National Children's Museum (Bal Bhavan)
Kotla Mg
Bahadur Shah Zafar Mg
CENTRAL RIDGE RESERVE FOREST
Mandir Marg
CONNAUGHT PLACE
Rajiv Chowk
Palika Bazaar
Barakhamba Road
National Museum of Natural History
Shankar's International Dolls Museum
IG Indoor Stadium
RAJENDRA NAGAR
Hanuman Mandir
Vikas Marg
Ind'a Mg
Mandir Lane
Kali Bari Rd
B.V. Singh Mg
Sacred Heart Cathedral
Barakhamba Rd
Triveni Kala Sangam
Satpura Ave
Hill Side Road
Shankar Road
Udyan Marg
Krishna Ashram Marg
B. Kharak Singh Mg
Jantar Mantar
Tolstoy Marg
Mandi Ho. Chowk
Mandi House
Akshardham Temple
Todapur Road
Ram Nath Vij Marg
Vandemataram Road
Rama Krishna Ashram Marg
Bangla Sahib Gurudwara
Ashok Rd
Sansad Mg
Ugrasen ki Baoli
Rabindra Bhavan
Mandi House
Supreme Court
Pragati Maidan
Mahatma Gandhi
Indraprastha
PUSA HILL FOREST
Park St
National Philatelic Museum
Patel Chowk
Janpath
Central Cottage Industries Emp.
Kasturba Gandhi Marg
Bhagwan Das Rd
Tilak Marg
Copernicus Mg
Mathura Road
PRAGATI MAIDAN
Upper Ridge Road
TALKATORA GARDEN
Talkatora Rd
P. Pant Mg
P. ment St
Windsor Place
Raisina Rd
Road
(Curzon Rd)
Purana Qila Rd
CENTRAL RIDGE RESERVED FOREST
Mother Teresa Crescent
North Ave
Church Rd
Sansad Bhavan (Parliament House)
Dr Rajendra Prasad Rd
Hyderabad House
Baroda House
George V Canopy
Crafts Museum
MUGHAL GARDEN
Central Secretariat
Indira Gandhi National Centre for the Arts
India Gate
Dhyan Chand
Bhairon Mg
National Science Centre Museum
Rashtrapati Bhavan
Central Vijay Chowk
Kidwai Mg
Rajpath
Singh
BUDDHA JAYANTI

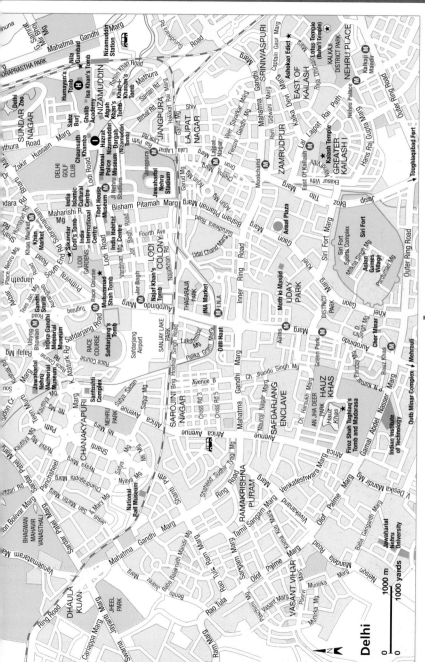

Delhi

0
0

1000 m
1000 yards

Chandni Chowk

Chandni Chowk is the main road leading through the heart of Shahjahanabad, the Moghuls' former capital. This now busy, crowded and noisy road was once an elegant boulevard with a canal running along its centre. Each street leading off the main road has its own speciality for sale: silver and gold at **Dariba Kalan**, wedding paraphernalia and theatrical props at **Kinari Bazaar**, and a fascinating wholesale spice market at **Naya Bazaar**, part of Khari Baoli. On Chandni Chowk itself is the **Digambara Temple**, the oldest Jain temple in Delhi, and the **Bird Hospital** (Jain Mandir), where injured birds are nursed back to health.

The Jama Masjid

Rising from an outcrop of rock southwest of Chandi Chowk is Shah Jahan's other landmark construction, the red-and-white striped **Jama Masjid** (Sat–Thur 8.30am–12.30pm and 2–4.30pm, Fri 8–11am and 2–4.30pm; free, cameras Rs200). Built in the mid-17th century, it's the largest mosque in India, with capacity inside its vast 100-sq-m (1,076-sq-ft) courtyard for

Delhi Transport

 Airports: Indira Gandhi International (IGI) Airport (**www.newdelhiairport.in**), the hub for both domestic and international services, lies 20km (12 miles) south of the centre. It has three terminals. The easiest route into town from all of them is to take the new high-speed metro line. Tickets for standard, non-a/c prepaid taxis (around Rs300) are on sale at counters inside the arrivals hall. The private firm Easycabs (tel: 011-4343 4343, www.easycabs.com) also has a counter for smarter a/c cars (Rs400–500).

 Metro and Tram: Delhi's ever-expanding metro network is generally the best way to get around the city (www.delhimetrorail.com). Single fares operate by means of a token which you hold by the reader at the start of your journey and feed into the machine at the automatic barrier when you exit the station. Tickets are cheap (Rs8–23), and services run from 6am to 11pm.

 Autorickshaws: While autorickshaws can be the most convenient way to get around the city centre, it is often hard for visitors to negotiate a fair price for their journey. The Delhi Government is wise to the problem and has put an extremely useful fare calculator online (http://delhigovt.nic.in/autofares/Transport.asp), which will give a good idea of what to pay the driver.

 Taxis: Delhi's yellow-and-black taxis are difficult to flag down on the street and are best picked up at their transport company's kiosks, which can be found close to all the main markets or commercial areas. Two companies that are reliable, honest and can be booked by phone are: Mega Cabs: tel: 1929/011-4141 4141 and Quick Cab: 011-4533 3333; http://quickcabs.in.

 Buses: Buses in Delhi are very crowded, if cheap. Stick to government-run services, safer and more reliable than other operators. The city authority recently ordered an entirely new fleet of modern vehicles to replace the old, rickety vehicles that used to ply the streets.

around 25,000 worshippers. Visitors are welcome to scale one of its magnificent 40m (133ft) -tall minarets (charge) for a stupendous view over the city.

NEW DELHI

Faithful to the policy of separating the British cantonment from the Indian quarters with a railway as the barrier, the new city built for the empire's Indian seat of government is separated from Old Delhi by the Amritsar to Agra line. British neoclassical architecture here is mixed with elements of the Buddhist, Hindu and Mughal past, and the geometry of its plan exudes the self-confidence of the empire. As a visiting statesman once said of it: 'What splendid ruins it will make!'

Connaught Place and Jantar Mantar

The circular shopping arcade of **Connaught Place** (properly Rajiv Chowk) **D** forms the heart of modern Delhi. The colonnaded corridors were built for the British to shop in style. Concentric roads create an Inner, Middle and Outer Circle lined with shops, restaurants, street stalls and cinemas. The underground **Palika Bazaar** has tiny shops overflowing with tourist tat and touts.

To the southwest along Sansad Marg (Parliament Street) stands the red sandstone **Jantar Mantar** (daily sunrise–sunset; charge ), an open-air observatory built by Maharaja Jai Singh I of Jaipur. Constructed in 1724, it was the first of several observatories the ruler subsequently built around India.

69

Delhi

Rajpath

The principal axis of the British imperial capital was **Rajpath**, a kilometre (half a mile) or so southeast of Connaught Place. Surrounded by lawns and shady trees, Delhi's 'Champs Elysées' has its own 'Arc de Triomphe' in the stately form of **India Gate E**, a 42m (138ft) -high archway built by Edwin Lutyens in 1931 to honour Indian soldiers who died during World War I and on the Northwest Frontier (there's also an 'eternal flame' to commemorate those killed in the 1971 war with Pakistan).

Rashtrapati Bhavan, the presidential residence (former Viceregal Lodge), can be seen at the western end of Rajpath with the circular **Parliament House** (Sansad Bhavan)

🚶 RED FORT

The mighty Red Fort (Lal Qila), inaugurated in 1648, was the most grandiloquent building erected by emperor Shah Jahan in his new capital. This walk leads you through the historic highlights of the complex.

Inside the red sandstone ramparts of the Red Fort survives a campus of beautiful colonnaded halls and domed apartments with cusp-arched windows overlooking the Jamuna, which, in spite of the depredations inflicted on them by Persian and British troops over the centuries, still bear witness to the refinement and sophistication of Mughal Delhi at its height. The complex was granted Unesco World Heritage status in 2007.

The main entrance is **Lahori Gate**, on the west side of the complex, facing Chandni Chowk. Each year on 15 August, Independence Day, prime ministers traditionally raise the Indian tricolour from a flagpole atop its crenellated ramparts. Once inside, you emerge at **Chatta Chowk**, formerly a covered bazaar where the Mughal nobility bought jewellery, silks and carpets; its stalls nowadays stock souvenirs.

At the far end of Chatta Chowk, the **Drum House** (Naubhat Khana) is where musicians used to regale guests and members of the royal household as they entered the fort. Walk around the building and follow the main pathway across the open space beyond it to the **Hall of Public Audiences** (Diwan-i-Am), in which the emperor used to hold court. Twelve marble panels inlaid with precious stones once surrounded the throne canopy, including one showing the god Orpheus, which was looted by a British soldier but later restored to its rightful place by the viceroy, Lord Curzon.

Follow the pathway arcing right from the Hall and you'll arrive at the **Mumtaz Mahal**, formerly the princesses' quarters, where a small archaeological

The elaborate Hall of Public Audiences

Tips

- Avoid weekends, when the fort gets uncomfortably crowded
- Time your tour to coincide with the dramatic sound and light show that takes place here nightly (except Mon), starting just after sunset (Nov–Jan 7.30pm, Feb–Apr and Sept–Oct 8.30pm, May–Aug 9pm; charge)
- Bring plenty of mosquito repellent if you come around dusk
- Don't discard your ticket on entering; you'll need it to enter the museums

Start your tour at the distinctive Lahori Gate

museum now displays Mughal manuscripts, miniature paintings, textiles, weapons and carpets.

Turn right out of the museum and follow the path running north, parallel with the fort's east wall, to reach the **Palace of Colours** (Rang Mahal), where the emperors' chief wives resided. Most of the exquisite gold leaf and mirror mosaic work embellishing the interior surfaces of the building were vandalised while it served as a British officers' mess in the 19th century, but the lotus-shaped marble carving on the central floor remains intact.

Next door stands the similar **Khas Mahal**, formerly the emperor's personal quarters, where he slept and prayed. Just beyond that on the same path lies the **Hall of Private Audiences** (Diwan-i-Khas), a white-marble pavilion in which Shah Jahan and his successors would consult with their ministers and nobles. This was where the famous solid-gold and gem-encrusted Peacock Throne rested until Nadir Shah carried it back to Persia as booty in 1739.

Turn right on leaving the Diwan-i-Khas and follow the path around to the white marble **Pearl Mosque** (Moti Masjid), built in 1659 by Shah

Jahan's son, Aurangzeb. From there you can continue north across the Hayat Bakksh Bagh, the last surviving formal Mughal garden in the fort, to the three-storey **Shahi Burj** pavilion at the top of the east wall, originally a pumping house supplying water from the river below.

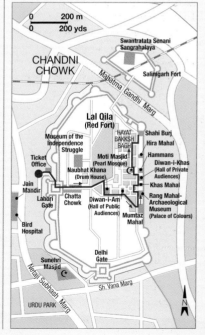

nearby. The huge formal Mughal-style gardens of Rashtrapati Bhavan are among the finest in Delhi but are only open to the public a few times a year (usually in Jan and Feb; ask at any local tourist office for precise dates).

The Museums

The area around Rajpath contains a wealth of museums. Just south of Rajpath, on Janpath, the **National Museum** ⑤ (www.nationalmuseum india.gov.in; Tue–Sun 10am–5pm; charge) is noted for its Indian sculpture and jewellery collections, Chola bronzes and a Buddhist gallery, including a carved Buddhist gateway from Sanchi. Among the most important artefacts here are those from the Harappan excavations at Mohenjadaro (including the famous small bronze statue of a dancing girl) and the holdings of Mughal manuscripts and miniatures.

Railway buffs will enjoy the open-air **National Rail Museum** (www. nationalrailmuseum.org; Tue–Sun 9.30am–5pm; charge), in the diplomatic neighbourhood of Chanakyapuri, southwest of Rajpath. Pride of place among its matchless collection of antique locomotives and carriages is the *Fairy Queen*, the world's oldest working steam engine.

The **Crafts Museum** (Tue–Sun July–Sept 9.30am–5pm, Oct–June 9.30am–6pm; free 🅜) on Bhairon Marg by Pragati Maidan holds fascinating displays of Adivasi art, woodcarving and textiles. The textile galleries are superb, with over 22,000 objects, as well as some astounding embroidery, especially the Kashmiri examples.

SOUTH DELHI

South Delhi's architecture charts the full span of the city's long history, from its prehistoric roots to the imperial grandeur of the British capital, and high-rise modernity of the present day. Made up of broad, tree-lined boulevards, it's a far more relaxing

Explore India's rich history at the National Museum

The Sher Mandal pavilion, in the grounds of the Purana Qila

proportioned Sher Mandal pavilion, set in beautifully maintained gardens, was used as a library by the Mughal emperor Humayun and was where he fell to his death in 1555.

Humayan's Tomb

Made from a delicate combination of buff-and-red sandstone and smart, grey-trimmed white marble, **Humayun's tomb** (daily sunrise to sunset; charge) ranks among the most splendid in Asia. It stands on a raised terrace amid walled, tree-shaded lawns, a short walk south of the Purana Qila. With a majestic dome uniting the four octagonal kiosks over the terrace's latticed arches, this is the first fully-realised masterpiece of Mughal architecture.

area to explore than the north, with numerous walled tomb gardens to lounge in during the heat of the day.

Purana Qila

The stately red ramparts of the **Purana Qila** , or fort (daily sunrise to sunset; charge) rise to the east of India Gate, on the site of what is thought to have been Indraprastha, the city featured in the ancient Sanskrit epic, the *Mahabharata*. The citadel surviving today was built by Afghan ruler Sher Shah Suri (1540–5) but taken over by the Mughal emperor Humayun when he regained the throne in 1555–6. Its Qila-e-Kunha Masjid is the best-preserved Lodi mosque in Delhi. The well-

Take a Breather

South Delhi holds a couple of delightfully atmospheric places to catch your breath between bouts of sightseeing. Ten minutes further west of the Nizamuddin *dargah*, the beautiful **Lodi Gardens** (sunrise–sunset; free) harbour a clutch of fascinating 14th- and 15th-century tombs set in well-maintained lawns, lined with flower beds and immense trees where people picnic in the shade. Nearby, at the end of Lodi Road, **Safdarjang's Tomb** (daily sunrise to sunset; charge) is a still more flamboyant specimen of late Mughal architecture, also set in beautiful gardens. It dates from 1753 and was the last significant tomb to be built in Delhi.

QUTB MINAR

The Qutb Minar victory tower is one of south Asia's most iconic landmarks, but is only one among a bumper crop of exquisitely decorated monuments, dating from the dawn of Indo-Muslim culture in the subcontinent.

Walk through the **main entrance** to the site and follow the walkway with the Mughal Garden to your right, keeping straight ahead when the road bends left. Stay on the main path, but when the lawn on your left ends, turn right to reach the decaying rubble core of the **Alai Minar**, a victory tower originally intended by its creator, Sultan Khalji Ala-ud-din, to be taller than the Qutb Minar, but which was never completed.

With the Alai Minar behind you, walk back across the four-lawned (*char bagh*) enclosure in the rough direction

of the Qutb Minar, but veer left before you reach it to the diminutive domed **Tomb of Imam Zamin**, in the bottom corner of the complex. Finished in polished white plaster, the interior is noteworthy for its splendid pierced-stone windows.

From the tomb, walk through the adjacent **Alai Darwaza**, a spectacular arched, domed gateway with intricately latticed stone *jali* screens and marble inlay, and out the other side, following the path until you reach an opening in the wall to your right. On the far side of this you'll see the **Qutb Minar** again. Tapering to a height of just over 72m (240ft), the edifice was built by Sultan Qutb-ud-din to celebrate his defeat of Delhi's last Hindu rulers in 1193. Each of its five storeys, ringed by projecting balconies and encrusted with elaborate Koranic inscriptions, was constructed at different times: the uppermost had to

The Qutb Minar victory tower

Tips

- Avoid weekends, when the site gets very crowded
- If you're a keen photographer, come soon after the complex opens, or towards the end of the day, to catch the red sandstone at its most alluring
- A new metro line runs as far as the Qutb Minar from central Delhi – this is the easiest approach
- Check with the tourist office on Janpath for the dates of the Qutb Minar Festival, a music and dance extravaganza held in late October– early November

be entirely rebuilt by the British in 1803 after an earthquake caused it to topple.

Diagonally opposite the Qutb Minar stand the crumbling remains of the **Quwwat-ul-Islam Masjid**, which served as Delhi's principal mosque for most of the 13th and 14th centuries. Go through its southern entrance to reach a spacious inner courtyard, where the famous **Iron Pillar** (Gupta) continues to draw crowds of admirers, even though it is these days enclosed behind a fence (an old saying asserts that anyone able to encircle the column with their arms would have their wish granted, which used to ensure a constant stream of eroding hugs).

Retrace your steps back towards the Qutb Minar, but before reaching the tower, turn to your right and head through the ruined perimeter walls of the **Allaudin Madrasa**, built in 1303 by Sultan Ala-ud-din Khilji as a religious college.

Inside the Quwwat-ul-Islam Masjid

Having explored the ruins, head across the lawns in front of them and continue north along the foot of the Quwwat-ul-Islam Masjid's west wall to the **Tomb of Iltutmish**, visible ahead, to the west of the Alai Minar. Behind the mausoleum's relatively plain exterior is hidden a wealth of ornately carved calligraphy, geometric patterns and lotus motifs – an appropriately impressive flourish on which to end this tour.

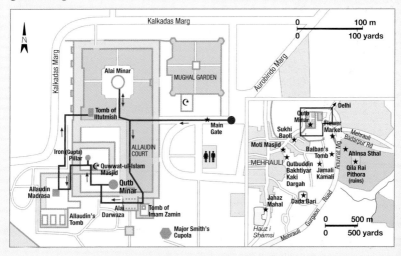

Hazrat Nizamuddin Dargah and Mughal Tombs

To the west of Humayun's Tomb lies the **Hazrat Nizamuddin Dargah** ❶, the shrine of the saint of the Chisti order, Sheikh Nizamuddin Aulia (1236–1325), after whom the surrounding colonies are named. A venue for all-night performances of Qawwali on Thursdays, the mausoleum forms an oasis of traditional Sufi culture in the thick of the modern metropolis. The actual grave of the saint is in a pavilion with beautiful marble screens (women are not allowed to venture beyond these into the inner shrine).

Qutb Minar

The remains of the first Muslim city constructed in the Delhi area stand 13km(8 miles) south of the modern centre in the **Qutb Minar** ❶ complex (daily sunrise to sunset; charge). Its centrepiece, acclaimed in Victorian times as one of the 'Wonders of the East', is a fluted, red sandstone victory tower; this is known as the actual Qutb Minar. Other famous monuments in the complex include an ancient **iron pillar** dating from the reign of Chandragupta II (375–413AD) and the building believed to be India's first mosque, the **Quwwat-ul-Islam Masjid**, built by Qutb-ud-din from the remnants of 27 temples. *(See p.74 for a walking tour of the site.)*

Akshardham Temple

The glittering new **Akshardham Temple** (www.akshardham.com; daily 9am–6pm; free 🅼), a Rs75 auto rickshaw ride from Connaught Place on the east side of the Yamuna River, is Delhi's most extravagant – and most visited – monument. Built in 2005 by the Gujarat-based Shri Swaminarayan sect, it's a modern take on traditional Hindu architecture, comprising a sumptuously carved pink-sandstone and white-marble shrine set in a huge walled garden. Once you've admired the temple, you can drift through a series of audio animatronic shows, mythological movies projected on giant screens, boat rides and musical fountains – a fascinating insight into contemporary Hinduism.

Akshardham Temple is one of Delhi's newest monuments

ACCOMMODATION

Delhi's hotels, which run the gamut from cheap guesthouses to five-star luxury temples, regularly sell out during the winter season, so if you are coming between September and March be sure to book your room ahead of time. Bear in mind that many of the more expensive hotels offer their best rates online.

Old Delhi

The Maidens Hotel
7 Sham Nath Marg, Old Delhi
Tel: 011-2397 5464
www.maidenshotel.com
A stately heritage hotel located in Old Delhi. Open since 1903, it was once the first choice of visiting bigwigs, before Lutyens developed the imperial capital. Large rooms, attentive service and competitive rates. **$$$$$**

Wongdhen House
15A New Tibetan Colony, Manju-ka-Tilla
Tel: 011-2381 6689
wongdhenhouse@hotmail.com
About 2km (1 mile) north of Old Delhi, the predominantly Tibetan colony of Manju-ka-Tilla offers a more peaceful range of backpacker accommodation than Pahar Ganj. This is the most popular place in the neighbourhood; its rooms are a bit gloomy, but clean and good value. **$**

New Delhi

The Aman
Lodi Road, Nizamuddin West
Tel: 011-4363 3333
www.amanresorts.com
Über-chic designer hotel with stone floors, *jali* screen windows, and private plunge-pools in some of the rooms, with a state-of-the-art spa on site. **$$$$$**

Bajaj Indian Home Stay
8A/34 WEA, Karol Bagh
Tel: 011-2573 6509
www.bajajindianhomestay.com
Promising an experience that's 'Indian, altogether', this place prides itself on its homely ambience. With 10 rooms it is a little bigger than the usual home stay but it still stands out from the crowd, and the rooms are spotlessly clean. **$$$$**

Imperial Hotel
1 Janpath, New Delhi
Tel: 011-2334 1234
www.theimperialindia.com
Built in 1933, this was the only hotel included in Lutyens' plans for the Imperial capital, and it still oozes high colonial style: huge palm trees flanking the entrance and lithographs from the owner's private collection on the walls. **$$$$$**

Lutyens Bungalow
39 Prithviraj Road
Tel: 011-2461 1341
www.lutyensbungalow.co.in
Set in a Lutyens-designed bungalow on one of the capital's most exclusive roads, this 15-room guesthouse retains the building's original charm, has a very friendly but unobtrusive feel and a swimming pool in the lovely gardens. A real chance to experience part of New Delhi's history at first hand; be sure to book well in advance. **$$$$$**

The Lutyens Bungalow is a great place to stay

Rak International
Tooti Chowk, 820 Main Bazaar, Paharganj
Tel: 011-2358 6508
One of the more dependable options in this
budget traveller enclave, with good-sized,
clean rooms and a pleasant rooftop terrace. **$**

YWCA Blue Triangle Family Hostel
Ashoka Rd
Tel: 011-2336 2975
www.ywcaindia.org
A recommended and safe place to stay for
both sexes, in a handy location. The spotless
a/c rooms come inclusive of breakfast at the
very good restaurant. Profits go towards a
project helping women in India. **$$$**

South Delhi
Ahuja Residency
193 Golf Links
Tel: 011-2462 2255
www.ahujaresidency.com
Clean, friendly, quiet and relaxing, this well-
located guesthouse is one of Delhi's hidden
gems. Great value; book well in advance. **$$$**

Amarya Haveli
P5 Hauz Khas Enclave
Tel: 011-4175 9268
www.amaryagroup.com
Stylish, French-owned boutique guesthouse
in a leafy district. The decor blends contemporary Indian chic with European comfort. **$$$$**

Jorbagh '27'
27 Jorbagh
Tel: 011-2469 8647
www.jorbagh27.com
Run more as a hotel then a guesthouse, this
18-room properly lacks some of the charm of
more homely places, but is well run, clean and
near the Lodi Gardens, a real bonus. **$$$**

LaSagrita
14 Sunder Nagar
Tel: 011-2435 9541
www.lasagrita.com
In a quiet residential area, this homely guest-
house offers en suite rooms with comfortable
beds. The staff are great, the food good and
rates excellent value. **$$$–$$$$**

Master Paying Guest House
R-500 New Rajendar Nagar
Tel: 011-2874 1089
www.master-guesthouse.com
Small and sweet with just four rooms, and
run by a very helpful couple. There is a nice
common area including a library created by
the guests. Recommended. **$$$**

RESTAURANTS

Regional cuisines from around India form
the backbone of the capital's thriving
and reasonably priced restaurant scene.
While you're in the city, be sure to sample
Delhi's own distinctive 'Mughlai' cooking
style, which makes use of the tandoor
oven and yoghurt and spice marinades.

Restaurant Price Categories

Prices are for a standard meal
for one, excluding alcoholic
drinks

$ = up to Rs200
$$ = Rs200–500
$$$ = Rs500–1000
$$$$ = over Rs1000

Old Delhi
Chor Bizarre
Hotel Broadway, 4/15A Asaf Ali Road
Tel: 011-4336 3600
www.chorbizarrerestaurant.com
Reliably delicious Mughlai and Kashmiri fare
in quirky surroundings, such as the salad

buffet being housed in a classic car. Reser-
vations recommended. **$$$**

Karim's
Gali Kebabiyan (just south of Jama Masjid)
Tel: 011-2326 4981
www.karimhoteldelhi.com

In the delightful Lodi The Garden Restaurant

'Secret of good mood, taste of Karim's food' says the menu, and judging by the number of satisfied customers, they can't be far wrong. This is hearty Mughlai cuisine for meat-lovers – vegetarians after anything more than *dal* will be disappointed. **$$**

New Delhi

Bukhara
Sheraton Maurya Hotel, Sardar Patel Marg
Tel: 011-2611 2233
Long-established king of Northwest Frontier cuisine, catering chiefly to the carnivore with melt-in-the-mouth dishes. Advance bookings essential, especially at weekends. **$$$$**

Havemore
11–12 Pandara Road Market
Tel: 011-2338 7070
One of the best of the handful of upmarket *dhabas* in Pandara Market, with a good selection of Indian veg dishes and a handy location just south of India Gate. **$**

Metropolis
Metropolis Hotel, 1634 Main Bazaar, Paharganj
Tel: 011-5154 1395
This popular rooftop restaurant is one of the most reliable places to eat in Paharganj, serving up north Indian fare, plus assorted European offerings and cheap cold beer. **$–$$**

Saravana Bhavan
46 Janpath
Tel: 011-2331 7755
One of a chain of excellent south Indian vegetarian restaurants, with good *dosas* and *thalis*. Very clean and good value. **$$**

The Spice Route
Imperial Hotel, 1 Janpath
Tel: 011-2334 1234
Superb restaurant, decorated with wooden carvings. Fabulous, if pricey, Sri Lankan and Southeast Asian food. **$$$–$$$$**

United Coffee House
E15 Connaught Place
Tel: 011-2341 1697
The food is only part of the attraction here – it's the original cake-icing decor and the ambience that set this place apart. Equally popular with locals and travellers. **$**

Véda
H27 Outer Circle, Connaught Place
Tel: 011-4151 3535
With decor from one of Delhi's leading fashion designers, the candlelit, Baroque-style interior sets this place apart. The food represents the whole of India rather than just the north. **$$$**

South Delhi

Lodi The Garden Restaurant
Lodi Gardens, Lodi Road
Tel: 011-2465 5054
This restaurant has a beautiful location in Lodi Gardens. The expansive terrace is the biggest draw, although the Mediterranean and Lebanese food comes a close second. **$$**

Punjabi by Nature
11 Basant Lok Complex, Vasant Vihar
Tel: 011-5151 6665
The ultimate in Punjabi and north Indian cuisine, the food at this place gets consistently rave reviews, and is hugely popular with local diners – worth booking ahead. **$$$**

Sagar
18 Defence Colony Market
Tel: 2433 3440
Delhi's most popular south Indian eatery, this place always sees lengthy queues at lunch time. The service is supreme, the food reliably excellent and the prices more than fair. **$$**

Listings

NIGHTLIFE

Delhi's boom generation has plenty of disposable cash to spend, and the city's nightlife reflects this fact, with an ever-increasing number of dance bars and lounge clubs to choose from – most of them in the five-star hotels of the suburbs. Bona fide clubs are more of a rarity, and tend only to open on weekends.

Hip Delhi-ites converge in Q'Ba

1911 Bar
Hotel Imperial, 1 Janpath
Tel: 011-2334 1234
www.theimperialindia.com
Sheer class (in the 'upper' sense), with comfortable sofas overlooking manicured lawns – the perfect spot for a sundowner of gin. Make sure you have your posh togs on.

Agni and Acqua
The Park, 15 Sansad Marg
Tel: 011-2374 3000
www.theparkhotels.com
The Park's fire-themed DJ bar, Agni, is super-stylish, while the poolside bar, Acqua, is more relaxing: have a drink reclined in a gazebo.

Elevate
Centre Stage Mall, Sector 16, NOIDA, on the east bank of the Yamuna River

http://elevateindia.com
Elevate is the only club in Delhi that wouldn't look out of place in the West. Expect a mix of commercial house, hip-hop and trance.

Q'Ba
E42/43, Inner Circle, Connaught Place
Tel: 011-4151 2888
www.qba.co.in
One of the hipper joints in town, with a Q-shaped bar downstairs and dining upstairs, outdoor terraces and a DJ most evenings.

Shalom
N18, Greater Kailash I
Tel: 011-4163 2282
www.shalomexperience.com
One of Delhi's hippest and best-known lounge bars, with chic interiors and great Mediterranean tapas and *meze*. Book on weekends.

ENTERTAINMENT

Film-going is a major pastime in Delhi, but the city also holds dozens of top performing arts venues where you can sample India's innumerable traditional dance and drama styles.

Dances of India
Parsi Anjuman Hall, Bahadur Shah Zafar Marg, near Delhi Gate, Old Delhi
Tel: 011-2623 4689
www.indianfolkdances.com
A mix of classical, tribal and folk dances, including Bharatnatyam and Kathakali.

India Habitat Centre
Lodi Road (near Safdarjang's Tomb)

Tel: 011-2468 2001
www.indiahabitat.org
This pioneering cultural centre hosts frequent performances of traditional and contemporary dance and music from around India.

The Kamani Auditorium
Copernicus Marg, near Mandi House metro
Tel: 4350 3351
www.kamaniauditorium.org

Performances of classical Indian dance and music by the country's leading artistes.

PVR Plaza
Radial Road, Connaught Place
Tel: 011-4151 3787
www.pvrcinemas.com
Gracious old cinema, dating from 1933.

Sangeet Natak Akademi
Rabindra Bhavan,
35 Firoz Shah Road
Tel: 011-2338 7246
www.sangeetnatak.com
Delhi's 'National Academy of Music, Dance and Drama', showcasing India's top classical musicians and dancers.

SPORTS AND TOURS

Delhi is vast, so if you're pressed for time joining an organised city tour makes sense. Individual, government-approved guides can be arranged through the tourist office on Janpath *(see p.64)*. The bagging of the 2010 Commonwealth Games was a major coup for Delhi and has raised the profile in the city of sports other than cricket.

Cricket
Firoz Shah Kotla Stadium
Bahadur Shah Zafar Marg
Tel: 011-2331 9323
One of the smaller and more historic venues for cricket in the country, and nowadays home to the local IPL team, the Delhi Daredevils.

Tennis
Delhi Lawn Tennis Association
R.K. Khanna Tennis Stadium, 1 Africa Avenue
Tel: 011-2619 3955
www.dltatennis.in
DLTA's 21 courts near Haus Khas are open to the public, along with its pool and gym.

Tours
Delhi Magic
Ground Floor, 2 Haus Khas Village
Tel: 98677 07414
www.delhimagic.com
Insightful group or personal tours of the city, by knowledgeable, articulate guides.

Delhi Tourism and Transport Development Corporation (DTTDC)
Baba Kharak Singh Marg
Tel: 011-2336 3607
www.delhitourism.nic.in
Runs tours of New Delhi (9am–2pm; Rs150) and Old Delhi (2.15–5.15pm; Rs150).

Listings

FESTIVALS AND EVENTS

There are hundreds of festivals in Delhi every year, often taking place in only one part of the city, or among one particular community. Those listed are the main events.

January–February
Republic Day
26 January
Marked by a huge parade of military might, folk dancing and bright floats down Rajpath.

Jahan-i-Khusrau
February
Sufi music festival by Humayun's Tomb.

August
Independence Day
15 August
Animated celebrations at the Red Fort.

October
Qutb Festival of Classical Music & Dance
Held at the Qutb Minar complex, with performances from some of India's best artists.

Northern Plains

The northern plains are one of India's most intense and unmissable regions. Between the discipline of Punjab and Haryana's proud Sikhs and the apparent lawlessness of much of Bihar lies Uttar Pradesh, held by many to be the heartland of India – its soul enshrined in the incomparable Taj Mahal, its political polygamy played out in Lucknow, and its religious sentiments laid bare on the burning ghats of Varanasi.

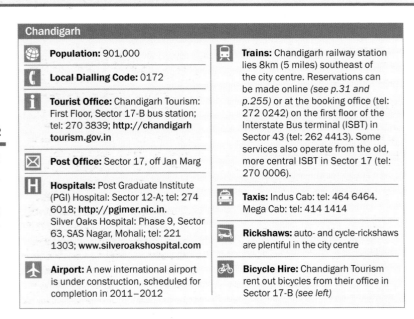

Chandigarh

Population: 901,000

Local Dialling Code: 0172

Tourist Office: Chandigarh Tourism: First Floor, Sector 17-B bus station; tel: 270 3839; http://chandigarh tourism.gov.in

Post Office: Sector 17, off Jan Marg

Hospitals: Post Graduate Institute (PGI) Hospital: Sector 12-A; tel: 274 6018; http://pgimer.nic.in. Silver Oaks Hospital: Phase 9, Sector 63, SAS Nagar, Mohali; tel: 221 1303; www.silveroakshospital.com

Airport: A new international airport is under construction, scheduled for completion in 2011–2012

Trains: Chandigarh railway station lies 8km (5 miles) southeast of the city centre. Reservations can be made online (see p.31 and p.255) or at the booking office (tel: 272 0242) on the first floor of the Interstate Bus terminal (ISBT) in Sector 43 (tel: 262 4413). Some services also operate from the old, more central ISBT in Sector 17 (tel: 270 0006).

Taxis: Indus Cab: tel: 464 6464. Mega Cab: tel: 414 1414

Rickshaws: auto- and cycle-rickshaws are plentiful in the city centre

Bicycle Hire: Chandigarh Tourism rent out bicycles from their office in Sector 17-B (see left)

Heartland of the great Mughal empire, India's northern plains are home to several of the country's most wondrous monuments – including the Taj Mahal and Fatehpur Sikri – as well as its holiest river, the Ganges. From the relative prosperity of Haryana-Punjab, the region grows noticeably poorer as you progress westwards across teeming Uttar Pradesh to the troubled state of Bihar, crucible of the Buddhist faith but nowadays a byword for corruption and poverty.

The rich alluvial soils of India's vast northern plains have nourished large, dense and highly stratified societies for literally thousands of years. Only the most scant remains survive of the ancient empires whose capitals once rose from the banks of the region's immense rivers. But the legacy of these lost civilisations endure in the languages and culture of Haryana-Punjab, Uttar Pradesh and Bihar – home to around 320 million people.

The principal natural feature of the northern plains – worshipped as a nurturing Mother Goddess by Hindus – is the river revered as 'Ma Ganga', the Ganges, which gushes out of the Himalayan foothills at Rishikesh and wends southeast towards its confluence with the region's other main artery, the Jamuna, at Allahabad. From there, the Ganga travels lazily west through the ancient city of Varanasi and to the former seat of the Mauryans, Patna, capital of modern-day Bihar.

PUNJAB AND HARYANA

Riven in two by Partition in 1947, the Punjab was named after the five major tributaries of the Indus flowing through it. Only a couple of these drain through the modern Indian state abutting the Pakistani border, but it still

In Chandigarh's Fantasy Rock Garden

The Hussainabad Imambara in Lucknow
(see p.93)

ranks among the most fertile parts of the country. The people of the region are largely from the Jat ethnic group. Tall, brawny and rugged, the Jats are renowned for their pugnacity and fierce attachment to the soil. Despite comprising only 2 percent of the national population, they have had a disproportionately wide-ranging influence on north Indian music, culture and cuisine, particularly that of Delhi, to which many Punjabi migrants fled in huge numbers from Pakistan after Independence. Neighbouring Haryana state, also a major agricultural contributor, has more recently come to prominence as India's industrial powerhouse. Half of the millions of cars and motorbikes made in India are manufactured here, while Gurgaon, a Singapore-styled satellite city to the south of Delhi, has emerged as a major IT sector player.

Chandigarh

Invited by the Indian government to create a new capital for the post-Partition Punjab, the Swiss-French architect Le Corbusier came up with a plan for a wholly modern city called

Chandigarh ❶, set on a windy plain at the foot of the Himalayas. He designed the leading public buildings and laid out a town of spacious boulevards and sweeping tree-lined avenues, inspired in part by Lutyens' ideas for New Delhi.

While some hail Le Corbusier's grand blueprint as one of the greatest influences on 20th-century urban design, Chandigarh has its fair share of detractors. Many still criticise its appearance as 'un-Indian' and the predominance of concrete as not only unsightly but also ill-suited to the intense heat of the Haryana plains. The buildings boast both geometric and amorphous shapes, with bright colours visible behind the sub-breaker grills.

The most striking modern buildings stand in Le Corbusier's **Capital Complex**, site of the state **Legislature Assembly** and **Secretariat**. Chandigarh's most visited tourist destination, however, is the famous **Fantasy Rock Garden** (daily 9am–6pm; www. nekchand.com; charge 🅼). Begun in 1965 by a Public Works Department

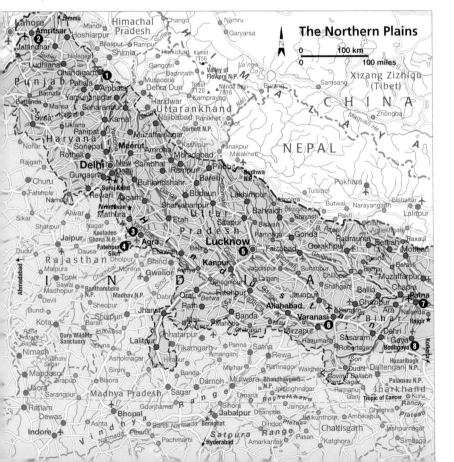

The Northern Plains

Amritsar's Golden Temple is the most important Sikh shrine

road inspector named Nek Chand, the site comprises a maze of walled enclosures, grottoes and flying walkways filled with outlandish sculptures of human figures and animals fashioned entirely from junk. It was originally intended as a small garden but its creator got carried away and his labour of love has since mushroomed into a giant 10-hectare (25-acre) complex, with thousands of statues made from discarded ceramic, rubber, scrap metal and industrial plastic.

Amritsar

The magnificent **Golden Temple** (dawn–about 10pm), holiest shrine of the Sikh faith, stands in the centre of **Amritsar ❷**, capital of Indian Punjab. Built by Guru Arjan Dev in the 16th century, the heart of the complex is the ornately gilded Harmandir. Every Sikh aims to make at least one pilgrimage to the shrine in their lifetime, but its doors are open to all: come early in the morning or around sunset, when the gold colour, reflected in the waters of the Amrit Sarovar (Pool of Immortality Giving Nectar), is most sublime.

In the 1980s, the Golden Temple became infamous as the site of two bloody sieges when Sikh militants agitating for an independent homeland fought pitched battles with the Indian

Border Rituals

The troubled Indo-Pak border runs barely 30km (18 miles) west of Amritsar. The long-standing antipathy between the two great nations is played out daily at the frontier village of **Wagah**, where a ritualised border closing ceremony is enacted each day at sundown. The tallest soldiers from both country's armies perform a series of provocative marches that culminate in the lowering of the flags and the banging shut of the gates, while the crowds on both sides shout patriotic slogans in an almost pantomime atmosphere.

The ceremony starts at 4.15pm sharp each afternoon. The best way to get to Wagah is to take a taxi (Rs600–700) from Amritsar. Cheaper shared taxis (Rs100 per person) run there from outside the Golden Temple Guru-Ka-Langar canteen at around 2.30pm.

Army. Thousands died in what Sikhs still regard as a terrible desecration of their most sacred site.

Amritsar is no stranger to mass violence. In 1919, it witnessed one of India's most appalling massacres, when British troops, under the command of General Dyer, opened fire on peaceful demonstrators at **Jallianwalla Bagh** gardens (summer 6am–9pm, winter 7am–8pm; free), killing between 400 and 1,500 innocent people. A memorial and martyrs' gallery at the site, not far from the Golden Temple, commemorates the atrocity, which kick-started Gandhi's movement for Home Rule.

UTTAR PRADESH

With close to 200 million inhabitants, Uttar Pradesh (UP) would be the world's fifth-most populous country if it were independent. As it is, the state forms the heartland of the world's largest democracy, and politics here are lively. Its name means 'northern state' and it is made up of two regions. The larger part comprises the rich, pancake-flat plain of the Ganges and its tributaries, while to the south, the Vindhya Hills rise to the edges of the Deccan Plateau. Although UP is famous worldwide for the Taj Mahal at Agra, it attracts devout Hindus to the many pilgrimage places along the River Ganges, which flows through the holy cities of Allahabad and Varanasi. Buddhists from all over the world are drawn to the deer park at Sarnath where the Buddha preached his first sermon.

Agra

Location of the Taj Mahal, **Agra ❸** is the most popular tourist destination in India. Even if the place had nothing

Agra

Population: 1.32 million

Local Dialling Code: 0562

Tourist Office: India Tourism: 191 The Mall; tel: 222 6378; www. incredibleindia.org. UP Tourism: Agra Cantonment Railway Station, Taj Road; tel: 222 6431; www.up-tourism.com

Post Office: The Mall; tel: 246 3886

Hospitals: District: Mahatma Gandhi Road, Cheopetola; tel: 246 6099. SN Medical College: Hospital Road; tel: 246 3318; www.snmcagra.in

Airport: Agra's Kheria airport lies 5km (3 miles) southwest of the centre. For timetable information contact Kingfisher airlines: tel: 240 0693; www.flykingfisher.com

Trains: Agra Cantonment train station (tel: 242 1202), on the southwest edge of the city, is the departure point for most long-distance services, including those to Delhi and Varanasi, though some leave from Agra Fort station, closer to the centre

Buses: An electric bus shuttles between the Taj and west gate of Agra Fort

Rickshaws/Taxis: Agra's green-and yellow-liveried auto-rickshaws run on cleaner CNG (natural gas). The best place to pick one up is the 24-hour prepaid booth outside Agra Cantonment train station, which stands alongside another booth for prepaid taxis. Cycle-rickshaws are easily found in Agra's centre.

One of the most famous monuments in the world, the Taj Mahal

else, it would be worth the trip: the exquisite Mughal mausoleum remains a spectacle for which no amount of pictures can adequately prepare you.

Some people assert the **Taj Mahal** (Sat–Thur sunrise–sunset; charge) looks at its best during Sharad Purnima, the first full moon after the monsoons. Others love to see it at the height of the rainy season. But in truth, the magic of the world's most beautiful building is irresistible at any time of year, and any moment of the day, or night. It was built between 1631 and 1648 by Shah Jahan to house the tomb of his beloved wife, Mumtaz Mahal, who died giving birth to their fourteenth child.

The gateway to the gardens of the mausoleum, whose graceful marble arches frame the first view of the monument, is something of a masterpiece in its own right, with domed kiosks on its four corner turrets and two rows of 11 small *chattri* (umbrella-domes). The *char bagh* (four-square) grounds inside are an integral part of the Taj Mahal, both spiritually, as the symbol of the Paradise to which Mumtaz Mahal has ascended, and artistically, to enhance the colour and texture of the mausoleum.

Exquisite harmony and refined symmetry are the keynotes of the tomb itself. The structure is clad in miraculously white marble from the Rajasthan quarries of Makrana. Standing protectively at the four corners of the raised terrace, the minarets are slightly lower than the sublime central cupola. Inside, the octagonal cenotaph-chamber

Northern Plains

Viewing the Taj: Practical Tips

- Remember the Taj is closed on Fridays
- Your ticket is valid for one full day, but only one entry
- Food, drink, books of any kind, electronics (aside from cameras) and mobile phones are not permitted inside the complex and have to be left in lockers near the entrance
- Try to time your visit to coincide with a full moon, when the Taj is open for two half-hour slots in the evening (8.30–9pm and 9–9.30pm); book tickets one day in advance from the Archaeological Survey of India office at 22 Mall Road (Mon–Sat 10am–5pm; tel: 0562-222 7261)
- Arguably the finest view of the Taj is to be had from the far side of the Yamuna River at Mehtab Bagh (daily sunrise to sunset; charge) – a wondrous location at dawn. Travel there by auto-rickshaw from the road bridge below Agra Fort.

contains the ceremonial marble coffins of Mumtaz Mahal and Shah Jahan, while muted beams of daylight filter in through the beautiful marble trellis screens (*jalis*). As was the custom of that time, the actual bodies are entombed in another chamber directly below. Sadly, vandals removed all of the Taj's precious stones, but they did leave the gentle beauty of roses and poppies in rich inlaid stones of onyx, green chrysolite, carnelian and variegated agate.

Elsewhere in the city stand plenty more sights to enthral travellers. Agra was the capital of Akbar the Great – the site of his fort, his tomb outside the city at Sikandra, and, several kilometres west at Fatehpur Sikri (*see right*), the marvellous, now-deserted town he built to celebrate the birth of a son.

Built by Akbar in 1565, **Agra Fort** (daily sunrise to sunset; charge) was conceived as a citadel with a moat on three sides and a river on the fourth. Pleasure palaces were a secondary consideration, and were in fact mostly added by Shah Jahan. The entrance from the south, at Amar Singh Gate, takes you up a ridged elephant's ramp to the long quadrangle of the pillared Hall of Public Audience (Diwan-i-Am). Just off the northeast corner of the pavilion, the harem had its very own mosque (the Nagina Masjida) and Hindu temple (the Mandir Raja Ratan) and a bazaar between the two where merchants sold silks and jewels. Near the *hammam* (baths), the Hall of Private Audience (Diwan-i-Khas) has rich carving and inlaid marble.

As in Delhi's fort, most of the private palace apartments face the Yamuna River. Among the most charming are the arcaded loggia and the gilt-roofed pavilions of the Private Palace (Khas Mahal). A minute staircase led to the Musamman Burj, a pavilion popularly known as the 'Prisoner's Tower' because Aurangzeb incarcerated his father Shah Jahan here, allowing him a view of his beloved Taj Mahal. The Palace of Jahangir is built around a square court with arches. There are Hindu motifs on the ceiling in the main hall, and in one on the western side, of peacocks holding snakes in their beaks.

Visible on the river bank opposite the fort is the **Tomb of Itimad-ud-Daulah** (daily sunrise to sunset; charge), often eclipsed by the Taj Mahal but still of exceptional beauty in its own right. The mausoleum was built 15 years earlier by Jahangir's

In the grounds of the Taj Mahal complex

wife, Nur Jahan, for her father, who served as Mughal *wazir* (prime minister). There's a fragile elegance to the white marble pavilion's silhouette, with a cupola and four octagonal turrets, topped by domed kiosks. The fine latticework on the arches and windows is superb, but its outstanding feature is the marble inlay, which is even more abundant than in the Taj, and better preserved.

Sikandra

Akbar also designed his own resting place. Completed in 1613, the tomb still stands at **Sikandra** (sunrise–sunset; charge ), 12km (7 miles) northwest of Agra, set in a garden roamed by langur monkeys and black-buck (*nilgai*). The mausoleum is four storeys high; the first three are of red sandstone, the fourth of white marble containing the false tomb of the emperor. The real tomb, as in all such mausoleums, is in a crypt below.

Fatehpur Sikri

After the mayhem of Agra city, it makes a refreshing change to travel 37km (22 miles) southwest to the ruins of **Fatehpur Sikri ❹** (daily sunrise–sunset; charge), former capital of Akbar the Great. The site, on an arid sandstone outcrop surveying the flat plains, was only occupied for a little under 15 years before being deserted. No one is quite sure why: water shortages are the explanation most often advanced.

Entering via the Agra Gate, at the northeast corner, you emerge at the Diwan-i-Am, the courtyard used for public audiences. In its southeast

Sikandra, the mausoleum of Akbar the Great

Northern Plains

corner stands the Turkish Sultana's House, or the 'Chamber of the Peerless Pool' (Hujra-i-Anup Talao), noted for its elaborate decorative carvings. Just in front of it, the Pachisi Court is a huge game board for which Akbar and his courtiers are said to have used slave girls as pieces. Dominated by a great central pillar supporting bridges to a balcony, the ornately decorated Diwan-i-Khas, at the north end of the same enclosure, is thought to have been where Akbar held his famous debates with Jesuits, Brahmins, Parsis, Sufi mystics, and Jain and Buddhist monks.

Separate from the palace complex on the southwest side of the ridgetop, Fatehpur's **Friday Mosque** (Jama Masjid) holds the much revered, marble-clad **Tomb of Shaikh Salim Chishti** – the mystic who prophesied that Akbar would have three sons. Flanking the southern side of the complex, the mighty **Great Gate** (Buland Darwaza) forms an appropriately grand entry and exit point

★ MUSIC OF THE NORTH

As the meeting point between indigenous Hinduism and the Muslim-Sufi traditions of Central Asia, the northern plains of India have served as the crucible for a highly expressive array of musical forms. Traditional types of patronage may have dwindled, but the old styles are still very much in vogue at the region's weddings, temples and concert halls. Thanks to the influence they exert on Bollywood cinema, they've also contributed in no small part to the soundtrack of India's vast, global diaspora.

Kirtan

The perfect complement to the serene vision of Amritsar's Golden Temple is the devotional music drifting from its central shrine, the Hari Mandir Sahib. Known as 'Kirtan' (or 'Shabad Kirtan'), Sikh hymns are sung in a style reminiscent of both Hindu and Sufi worship – though they're more formal and restrained than either. Verses from the Sikh holy book, the Guru Grant Sahib, provide the words, while accompaniment comes from a trio of specially trained *raagis* (temple musicians) on tabla drums and harmonium. Listening to these intensely spiritual songs of praise to God and the Gurus while pilgrims file reverently around the complex can be deeply moving.

Ghazal

The solemnity of Sikh Kirtan is not as far removed as you might imagine from the

Kirtan musicians perform devotional Sikh hymns

overtly passionate, romantic song form popularised by the Nawabs of Avadh in their court at Lucknow. *Ghazal* also has its roots in the devotional music of the Sufi dervishes, which spread through the region in the 12th century and soon blended with the sensuousness of Krishna worship. In Sufism, love of God is often phrased in terms of soulful longing of an earthly kind – that of the lover for his absent beloved. Thus pain, loss and sensuality came to provide the emotional substance of *ghazals* sung in Urdu at the courts and *mehfils* (private gatherings) of Lucknow, where high-class courtesans, or *tawaifs*, would perform for select audiences of wealthy patrons.

These days, both Nawabs' courts and *mehfils* are a thing of the past, but *ghazal* is alive and well, and you can be sure of hearing Lucknow's finest singers at the city's Mahotsa festival, held annually in December.

Playing the tabla drums

Bhojpuri

One type of music you're certain to hear while travelling through Uttar Pradesh and Bihar is Bhojpuri folk. Played at top volume in buses and shops everywhere, Bhojpuri is an unashamedly upbeat, energetic and often bawdy style, traditionally sung at weddings when the groom's party *(bharat)* arrives at the bride's house. Women from the latter's family would use Bhojpuri songs to taunt and tease the men from the boy's side, criticising their appearances and even their sexual potency. These days, such 'item songs', with their hilariously ribald double-meaning lyrics, dominate the scores of hit Bhojpuri films.

Kirtan music makes use of the harmonium

for the imperial city. It was erected in 1576 to celebrate Akbar's triumphant conquest of Gujarat and rises to a height of 54m (177ft). Visible for kilometres, an inscription from the Koran carved over the archway reads: 'Said Jesus son of Mary (Peace Be Upon Him): the world is but a bridge. Pass over without building houses on it. He who hopes for one hour hopes for eternity; the world is an hour – spend it in prayer for the rest is unseen.'

Lucknow

Uttar Pradesh's state capital, **Lucknow ❺**, stands on the Gomati River, a tributary of the Ganges. As the seat of the Nawabs of Avadh (Oudh), it was once a city of unparalleled sophistication, famous for its sumptuously decorated palaces and pleasure gardens, and its skyline of gilded domes, cupolas and minarets, and for the skills of its Urdu poets and craftsmen. Tales of 700 women harems and troupes of glittering dancing (*nautch*) girls swirled around the royal court, which was the most decadent in the subcontinent during the 18th century.

Partition, however, had a devastating impact on Lucknow. When its cultured Muslim aristocracy all fled to Pakistan in 1947, the city went into sharp decline. Marred by unsightly industrial complexes, it's now better known for poverty, backwardness and violence than Islamic calligraphy or sybaritic cuisine, but does retain some of the finest Muslim architecture in India.

Since the Uprising of 1857, however, Lucknow has above all been synonymous with the bloody and protracted siege of the former Residency, in which thousands of lives were lost. Set in formal gardens, the **Residency Compound** (daily sunrise–sunset; charge) still stands on the northwest side of the city, little changed in over a century. The main building itself, where around 3,000 Europeans held off a vastly superior native force for a total of 147 days, has been left almost exactly as it was at the end of the fateful events of November 1857 – a burnt-out, derelict shell. A small **museum** (daily 9am–4.30pm; free) recounts the story.

About 2km (1¼ miles) west, beyond the Residency, the **Bara Imambara** (daily 8.30am–6pm, closed during Muharrum; charge) is the most splendid of all the Nawab of Avadh's tombs. Built in the time of famine in 1784 as a food-for-work programme, it is an architectural marvel built without pillars, and contains a hall 50m (163ft) long with acoustics so good you can hear a paper tear at the other end. There is an entertaining maze on the upper floor. The entrance ticket also gives access to the **Hussainabad Imambara** next door, with its fabulous chandeliers and silver pulpit, the Picture Gallery housing portraits of the nawabs, the Hussainabad Clock Tower and the Friday Mosque (Jama Masjid).

Varanasi

The most sacred stretch of the Ganges is at **Varanasi** (Benares) , one of the oldest living cities in the world and arguably the most intense, atmospheric place in the whole of India. Hindus believe that to die here on the banks of the holy river is to achieve *moksha*, liberation from the cycle of life and death, and a regular sight in the twisting

> ### Triveni Sangam
>
> One of the holiest places in India lies on the southeast edge of the city of Allahabad, in central UP, where the blue waters of the Yamuna flow into the shallower, silty yellow waters of the Ganges. Another invisible, mythical river, the Saraswati, also joins the confluence here, hence its name: **Triveni Sangam**, or 'Place Where Three Rivers Meet'.
>
> A dip in the Sangam, believed by Hindus to be where the gods spilt a drop of the elixir of immortality, is supposed to wash away the accumulated sins of a lifetime – or several lifetimes if the immersion is performed during the astrologically auspicious period of the **Kumbh Mela**, held here every 12 years. In 2001, an estimated 60 million pilgrims and naked sadhus bathed at the confluence over a period of six weeks – the largest gathering of people ever recorded. Each year in January– February, a smaller, but no less fervent, pilgrimage called the Magh Mela takes place on the site, attracting legions of ash-smeared sadhus from around India.

Looking out over Lucknow from the Bara Imambara

Varanasi

 Population: 1.22 million

Local Dialling Code: 0542

 Tourist Office: UP Tourism, Tourist Bungalow, Varanasi Junction Railway Station: tel: 250 6670; **www.up-tourism.com**

Post Office: Kabir Chaura Road (ask for the 'GPO')

Hospital: Heritage Hospital, Lanka: tel: 206 8888; **www.heritagehospital.in**

 Airports: Varanasi's Babatpur airport (tel: 250 2527) lies 22km (14 miles) northwest of the city

Trains: Varanasi Junction, also known as Varanasi Cantonment, is the main rail hub; the Foreign Tourist Centre, for tourist quota bookings, stands on the ground floor near the UP Tourism information counter

Buses: Long-distance buses work out of the hectic city bus stand, just east of Varanasi Junction train station

Rickshaws/Taxis: prepaid taxi and auto-rickshaw booths are located outside the train station

alleyways of the Old City is that of a muslin-wrapped body being carried to the cremation ghats on the riverbank. Perhaps nowhere else in India can offer the visitor such an explicit crash course in the tenets of the Hindu faith.

The river flows south to north, with the city on the west bank, and fields and trees to the east. Dawn is the best time to venture on to the water. Rowing boats take visitors from Assi in the north to Raj Ghat – a highly recommended experience. As the sun rises, the golden rays illuminate countless temples and 70 bathing ghats, priests plying their trade under tilted umbrellas, and devout Hindus taking a purifying dip.

Within the city itself, the **Vishvanath Temple**, built in the late 18th century, is the main Shiva sanctuary. It is closed to non-Hindus, but visitors can climb surrounding buildings to see the gilded dome. Across the river, **Ramnagar** is home of the Raja of Benares, whose fort houses a private **museum** (daily

Early morning sees prayers and ablutions carried out at the Varanasi ghats

Sculpture of the Buddha at Sarnath

by an excellent **museum** (Sat–Thur 10am–5pm; charge) – a treasure trove of superb early Indian sculpture.

BIHAR

The state of Bihar lies in the eastern Gangetic plain, occupying the area that was the seat of several of the most famous ancient Indian dynasties, as well as being the cradle of Jainism and Buddhism. Although the state is situated on the fertile alluvial soils of the flood plain of the Ganges, this is one of the very poorest parts of India, all but untouched by the economic boom taking place in other parts of the country. Bihar is notorious for its rampant corruption, decrepit infrastructure and extreme divisions of caste, manifested in sporadic outbreaks of violence.

9am–noon and 2.30–5pm; charge). He is the patron of the Ramnagar Ram Lila, a traditional month-long enactment of the *Ramayana*, performed in October and November.

Sarnath

About 10km (6 miles) from the centre of Varanasi, **Sarnath** is where Buddha gave his famous Deer Park sermon to five disciples around the year 530BC – regarded by Buddhists the world over as the founding moment of their faith. The site quickly became a leading place of pilgrimage, and still today attracts streams of devotees from Japan, China and Southeast Asia. Emperor Asoka commanded his edict-pillars to be built within the monasteries and stupas (hemispherical sculptures symbolising Buddha's Enlightenment), of which he had thousands constructed. But just like Varanasi, Sarnath suffered at the hands of Qutb-ud-din in 1194. Today the ruins have been well restored, and are accompanied

Patna

Patna ❼, the capital of Bihar, is a city of more than 1 million people, lying beside the Ganges, but it feels more like a rural town run wild. Under the name of Pataliputra it was the capital of the Magadha Empire, of which only a desultory scattering of partly submerged ruins on the eastern outskirts of town has survived. Some hint of the former splendour from more than 2,500 years ago can be found at the **Patna Museum** (Tue–Sun 10.30am–4.30pm; charge) near the High Court, which houses a collection of superb ancient Mauryan and Gupta stone votive statues, bronzes and terracotta sculptures, 18 of which were stolen in 2006 (although the police station is next door).

Also of interest is the bizarre **Golgar** granary (daily 24 hours; free), just south of the river overlooking Gandhi Maidan. Built by the British as a precaution against famine, the giant dome can be climbed via a spiral staircase for a spectacular view over the Ganges. Old Patna, the hectic bazaar district, lies to the east of the Maidan. In its midst stands the **Khuda Baksh Oriental Library** (Sat–Thur 9.30am–5pm; free), worth a visit for its collection of rare Persian, Arabic and Mughal manuscripts and miniature Rajput paintings.

Bodhgaya

Gaya, 90km (56 miles) southwest of Rajgir, is an important Hindu site, where pilgrims come to perform last rites for recently departed relatives. For most foreign travellers, however, it's primarily a staging post on the journey to **Bodhgaya** ❽ 12km (7 miles) further south on the Phalgu River, where the Buddha is believed to have attained Enlightenment. The exact site of this momentous occurrence was a ficus, or bodhi tree, a descendant of which still grows on the same spot. Buddhists travel here from all over the world to worship in the sacred garden, the centrepiece of which is the resplendent, Unesco World Heritage-listed **Mahabdodhi Temple** (daily 5am–6pm; charge), built in the 6th century AD on top of the original shrine erected by Emperor Ashoka more than 800 years before.

Bihar's Floods

More than one fifth of all those gravely affected by flooding in India live in Bihar, and practically the whole of the northern half of the state is at risk during the southwest monsoon period between July and October. Embankments have been built in an attempt to keep the floodwaters of the Kamla Balan River at bay, but 2009 was the fifth year in succession that the embankments failed; with over 2 million people affected, these were the worst floods in northern India for half a century.

As ever in Bihar, political power dictates who is most likely to suffer; even the embankments themselves swerve to ensure that the houses of the most influential residents – including those of its top politicians – remain untouched.

A pilgrim makes her way to Bodhgaya, which is highly significant to Buddhists

ACCOMMODATION

Accommodation in the states of the northern plains covers every conceivable kind, from grubby flea-pits to glamorous boutique hotels with views of the Taj. As with the rest of the country, advance booking is strongly recommended, especially during busy holiday periods.

Haryana and Punjab
Chandigarh Divyadeep
Himalaya Marg Sector 22-B, Chandigarh
Tel: 01272-270 1179
Along with the jointly owned Satyadeep (tel: 01272-270 3103) this is the most dependable and best-value option at the bottom end of the scale. The rooms are all clean, with windows and running hot water. **$**

Hotel Mountview
Sector 10, Chandigarh
Tel: 0172-274 0544
www.citcochandigarh.com
A big, luxury hotel set in landscaped grounds. Large, airy rooms and good business and leisure facilities including a pool.
$$$$–$$$$$

Mrs Bhandari's
10 Cantonment, Amritsar
Tel: 0183-222 2390
http://bhandari_guesthouse.tripod.com
Highly recommended, unusual lodging in a family-run colonial house, with three-course meals (only for residents), garden and pool, slightly out of town. **$$**

Sita Niwas
Off Mahna Singh Rd, nr Golden Temple, Amritsar
Tel: 0183-254 3092
Good budget option which is central, with a range of small but very cheap rooms, with or without bathroom. **$**

Uttar Pradesh
Atithi
Tourist Complex Area, Fatehabad Road, Agra
Tel: 0562-233 0880
www.hotelatithiagra.com
Forty-four clean a/c rooms in modern hotel with pool and attentive staff; this is good value for Agra. **$$$**

Carlton Hotel
Ranapratap Marg, Hazratganj, Lucknow
Tel: 0522-222 2413
A long-established, legendary hotel, somewhat faded, with old-fashioned rooms and baths (non-a/c much cheaper). An impressive colonial building with a lovely garden, restaurant and bar; good value. **$$**

Gateway Hotel Ganges
Nadesar Palace Grounds, Nadesar, Varanasi
Tel: 0542-250 3001
www.tajhotels.com
One of the top hotels in town. Comfortable rooms, two good restaurants and a nice swimming pool. **$$$$$**

The Grand Imperial
M.G. Road, Agra
Tel: 0562-225 1190
www.hotelgrandimperial.com
Beautifully restored heritage property, slightly further from the Taj Mahal than other five-stars but oozing charm and sophistication. **$$$$$**

Hotel Ganges View
Assi Ghat, Varanasi
Tel: 0542-231 3128
www.hotelgangesview.com
An old mansion converted into an atmospheric and well-run hotel. Comfortable, very clean a/c rooms with good attached

A bedroom at the Hotel Ganges View

baths. Great views from an upstairs terrace. Drinks and snacks available, vegetarian dinner (ask in advance) served at 8pm. **$$$**

Hotel Maya
Purani Mandi Circle, Fatehabad Road, Agra
Tel: 0562-233 2109
www.mayainmagic.com
Extremely friendly and well-run hotel in good location. Great food, good value. **$$**

Hotel Pradeep
C-27/153 Jagatganj, Varanasi
Tel: 0542-220 4963
www.hotelpradeep.com
A friendly hotel with well-maintained and clean a/c rooms. Very good value for money. **$$–$$$**

Mrs Sharma's Guest House
Mall Avenue, Sudharshan Seth, Lucknow
Tel: 0522-223 9314
A highly recommended small guesthouse run by the widow of a retired brigadier. Very clean and friendly, with good home-cooked meals available on request. **$**

Tourist Rest House
Kachahari Road, Baluganj, Agra
Tel: 0562-246 3961
www.dontworrychickencurry.com
The best low-cost place to stay in Agra. Clean rooms with attached bath around a courtyard. Friendly owners and good vegetarian food; recommended. **$**

Bihar
Amar
Fraser Road, Patna
Tel: 0612-222 4157
Basic but pleasant rooms with attached baths. **$–$$**

Hotel Maurya
South Gandhi Maidan, Patna
Tel: 0612-220 3040
www.maurya.com
Patna's top (and most expensive) hotel, with decent rooms, a pool and a couple of restaurants. **$$$$$**

Root Institute
Near the Thai Temple, Bodhgaya
Tel: 9631-332648
www.rootinstitute.com
The Root Institute is an organisation that runs a Buddhist meditation retreat. As well as attending courses, it is possible to stay in the huts and dormitories as an independent visitor. Consistently good vegetarian meals are provided; note that retreat rules must be followed at all times. **$$**

RESTAURANTS

The food changes as you travel along the Ganges from west to east. Starting in the Punjab, the meat dishes of the Sikhs are spicy and rich, exemplified in concoctions such as butter chicken. There is, however, a vegetarian tradition, too, with tasty dishes such as *alu gobi* (potato and cauliflower curry) and wonderful *dals*. The food of UP is very similar but generally a bit lighter; the lightly spiced vegetarian food of strict UP Brahmins, with its avoidance of onions and garlic, is worth seeking out. The Muslim food of Lucknow is another speciality, with delicious grilled kebabs and meat stews.

Haryana and Punjab

Bhiranwan-da-dhaba
Near the City Hall, Amritsar
Excellent vegetarian *dhaba*, famed for its melt-in-the-mouth *parathas* and *dals*. Small menu, but very good *thalis*. **$–$$**

Bhoj
Sector 22-B, Chandigarh
Recommended for Indian vegetarian food, including good *thalis*; great value. **$**

Khyber
Sector 35-B, Chandigarh
Frontier-style cuisine on the ground floor, but the real gem is the 'Wild West' basement, complete with cowboy-styled waiters and draught beer. **$$**

Makhan Dhaba
Lawrence Road, Amritsar
This inexpensive *dhaba* is the place to come for an elusive local delicacy, Amritsari fish – freshwater sole in a crisp white batter flavoured with fragrant *ajwain* seeds (lovage). **$**

Uttar Pradesh

Brown Bread Bakery
D-5/17 Tripura Bhairavi, Varanasi
Tel: 0542-240 3566
www.brownbreadbakery.com
This wonderful wholefood and organic bakery serves delicious Western, Chinese, Tibetan, Nepali and Indian dishes, in hygienic surroundings close to the river front. They're deservedly proud of their cakes, pastries and many varieties of cheeses, and there's live classical music in the evenings. **$–$$**

Dasaprakash
Meher Theatre Complex, 1 Gwalior Road, Cantonment, Agra
Top-notch south Indian restaurant, renowned for its real *dosas* and ice-cream desserts. **$$**

Esphahan
Amarvilas Hotel, Taj East Gate End, Agra
Tel: 0562-233 1515
Sumptuous Mughlai cuisine served in an ornate hall that's like something out of *Arabian Nights*. Dinner is served in two sittings (7pm and 9.30pm); reserve ahead. **$$$$**

Falaknuma
Rooftop of Clark's Hotel Avadh, 8 MG Road, Lucknow
tel: 0522-262 0131
Traditional Nawabi cuisine served by candlelight to the sound of superb live *ghazals*. **$$$**

A delectable *thali* at Dasaprakash

Dasaprakash *(see p.99)* is a popular spot

Joney's Place
Taj Ganj, Agra
The original and best of the area's cheap eateries, serving travellers' breakfasts and chickpea curries with *puri* from dawn – handy if you're up early to visit the Taj. **$**

Keshari
D-14/8 Teri Neem, off Dasasvamedha Ghat Road, Varanasi
Tel: 0542-240 1472
Tomato *paneer* and mushroom curry are the specialities at this enduringly popular restaurant, hidden away down a narrow alley in the Old City, which also does filling, good-value *thalis* and legendary *lassis*. **$$**

Madhu Milan
Dasawamedh Ghat Road, Varanasi
Recommended for light, south Indian rice meals, quick bites such as paper *dosas* and *idli*, as well as more substantial *thalis*. **$**

Tunday Kabab
In the Chowk, Lucknow
A Lucknow institution: try the spicy mutton kebabs, *biriyanis* and tandoori specialities, served with tasty *naan* breads. **$$**

Zorba the Buddha
E13 Shopping Arcade, Gopi Chand Shivhare Road, Sadar Bazaar, Agra
A very clean and popular vegetarian restaurant serving tasty and imaginative dishes. **$$–$$$**

Bihar
Bellpepper
Hotel Windsor, Exhibition Road, Patna
Tel: 0612-220 3250
The Windsor's plush, air-con restaurant serves mainly Muslim-accented, Mughlai cuisine, as well as kebabs and spicy marinated chicken piping hot out of the tandoor. **$$**

Takshila
Beerchand Patel Marg, Patna
Tel: 0612-222 3141
The Takshila serves some of the tastiest northwest cuisine in the city, to enjoy with a cool Kingfisher beer. Upstairs in the same hotel, the multi-cuisine Samarat has a family-friendly atmosphere. **$$–$$$**

SPORTS AND TOURS
The Northern Plains contain many major sites and attractions, so visiting them can be hectic; many local tourist offices organise tours to minimise hassle.

Cricket
Punjab Cricket Association Stadium
Mohali, near Chandigarh
www.kxip.in
The Punjab has its own IPL Twenty20 cricket team, the Kings XI Punjab. Owned by Bollywood starlet, Preity Zinta, it's one of the most glamorous line-ups on the circuit, boasting the services of the flamboyant Yuvraj Singh, who once hit six sixes in a single over for the team, and Sri Lankan batting legend Jayawardene.

Swimming
Hotel Surya
20/51 The Mall, Varanasi
Tel: 0542-250 8465
www.hotelsurya.com
The swimming pool is open to non-residents.

Tours

Bihar State Tourism Development Corporation
Bir Chand Patel Path, Patna
Tel: 0612-222 5411
http://bstdc.bih.nic.in
Operating a range of different themed tours to key religious sites around the state (Buddhist, Jain and Sikh). Full details are published online at their website, or you can contact the head office here.

Chandigarh
From the Hotel Shivalik View Sector 17-E)
Tel: 01762-270 3839
Half-day double-decker tours of Chandigarh taking in the city's main highlights, including Nek Chand's Fantasy Rock Garden and government museums. Tickets are sold in advance from the Shivalik View's reception.

Uttar Pradesh Tourism
Headquarters: Rajarshi Purshottam Das Tandon Paryatan Bhavan,C-13, Vipin Khand, Gomti Nagar, Lucknow
Tel: 0522-230 8916
www.up-tourism.com
Various package tours of tourist destinations around the state are offered by UP Tourism; or contact any of their offices. Guided tours of Varanasi and the ghats may be arranged through UP Tourism's information office at Varanasi Junction train station (daily 7am–7pm). They can also arrange boat rides on the Ganges.

FESTIVALS AND EVENTS

The world's largest religious gatherings – notably the Kumbh Mela at Allahabad – are the highlights of this region's festival calendar. Smaller, but no less colourful, celebrations are staged throughout the region year round.

January–February
Magh Mela
Allahabad
Mass bathing at the Triveni Sangam on the city's outskirts.

August
The Teej Festival
Chandigarh
Hindu women adorn their arms with special henna tattoos and bangles, and perform folk dances. The famous Rock Garden assumes a festive look for the occasion.

September–October
Ram Lila
Varanasi
The 'City of Light' on the banks of the Ganges is the best place in the country to watch colourful re-enactments of the Hindu epic the *Ramayana*, the culmination of which is the burning of giant effigies.

Muharram
Lucknow
Shia Muslim mourning for Imam Hussein, grandson of Mohammed. Spectacular illuminated bamboo and paper replicas of the martyr's tomb are paraded through the town in fervent processions.

November
Sonepur Cattle Fair
near Patna
On the banks of the Ganges, this month-long cattle and elephant market is one of the world's biggest, with more than 700,000 visitors.

December
Lucknow Mahotsa
Lucknow
Superb 10-day cultural festival featuring kathak dance performances, recitals of *ghazals* (romantic song) and traditional kite flying.

Listings

The Northwest Himalaya

From the lush Kullu Valley to the arid heights of Ladakh, India's northwest Himalaya are much loved by walkers, climbers and those in search of tranquillity or simply incredible views. The area is also imbued with spirituality: just as Islam dominates Kashmir, Buddhism has a bearing on large swathes of Ladakh and Himachal Pradesh, while the area is home to some of the holiest Hindu sites.

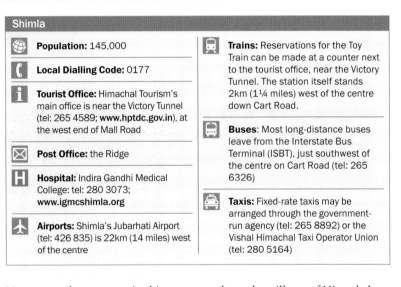

Shimla

Population: 145,000

Local Dialling Code: 0177

Tourist Office: Himachal Tourism's main office is near the Victory Tunnel (tel: 265 4589; www.hptdc.gov.in), at the west end of Mall Road

Post Office: the Ridge

Hospital: Indira Gandhi Medical College: tel: 280 3073; www.igmcshimla.org

Airports: Shimla's Jubarhati Airport (tel: 426 835) is 22km (14 miles) west of the centre

Trains: Reservations for the Toy Train can be made at a counter next to the tourist office, near the Victory Tunnel. The station itself stands 2km (1¼ miles) west of the centre down Cart Road.

Buses: Most long-distance buses leave from the Interstate Bus Terminal (ISBT), just southwest of the centre on Cart Road (tel: 265 6326)

Taxis: Fixed-rate taxis may be arranged through the government-run agency (tel: 265 8892) or the Vishal Himachal Taxi Operator Union (tel: 280 5164)

No matter where you are in this spectacular corner of the world, you're never far from a stunning view of a snowcapped mountain. These can be enjoyed in the company of thousands – Manali is still top of every Indian honeymooner's and snow-seeker's wish list – or entirely alone. With its Buddhist monasteries set against gleaming ice peaks, the high-altitude desert of Ladakh is guaranteed to fulfil every fantasy about the Himalaya, while the flower meadows

and wooden villages of Himachal Pradesh provide a dreamily bucolic backdrop for explorations on foot.

Closed for decades by the civil unrest, Kashmir – long considered since the time of the Mughals as the Jewel in the Crown of all India's mountain regions – has also begun to attract visitors again. But for sheer exoticism, it's hard to top the Hindu pilgrimage sites of Garwhal and Kumaon in Uttarakhand, where ancient temple towers are framed by the dazzling white giants of the Inner Himalaya.

HIMACHAL PRADESH

The picturesque state of Himachal Pradesh straddles the Himalaya from the foothills to the high, remote valleys of Lahaul and Spiti, with a swathe of snowy peaks in between. In early summer (May–June) – the best period to visit – the coolness of melting snow tempers the heat in the myriad wood- and stone-built villages perched on terraces high above the valley floors.

The majority of Himachalis are Hindus, but Buddhism is also a major influence, particularly with the presence of the exiled Dalai Lama at Dharamsala and the large settlements of Tibetan refugees.

The town of Shimla was a favourite retreat of the British Raj

The dazzling scenery of Ladakh

Shimla

Now the capital of Himachal Pradesh, the town of **Shimla ❶** was built in the early 19th century when the British colonial settlers were searching for a summer refuge from the heat of the plains. At an altitude of 2,130m (6,755ft), the site was first discovered by British troops returning from the war with the Gurkhas of Nepal in 1819. They returned soon after to build little holiday bungalows with fabulous views of the mountains. Within a decade Shimla had become the most prestigious hill station in India – and the summer capital of the entire Raj.

In town, visitors can retrace the favourite promenades along the Mall and see the old administrative offices of the Ridge, which leads past the neo-Gothic, Anglican **Christ Church**, where the bells are made from the brass of cannons captured from the Sikhs. At the end of the Ridge, you'll find the baronial pile of **Viceregal Lodge**, where

The Northwest Himalaya

Mountbattan, Gandhi, Nehru and Jinnah held their crucial negotiations in the run-up to Partition in the 1940s.

The most popular walk out of Shimla begins just behind Christ Church, from where a lane strikes steeply up to the **Jakhu Temple**. Famous for its monkeys – be sure to keep all food items out of sight, as they are quite brazen about stealing them – it is also a good vantage point for magnificent early-morning views of far-off Himalayan mountains.

The Kullu Valley

The legendary **Kullu Valley** ❷ on the River Beas is renowned for its beautiful scenery, apple orchards, wooden temples, and music and dances. The district headquarters, **Kullu** town itself, holds few attractions to detain travellers beyond its two main temples: **Raghunathji**, seat of the valley's chief deity; and the cave-temple of **Vaishno Devi**. The former plays the presiding role in the annual Dussehra festival, when tourists and locals flood into the

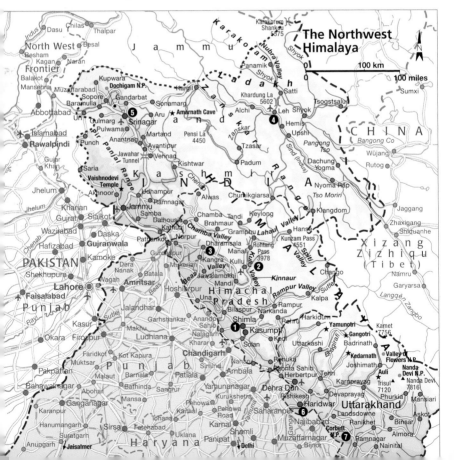

Prayer flags outside a Buddhist monastery in Ladakh

centre, it now serves as a popular resort for Indian honeymooners, as well as Western and Israeli backpackers.

Three kilometres (2 miles) up the valley from Manali lie the hot springs of **Vashisht**. The temple complex here has separate outdoor baths for men and women. The Kullu Valley ends as the road winds up through rocky ranges to the **Rohtang Pass** (3,978m/13,260ft), gateway to the enchanting Lahaul and Spiti valleys. Marking the line of the Great Himalayan Watershed, it forms a stark divide between the lush Kullu Valley and the arid mountains beyond, which lie in the vast rain shadow of the world's highest range of peaks.

town to see spectacular processions of gold-faced temple deities, carried from the surrounding villages on the shoulders of devotees.

Circled by beautiful glades of deodar cedars, **Manali** makes an ideal base for walks, climbs, treks and picnics. Once an important trading

Dharamsala and McLeod Ganj

West of Manali at the foot of the Dhauladhar Range in the beautiful Kangra Valley lies **Dharamsala** ❸. Consisting of a lower and an upper town, its altitude varies from 1,000 to 2,000m (3,250–6,500ft).

The Mountain Railways of Himachal Pradesh

Since 1903, the most memorable way to travel to Shimla has been via the narrow-gauge line from Kalka (26km/16 miles northeast of Chandigarh). Diesel locomotives rather than steam engines nowadays haul the famous **Viceroy's Toy Train** up the winding 96km (60 miles) to the Himachali capital, but the journey remains as spectacular as ever, featuring 103 tunnels, 26 bridges and 18 stations 🅼.

The state's other, lesser-known narrow-gauge mountain line runs further northwest in the **Kangra Valley.** Covering 163km (102 miles), it's much longer than the one to Shimla, and affords even more astonishing views, thanks to the predominance of bridges (950 in total) rather than tunnels, and the proximity of the Dhauladhar Range's glistening snow fields.

Herding goats in an otherworldly-looking Ladakh valley

Upper Dharamsala, better known as **McLeod Ganj**, is the home of His Holiness the Dalai Lama and the Tibetan Government in Exile. The large Tibetan population supports many organisations, including **TIPA** (Tibetan Institute of Performing Arts), which preserves and arranges performances of traditional Tibetan music and dance, particularly the drama, lhamo. In the lower town is the **Museum of Kangra Art**, housing a collection of miniature paintings and other local artefacts.

The nearby ancient town of **Kangra** is well known for its temples whose riches were plundered by a number of invaders – the most popular being the one dedicated to the goddess Vajresvari.

Leh

Population: 29,000

Local Dialling Code: 01982

Tourist Office: J&K Tourism's main office is on Ibex Road (tel: 253 482; www.jktourism.org), just west of Main Bazaar

Post Office: Main Bazaar

Hospital: Sonam Norbu Memorial Hospital: tel: 252 012

Airport: Leh's Kushok Bakua Rinpoche airport stands 5km (3 miles) southwest of town

Buses: The main bus stand is 10 minutes' walk south of the main bazaar, though Himachal Pradesh Tourism Development Corporation (HPTDC) buses to Manali (0945-1846 0071) leave from Fort Road

Taxis: Ladakh Taxi Operators Cooperative (tel: 252 723)

LADAKH

Although officially within the boundaries of Jammu-Kashmir state, the remote Himalayan region of Ladakh is a world apart, in every sense. Encircled by some of the world's highest mountains, the geography and culture of the 'Land of High Passes' has more in common with neighbouring Tibet than Muslim Kashmir. The majority of its inhabitants are Buddhists, and from the moment you first enter the region, the brightly coloured prayer flags and monasteries perched on hillsides of parched scree reinforce the impression that you have arrived on the margins of Indian influence.

Only opened to tourists in 1975, Ladakh is centred on the stunning Indus Valley. Along its floor, at a base altitude of around 3,500m (11,600ft), a string of picturesque villages cowers beneath vast, ice-capped mountains. These form an all but impregnable barrier to the monsoon clouds sweeping north off the Indian plains, with the result that rainfall is minimal.

For thousands of years, the Indus Valley formed an important trade artery connecting Central Asia and Tibet with Kashmir and the Indian lowlands. Along it, tea, silk, pashmina, semiprecious stones – and the Buddhist religion – were imported in caravans of yaks and ponies. The fragile – and still disputed – borders with China and Pakistan that now enclose Ladakh have effectively blocked these ancient trans-Himalayan routes, but the region still thrives as an important military base and tourist destination.

Leh and the Indus Valley

Despite its remoteness, **Leh ❹**, the capital of Ladakh, is a developed town boasting most modern amenities. Spilling from the foot of a ruined Tibetan-style palace, its broad bazaar and jam of ancient mud houses look south across the Indus Valley to the snowy peaks of the Stok Kangri massif.

Most visitors use the town as a base for excursions into the valley, travelling by taxi or local bus to the monasteries (*gompas*) of **Shey**, **Tikse**, **Stok** and **Likkir**. With a few more days at your disposal, you could consider a longer trip west towards Kashmir, taking in the spectacular **Lamayuru** *gompa* and the Unesco World Heritage monument of **Alchi**,

Local children in Ladakh, where the Buddhist tradition is strong

Getting to Ladakh

Cut off for months behind snowbound passes, Ladakh may be among the most remote inhabited regions on the planet, but it's surprisingly easy to reach thanks to the presence outside its capital, Leh, of the highest civil airport in the world, **Kushok Bakula Rinpoche**. Served by five daily flights from Delhi (with Air India, Kingfisher and Jet Airways), it functions year-round, even in the depths of winter. From July through October, when the motorable passes into Ladakh are open, you can also travel there overland from Manali or from Srinagar. Requiring overnight halts, both routes take you through staggeringly beautiful country, but the one from Manali has the edge as the road reaches a high point of 5,360m (17,860ft) at Tanglang La, from where you can gaze across the Indus Valley to the Karakoram Range.

whose architecture, murals and devotional statues date from the first spreading of Buddhism in the 11th and 12th centuries.

KASHMIR

The Vale of Kashmir, 1,700m (5,000ft) above sea level, has historically offered much-needed respite for conquerors and travellers alike. With its meadows, forests, fruit orchards and lakes, it remains the undisputed treasure of South Asia – though one that's perennially troubled.

Continuing conflict between the Indian army and Pakistani-backed insurgents in the region has rendered Kashmir a dangerous place for travellers for the past couple of decades. However, the situation has improved significantly in recent years and – in spite of advice to the contrary from their governments

– foreign travellers are now returning to the area. Even so, check the latest security situation carefully before visiting, especially if you're planning to venture out of Srinagar itself into the surrounding mountains.

Srinagar

Kashmir's capital, **Srinagar ❺** extends along the banks of the serpentine Jhelum River on the southern shore of Dal Lake. Few monuments have survived its troubled history, but the city's legendary beauty endures in its numerous waterways and gardens. A fleet of hand-paddled *shikharas* (canoe taxis) is on hand for excursions on the lake. From the western shore rise the large white dome and minarets of **Hazratbal Mosque** (Hazratbal Masjid), famous for its relic – a hair from the beard of the prophet Mohammed.

Of the formal **Mughal Gardens** spread in steep terraces over the surrounding hillsides, **Shalimar Bagh** (Apr–Oct daily 9am–dusk; charge) is the most famous. Dotted with exquisite marble pavilions, it was originally laid out by Emperor Jehangir as a summer retreat for his wife, Nur Jahan. For spellbinding panoramic views over the town, take an autorickshaw up to the **Pari Mahal** (dawn–dusk; free), a ruined Mughal astrological college now converted into a tourist village. In the atmospheric **Old City** of Srinagar itself, the **Khanqah of Shah-Hamadan Mosque**, on the banks of the Jhelum, is the most impressive monument, with a tapering tower and facade

The elegant gardens of Shalimar Bagh

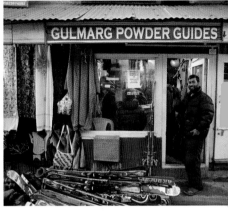
Gulmarg is a resort area with an increasing number of ski facilities

The Northwest Himalaya

covered in elaborately painted wood-carvings. It's closed to non-Muslims, but you can peek at the building through its main gateway.

Gulmarg and Sonamarg

An hour by road from Srinagar lies the ski and summer resort of **Gulmarg**, familiar to Indians the world over as a backdrop for Bollywood song sequences. Surrounded by verdant flower meadows and high mountains, the town is experiencing something of a renaissance following the completion of an 8km (5-mile) ski lift, the highest gondola in the northern hemisphere *(see box, p.112)* – which trekkers use in the summer months to access the high ridges overlooking the resort offering views of the Karakoram range.

Thanks to its spectacular Alpine landscape, **Sonamarg**, 87km (54 miles) northeast of Srinagar on the road to Leh, is also seeing an increase in visitor numbers. A stopover on the

⭐ THE CHOTA CHAR DHAMS

The headwaters of India's most hallowed rivers all lie in the high mountains of Uttarakhand, and their sources form the cardinal points of a famous pilgrimage circuit known as the *Char Dhams* ('Four Holy Abodes'), also called the 'Chota (Little) Char Dhams' to distinguish it from a longer, all-India pilgrimage of the same name.

Reaching the Rivers' Source

Open between mid-April and October, the Hindu shrines marking the rivers' official wellsprings used only to be accessible in a two-month trek, undertaken by committed sadhus (wandering ascetics) and pilgrims wealthy enough to afford the necessary entourage. Since roads to them were built in the 1960s, however, the route has grown hugely in popularity, and now attracts an annual average of 250,000 worshippers, the majority in the 6- to 8-week period preceding the monsoon, when a trip to the hills comes as a welcome break from the oppressive heat of the northern plains. Few foreigners do the full loop, but it's worth taking in one or two of the Chota Char Dham's temples to sample the unique atmosphere of high-altitude Hinduism. The shrines are traditionally visited in a set order.

Yamunotri

A hotchpotch of yellow and pink concrete at the foot of a steep ravine, the temple of Yamunotri (3,293m/11,000ft), marking the source of the River Yamuna, is reached via a 13km (8-mile) trek from the village of Hanuman Chatti. Pilgrims

Trekkers make their way to Gangotri

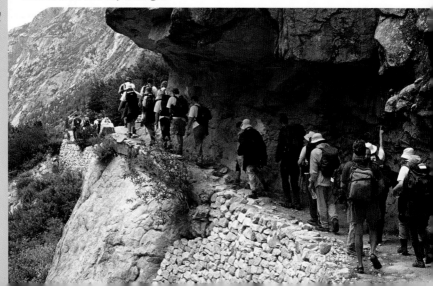

cook rice and potatoes in a hot spring near the temple and offer them to the goddess, depicted here in black marble.

Gangotri

A motorable road runs all the way to the whitewashed 18th-century temple dedicated to the Goddess Ganga at Gangotri (3,200m/10,660ft), reached after a two-day drive from Yamunotri. For a taste of the Inner Himalaya, devout pilgrims press on a further 17km (6¼ miles) up the valley to the true source of the Ganges: the snout of a massive glacier, Gau Mukh. This 40km (28-mile)-long river of ice carves its way through the mountains, a skyline dominated by the impressively pointed Bhagirathi Peaks (6,856m/22,493ft). The freezing pool where the source gushes out of the ice is a place of great sanctity for Hindus.

Kedarnath

A two-day drive away from Gangotri at the head of a sweeping valley, the Shiva temple at Kedarnath (3,581m/ 11,936ft), source of the River Mandakini, is the most remote and spectacularly situated of the Chota Char Dhams. Horses and ponies are on hand to help the less able with the 13km (8 mile) trek from the nearest roadhead.

Badrinath

Dedicated to the God Vishnu, the Badrinath temple (3,133m/10,440ft), where the Alakanda first sees the light of day, is regarded as the most auspicious of the four shinres. Accessible by road, it's painted in multicoloured designs reminiscent of Tibetan monasteries.

The Goddess Ganga temple at Gangotri

A Hindu pilgrim on the rocky way up to Gangotri

The Chota Char Dhams

India barely registers on the radar of most international skiers, but that may well change over the coming decade.

Some of the most compelling powder snow on the planet is to be had in Kashmir, on a plateau at 2,600m (8,660ft) above the former British hill station of **Gulmarg**. A superb new French-built gondola drops skiers at a dizzying 4,000m (13,330ft), and you won't have to queue to get on it. Guided trips are organised by IMFGA-qualified Mountain Tracks (www.ski-gulmarg.co.uk).

Other Indian ski stations worth a spin include **Auli**, near Joshimath in Uttarakhand, which has seen major investment recently. Uttarakhand Tourism (www.uttaranchaltourism.in) offers packages. In Himachal Pradesh, the possibilities for skiing virgin powder are endless around **Manali**, and there are a few basic surface tows in nearby **Solang Nala** during the winter.

popular Hindu pilgrimage to **Amarnath**, where a remote cave harbours a ice stalagmite held by Hindus to resemble a Shiva lingam, the town is also an internationally renowned fishing destination thanks to the presence in its glacier-fed rivers and lakes of Himalayan snow trout.

UTTARAKHAND

The spectacular mountain tract to the north of Uttar Pradesh, sandwiched between Tibet, Nepal and Himachal, is encompassed within the boundaries of Uttarakhand, territory which acceded from UP in 2001 after decades of agitation. The young state has two administrative divisions: Garwhal to the northwest and Kumaon to the southeast. Home to some of India's holiest Hindu pilgrimage places, the former is the more visited of the two. Its high glacial valleys hold the headwaters of both the Ganges and Yamuna rivers, as well as the highest massif entirely within India – Nanda Devi, rising to 7,816m/25,646ft (Kanchenjunga is loftier, but straddles the Nepali border).

Haridwar and Rishikesh

Haridwar ❻, where the Ganges flows out of the mountains into the plains, is one of the seven most sacred cities of India. Every 12 years, like the Treveni Sangam on the outskirts of Allahabad, it plays host to the Kumbh Mela, a great religious festival. The evening *aarati* (worship) of the River Ganges is held every day at **Har-ki-Pauri**, the main ghat.

Skiing in the Himalaya

Devotions are held every evening on the ghats at Haridwar

The Northwest Himalaya

Rishikesh, a town of temples and ashrams surrounded by forest, lies 25km (15 miles) upstream. Its northern part, Muni-ki-Reti, is very attractive, though the best views are to be had from the two footbridges suspended across the river: Ram Jhula and Laksman Jhula. This is where the Beatles and their entourage came to study yoga and meditation with the Maharishi Yogi in 1967, and the town remains India's prime destination for spiritual tourists, with scores of ashrams and yoga schools.

Corbett National Park

At the foot of the Himalayas, some 300km (180 miles) northeast of Delhi and accessible from the capital either by train or road, is the **Corbett Tiger Reserve ❼** (daily 6.30–9.30am and 1.30–5.30pm; charge). Among India's nature reserves, this is the best known because of Jim Corbett, the audacious hunter of the man-eating tigers of Kumaon. The park was established in 1935 and was given Corbett's name after India became independent.

The lovely expanse of forest and meadows by the Ramganga River remains a home to tigers, leopards and elephants, as well as cheetahs, sloth bears, wild pigs, jackals and hyenas. The river abounds with mahseer and trout, as well as two kinds of crocodile and the occasional blind freshwater dolphin. Birdwatchers should look out for stork, red jungle-fowl and black partridge. Safaris are conducted by Jeep and elephant back. Rest at midday in the lodge at Dhikala and watch the elephants head down to the river.

ACCOMMODATION

Accommodation Price Categories

Prices are for one night in a standard double room (unless otherwise specified)

$ = Up to Rs1000
$$ = Rs1000–2000
$$$ = Rs2000–4000
$$$$ = Rs4000–7000
$$$$$ = Rs7000 and above

Himachal Pradesh is these days the prime hot-season retreat for well-heeled Delhi-wallahs, and prices soar during the heat of late- April and May, when advance booking is essential. Ladakh does most of its tourist business from July to September, when the roads from Manali and Srinagar are open. Most first time visitors to Kashmir opt to stay in a houseboat on Srinagar's Dal Lake; ask the Houseboat Owners Association (tel: 0194-245 0872) to arrange a *shikhara* (taxi canoe) for you to look around before booking. Beds are only hard to come by in Uttarakhand at the peak of *yatri* (pilgrimage) season, from May to September. Out of the region's main season, you can usually negotiate discounts on rooms. As a rule of thumb, the further into the mountains you go, the more basic the amenities become.

Himachal Pradesh

Chapslee House
Lakkar Bazaar, Shimla
Tel: 0177-280 2542
www.chapslee.com
A Simla institution. A very elegant, typically British manor house with wonderful suites, period furnishings and antiques, as well as excellent food. **$$$$$**

Dreamland
The Mall, Shimla
Tel: 0177-265 3005
http://hoteldreamlandshimla.com
Reliable budget hotel on the spur high above the Mall, with great Himalayan panoramas from its well-kept rooms. **$–$$**

HPTDC Hotel Rohtang Manalsu
The Mall, Manali
Tel: 01902-252 332

The Pema Thang guesthouse in Dharamsala

http://hptdc.nic.in
A quiet hotel set in lovely grounds, out towards the Hadimba Temple. The large rooms have sweeping vistas across the valley. **$$**

Johnson's Lodge
Circuit House Road, Manali
Tel: 01902-253 023
www.johnsonslodge.com
Well-maintained self-catering cottages or luxury doubles in a Himachali-style hotel, built using traditional materials, but with modern interiors. **$$$–$$$$**

Norbulingka Guest House
Norbulingka Institute, Sidhpur
Tel: 01892-246 406 418
www.tibet.org/norling
Beautiful rooms, decorated with Tibetan handicrafts and murals, in a delightful garden setting 6km (4 miles) south of Dharamsala. **$$–$$$**

Pema Thang
Bhagsu Road, Dharamsala
Tel: 01892-221 871
www.pemathang.net
Friendly and well-run guesthouse, tucked away down a quiet side street; many of the rooms have small kitchens. There's also a great restaurant. **$–$$**

YMCA
The Ridge, Shimla
Tel: 0177-225 0021
Very popular. Dining hall and large, old-fashioned rooms with shared bathrooms. **$**

Ladakh
Omasila
Changspa Lane, Leh
Tel: 01982-252 119
www.hotelomasila.com
Fabulous views over the Indus Valley to Stok Kangi from the terrace of this comfortable hotel, done up in traditional Ladakhi style. **$$**

Oriental
Changspa Lane, Leh
Tel: 01982-253 153
www.orientalgueshouse.com
Below the Shanti Stupa at the end of Chang-spa Lane, this family-run guesthouse ticks all the boxes: lovely Ladakhi-style rooms, warm hospitality and great local food.  **$–$$**

Kashmir
Lalit Grand Palace
Gupkar Road, Srinagar
Tel: 091-194-250 1001/250 1002
www.thelalit.com
Visiting dignitaries and Bollywood stars stay at this former Maharaja's palace on the outskirts of town – the most grandiloquent address in this corner of the Himalayas. Its period architecture and interiors, indoor pool and spa are the main attractions. **$$$$$**

Swiss Hotel
172 Gagribal Road, Nehru Park, Srinagar
Tel: 0194-247 2766
www.swisshotelkashmir.com
Impeccably clean, professionally managed mid-range hotel in a quiet suburb at the foot of Shankacharya Hill. Cycle hire and free internet available on request. **$$**

Uttarakhand
Ananda in the Himalayas
Palace Estate, Narendra Nagar, Rishikesh
Tel: 011-2656 8888
www.anandaspa.com

Norbulingka Guest House in Sidhpur

A very expensive but fabulous spa hotel 18km (11 miles) from Rishikesh. Set in an old palace, it has elegant rooms with lovely views. The spa has a wonderful pool. **$$$$$**

Bhaj Govindam
Nr Bhimgoda Jhula, Haridwar
Tel: 01334-261 682
At a prime location slap on the riverbank, this little campus of bamboo 'cottages', set in an enclosed garden, is a comfortable mid-price option. All of the huts are en suite, and fitted with fans or air coolers. **$$**

Corbett Hideaway
11km (7 miles) north of Ramnagar
Tel: 9810-396 848
www.corbetthideaway.com
Luxury cottages dotted around a shady mangrove orchard on a spur overlooking the river. Well placed for early-morning safaris, and with a quality restaurant and pool on site. **$$$$$**

Corbett Motel
Corbett Tiger Reserve, Ramnagar
Tel: 9837-468 933
The best of the budget places within easy reach of the park, close to the train station. Complimentary pick-up on request. **$–$$**

Haveli Hari Ganga
Pilibhit House, 21 Ramghat, Haridwar
Tel: 01334-226 443
www.havelihariganga.com
A beautifully restored, atmospheric *haveli* with 20 characterful rooms overlooking the Ganges, and a good vegetarian restaurant: easily the best place in town. **$$$$–$$$$$**

RESTAURANTS

As with accommodation, restaurants grow increasingly basic the further from the major resorts you venture. In big tourist towns such as Shimla, Manali and Leh, by contrast, three or more decades of catering for visitors have spawned enormous choice, with plenty of Western alternatives to the spicy, Punjabi-oriented dishes served up throughout the region, as well as healthier, lighter Tibetan soups and *momos* (steamed dumplings).

Himachal Pradesh

Chocolate Log
Jogibara Road, McLeod Ganj, Dharamsala
Cakes, pies and quiches are the stock-in-trade of this established travellers' bakery, which has a pleasant roof-terrace café. **$**

Chopsticks
The Mall, Manali
Excellent Chinese and Tibetan food, including great *momos*; opens early for breakfast. **$$**

Indian Coffee House
The Mall, Shimla
Shimla's ICH is a classic of its type: lost in a faded colonial time warp and full of old-school atmosphere. Most people just come for tea, but they serve tasty, inexpensive biriyanis, *dosas* and egg curry. **$**

Johnson's Café
The Mall, Manali
Classy garden restaurant en route to Old Manali (before Johnson's Lodge). Excellent food, including exceptional trout. **$$–$$$**

Nick's Italian Kitchen
Bhagsu Road, McLeod Ganj, Dharamsala
Authentic Italian dishes served on an open roof terrace with superb views. **$$**

Ladakh

La Pizzeria
Changspa Lane, Leh
The crusty, flavoursome pizzas served in this lovely garden restaurant are hot contenders for the best in the Himalaya, and they also offer a range of equally good soups, Moroccan tagines and Tibetan specials. **$$–$$$**

Pumpernickel German Bakery
Main Bazaar, Leh
A large range of breads, pasta, muesli, cakes and pastries, and wonderful apple pie. A travellers' favourite. **$–$$**

Kashmir

Mughal Darbar
Residency Road, Srinagar
Tel: 0194-257 6998
One of the few places in town where you can order proper Kashmiri *wazwan* (cuisine) in authentic surroundings. The dishes are heavy, meat-based and come in huge portions. **$$**

Uttarakhand

Chotiwala
Swarg Ashram, Ram Jhula, Rishikesh
Chotiwala is the most famous restaurant in town, serving extensive multi-cuisine menus. Their *thalis* are especially popular. **$–$$**

Hoshiyar Puri
Upper Road, Haridwar
Old-established *dhaba*-style place which has done a brisk trade since the 1930s in tasty Punjabi dishes, such as stuffed *parathas*, creamy *dal makhani* and aubergine curry. **$**

Madras Café
Ram Jhula, Rishikesh
It's legendary for its filter coffee, but also whips up tasty wholefood curries and its signature 'Himalayan Health Pulau'. **$**

SPORTS AND ACTIVITIES

The Northwest Himalaya is, of course, one of the finest trekking destinations in the world *(for companies, see p.45)*, but it also offers a range of other adventure sports.

Paragliding

Billing Meadow
Bir, Kangra Valley, Himachal Pradesh
For confirmed enthusiasts, this celebrated field is the place to head for, with powerful thermal uplifts and flight times of up to half an hour in good conditions.

Solang Nala
14km (9 miles) from Manali, Himachal Pradesh
As well as being a low-key ski resort, Solang Nala, at the head of the Kullu Valley, is a renowned paragliding hot-spot from April–September, with around 100 trained pilots offering tandem flights over the snowy peaks of the Dhauladhar Range. All equipment is available for rent on site.

Whitewater Rafting

Garwhal Mandal Vikas Nigam
Devprayag, Uttarakhand
www.gmvnl.com
Whitewater rafting is also popular along the 70km (44-mile) stretch of the Ganges south of Devprayag. The state tourism corporation offers a range of packages and courses.

Tsomori Tours
Fort Road, Leh, Ladakh
Tel: 9419-178 029
www.ladakhinfo.com
The Indus River provides some wonderful whitewater rafting: the area near the capital, where the river is broad and less fierce, is good for beginners, while the Zanskar River, rushing through the deepest canyon in the world, offers compelling 4- to 5-day expeditions.

FESTIVALS AND EVENTS

Although the majority of Buddhist monastery festivals take place during the freezing winter months, when much of the region is cut off behind snowbound passes, the summer sees the descent of the Himalaya's many Hindu gods and goddesses from their village shrines to market towns lower down the valleys for fervent celebrations.

January–February

Makar Sankranti
Uttarakhand
Deities descend from mountain villages in palanquins to the region's hub temples.

McLeod Ganj
Losar
The Tibetan New Year is celebrated in the Dalai Lama's home town with masked *cham* dances in local Buddhist monasteries.

Magh Mela
Haridwar
Smaller version of the Kumbh Mela; Hindu pilgrims take sin-cleansing dips in the Ganges.

May

Himalayan Hang-Gliding Rally
Billing, Kangra Valley
International hang-gliders and parascenders come for a week of high-altitude flying.

July–September

Shri Amanarth Yatra
Kashmir
Pilgrims trek for three days to a cave in the Himalayan range to worship an ice lingam.

October

Dusshera
Kullu Valley
Gathering of Kullu's gods for music and dance.

Rajasthan and Gujarat

The states of Rajasthan and Gujarat are where India's orientalist clichés – from painted elephants to onion-domed palaces dripping with bejewelled treasures, romantic forts and icing-white hilltop shrines – form the setting for everyday life. Framed by the backdrop of sunburnt deserts, the vivid colours of local cities, festivals, crafts, saris and turbans are all the more mesmerising.

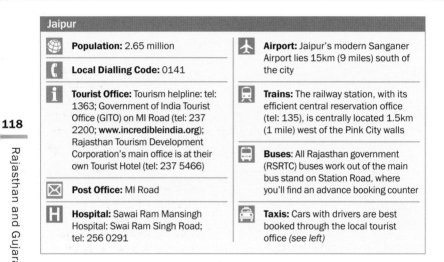

Jaipur

Population: 2.65 million

Local Dialling Code: 0141

Tourist Office: Tourism helpline: tel: 1363; Government of India Tourist Office (GITO) on MI Road (tel: 237 2200; **www.incredibleindia.org**); Rajasthan Tourism Development Corporation's main office is at their own Tourist Hotel (tel: 237 5466)

Post Office: MI Road

Hospital: Sawai Ram Mansingh Hospital: Swai Ram Singh Road; tel: 256 0291

Airport: Jaipur's modern Sanganer Airport lies 15km (9 miles) south of the city

Trains: The railway station, with its efficient central reservation office (tel: 135), is centrally located 1.5km (1 mile) west of the Pink City walls

Buses: All Rajasthan government (RSRTC) buses work out of the main bus stand on Station Road, where you'll find an advance booking counter

Taxis: Cars with drivers are best booked through the local tourist office *(see left)*

Rajasthan – literally 'Land of Kings' – conforms to a popular ideal of romantic India, boasting more maharajas' palaces, camel treks and colourful festivals than you could experience in a lifetime. Itineraries tend to revolve around the state's main cities, each of which is distinguished by a different hue: the salmon pink of the capital, Jaipur; the cobalt blue of Jodhpur's old city; the yellow ochre of Jaisalmer's desert citadel; and the white alabaster of Udaipur.

Although far less visited, Gujarat holds no less interest, boasting a distinctive Indo-Muslim culture, at its most striking in the modern capital Ahmedabad, where elaborately carved mosques and shrines huddle in the packed streets of the old city. Vibrant handicrafts traditions and some superbly atmospheric Jain and Hindu temples form the focus of forays further afield.

Big cats tend to be high on the agendas of most visitors to this region, thanks to the presence in Rajasthan of one of India's foremost tiger reserves, Ranthambore, and in the Sasan Gir Sanctuary in the Saurashtra region of Gujarat – the last stronghold of the Asiatic lion.

JAIPUR

Jaipur ❶, the capital of Rajasthan, was not always pink. The original city was in fact light grey, edged with white borders. It only acquired its characteristic salmon hue – the traditional colour of welcome – ahead of the visit in 1883 of the Prince of Wales. Comprising rectangular blocks divided by broad, tree-lined avenues, the regular grid plan at the heart of the old city was devised in 1728 by Majharaja Jai Singh. Its design was supposed to replicate the form of an auspicious *mandala*, or sacred Tantric diagram, the aim being to create a framework that would infuse Jaipur's daily life with 'the overarching

The gateway to Jaipur's City Palace

harmony of the Cosmos'. As well as proving an aesthetic triumph, the streamlined layout and its fortifications successfully repelled would-be invaders for decades, ensuring a lasting prosperity that has continued into the modern era.

The City Palace

Occupying the most auspicious central portion of Maharaja Jai Singh's grid, the **City Palace** (daily 9.30am–5pm; charge) formed the political hub of Jaipur, and remains the residence of the royal family. Although its innermost enclosures date from the 18th century, other wings were added in subsequent eras, fusing Mughal and Rajput architectural motifs.

A series of ornamental gateways leads to the interlocking courtyards inside the palace, many of whose pavilions are given over to the **Sawai Man Singh II Museum**. Armour, weapons, priceless carpets, state regalia, jewellery, miniature paintings, manuscripts and precious ritual paraphernalia make up the bulk of the collection, all lavishly

The Palace of the Winds is the city's most celebrated landmark

Rajasthan and Gujarat

decorated by craftsmen whom the Jaipur maharajas recruited from the courts of the Mughals as the empire lapsed into decline.

Palace of the Winds and Jantar Mantar

At the eastern perimeter of the palace, overlooking the bazaar, stands Jaipur's most photographed monument, the **Palace of the Winds** (Hawa Mahal; daily 9am–4.30pm; charge 🅜). A five-floored confection of domed balconies, delicate cupolas and pierced stone *jali* screens, it is not in fact a palace, but a hollow facade of 953 airy niches and windows, used by the royal women in *purdah* (secluded from the public) to watch the streets below.

Immediately behind it, the **Jantar Mantar** (daily 9am–4.30pm; charge 🅜) consists of 16 colossal geometric structures which Maharaja Jai Singh – a keen astronomer – used to calculate celestial latitudes and planetary movements; it is one of five such complexes built at Hindu cities across India.

A popular way up to the stunning Amber Fort is on the back of an elephant

Amber and Jaigarh Forts

Sitting astride a ridge at the head of narrow mountain valley 11km (x7 miles) north of Jaipur, **Amber Fort** (daily 9am–5.30pm; charge ) is the jewel in the crown of Rajput fort-palaces. Painted elephants take visitors up the hill to admire the massive gateways, pillared pavilions and palaces that recall the glory and wealth of Amber's association with the Mughals.

A 20-minute walk further uphill stands **Jaigarh Fort** (daily 9am–4.30pm; charge), opened to the public in the late 1980s after being sealed for decades following a rumour that an enormous quantity of gold was buried in vaults under deep reservoirs. This forced isolation ensured the complex's many palaces and temples remained better preserved than those below it.

EASTERN RAJASTHAN

The scrub-covered countryside east of Jaipur is one of the least-visited corners of the state. Those travellers who do cross it tend to do so en route to the Unesco-listed Keoladeo Ghana National Park, near Bharatpur, before veering south towards the famous Ranthambore tiger reserve.

Keoladeo Ghana National Park

Spread over 29 sq km (11 sq miles) of marshes and lakes, **Keoladeo Ghana National Park ❷** (Apr–Sept 6am–6pm, Oct–Mar 6.30am–5pm; charge), 6km (3¾ miles) south of Bharatpur, once served as the Maharaja's hunting reserve; today, despite a recent fall in nesting numbers, it serves as a sanctuary for 220 resident bird species and a further 146 migrants, some of which fly across the Himalayas from the Central Asian and Russian steppes to nest. Sadly, the super-rare Siberian cranes for which Keoladeo has traditionally been a breeding ground appear to have stopped returning to the park from their summer home on the shores of the Caspian Sea in Iran.

Ranthambore National Park

Great concern surrounds the future of the 30 or so tigers surviving at **Ranthambore National Park** ❸ (tel: 0120-405 2615; www.ranthamborenationalpark.com; Oct–June; charge 📷), but for the time being, at least, the reserve's beautiful big cats are sufficiently numerous to justify the lengthy trip to this remote corner of the state.

Moreover, the scenery is magnificent. Spread over nearly 400 sq km (155 sq miles) of rolling grasslands, mixed deciduous forest and scrub, Ranthambore encompasses a former royal hunting reserve, set around an estate of artificial lakes dotted with pavilions and *chatris*. To complete the scene, a rambling Rajput fort perches on top of a sandstone outcrop in the centre of the park, where monkeys scamper around ruined temples like a scene from the *Jungle Book*. Safaris take place in the mornings and evenings. Unless you're staying in a hotel with pre-booked places, tickets have to be arranged a day in advance through the RTDC Vinayak Tourist Complex in **Sawai Madhopur**, Ranthambore's main road- and rail-head, 14km (9 miles) east. The best period to visit is between October and March; the park is closed during the monsoons.

WESTERN RAJASTHAN

Across the west of Rajasthan, from the far side of the Aravalli hills as far as the sensitive India-Pakistan border, sprawl the wastes of the Thar, or 'Great Indian Desert'. Known since ancient times as

Inside one of the apartments in Jodhpur's Meherangarh Fort

Junagadh Fort glows in the late afternoon sun (see p.124)

funeral pyre in 1843. The core of the palace, a complex of sumptuously decorated apartments overlooking enclosed courtyards, is given over to the excellent **Meherangarh Museum** (admission included with fort entrance ticket), where royal artefacts spanning five centuries are displayed.

After three successive droughts, with millions of his subjects on the verge of starvation, Maharaja Umaid Singh embarked in 1929 on the construction of a massive new palace as a famine relief project. Rising from the scrubby southern outskirts of the city, **Umaid Bhavan** took 3,000 workers 15 years to complete. With 347 rooms, a vast central domed hall and

'Marusthali' – or 'Land of Death'– this drought-prone region is in fact neither entirely barren nor uninhabited, but home to some extraordinary medieval monuments and an equally distinctive agro-pastoralist culture.

Jodhpur

If any sight could be said to epitomise the indomitable pride and swagger of old Rajputana, it's the **Meherangarh Fort** in **Jodhpur ❹** (daily 9am–5pm; charge). The walls and huge bastions of Rao Jodha's citadel, begun in the 15th century, float 125m (420 ft) above the surrounding sea of blue houses and dusty plain. The main approach is a zigzagging ramp through a series of fortified gateways, the innermost of which, **Loha Pol**, bears carved handprints representing the 13 wives and concubines who committed *sati* on their husband's

---

Jodhpurs

The famous tapered riding breeches named after the Marwari capital were invented by Regent Pratap Singh, who disliked the usual *puttis*, or cloth wrappings, worn around the shins when riding. Instead he devised an all-in-one trouser alternative, based on traditional Rajput garb. The fashion spread to London after the Marwari ruler's visit to Queen Victoria's Diamond Jubilee in 1887. En route to England, his ship sank at Suez while he was ashore and the Regent, who lost his entire wardrobe in the accident, had to instruct a London tailor to make replicas of his Durbar outfits. For want of a more accurate name, the tailor dubbed the curious trousers he was charged with making for Pratap Singh as 'jodhpurs'.

The sandstone city of Jaisalmer is famed for its amber hue

the most fabulous Art Deco interiors money could buy, the palace emerged as a folly of breathtaking proportions. One third of the building is today occupied by the present royal family; the rest is given over to a luxury hotel.

Bikaner

Founded in 1486, **Bikaner** , Rajasthan's fourth city, is surrounded by 6km (3¾ miles) of rich pink sandstone walls. Its medieval heart today holds plenty of desert atmosphere, with ancient Jain temples and late 19th-century *havelis* lining dusty backstreets. Chief among the attractions here is the late 16th-century **Junagadh Fort** (daily 10am–4pm; charge). The palace complex inside is justly famed for its interiors, which rank alongside those

Jaisalmer

 Population: 58,300

 Local Dialling Code: 02992

 Tourist Office: Tourist Reception Centre: Gadi Sagar Road; tel: 252 406

Post Office: Hanuman Circle Road, west of the walled fort

H Hospital: Shree Mahshwari Hospital: 35 Barmer Road; tel: 250 024; www.maheshwarihospital.net

 Airport: Jaisalmer's tiny airport, 9km (5½ miles) west of town, handles a limited schedule of flights to cities across the northwest, including Jodhpur, Delhi and Udaipur

Trains: The train station lies 2km (1¼ miles) east of town on the Jodhpur Road

Buses: Buses depart from a stand below the southwest end of the fort and from the main RSRTC bus stand (tel: 251 541) out near the train station

 Car Hire: Jeeps for explorations of the surrounding desert are best hired through the tourist office *(see left)*

of Amber, Udaipur and Jodhpur and contain a wealth of royal treasures.

The present royal family resides in the more modern **Lalgarh Palace**, 3km (2 miles) north, parts of which function as a luxury hotel. It's less alluring than its predecessor, but harbours a fascinating collection of old photographs and royal memorabilia in the **Shri Sadul Museum** (Mon–Sat 10am–5pm; charge).

Jaisalmer

Sailing above the ochre sand flats of the Thar on a long, low ridge, the amber-coloured walls of **Jaisalmer**  exude a molten glow at sunset, generating an atmosphere that has entranced travellers for centuries. Founded in 1156, it was the oldest of Rajasthan's fortified towns, protected by an imposing double set of bastions and crisscrossed with narrow streets and alleyways. Around this stretches the more modern town, fashioned out of the same honey-coloured sandstone and home to numerous spectacularly carved *havelis* (merchants' houses), many of which now accommodate atmospheric hotels.

The elaborate sculpture decorating the four 15th-century **Jain temples** inside the fort finds its counterpart in the finely carved facades of the merchants' *havelis*, built 200 years later. But much more than the individual monuments, it is the general ambience of the town that gives it its special allure. Everything here is bathed in a serene desert light that adds a shimmer to the stone and a translucence to the shadows.

Rajasthan and Gujarat

Gadi Sagar lake, in Jaisalmer

SOUTHERN RAJASTHAN

The lake city of Udaipur, with its fairy-tale whitewashed palaces, lures most visitors to the far south of Rajasthan at some stage. En route, Pushkar, a gem of a temple town rising improbably from the desert around the shores of a sacred lake, and its neighbour, Ajmer, where Muslim pilgrims flock to worship at the shrine of India's most revered Sufi saint, deserve at least a couple of days' stopover. Once you're in the deep south, it's also worth making time for the quirky hill station of Mount Abu – the only one in the state.

Ajmer and Pushkar

Ajmer ❼ was one of the most important cities of the Mughal empire during the 16th and 17th centuries,

and for 2,000 years before that its hillfort – the Taragarh – was one of the most strategically important in all of India. However, the town's historic prominence is these days eclipsed by its significance as the site of Islamic India's most revered shrine: the tomb (*dargah*) of **Khwaja Muin-ud-din Chishti**. Visitor numbers, always high, reach their peak at the time of the saint's *Urs*, or death anniversary, in October/November, when millions from across the subcontinent converge here to pray at the shrine.

Hindu mythology identifies **Pushkar**, just across the hills from Ajmer, as the spot where a lotus flower dropped by Brahma, the Creator, fell to earth. A gorgeous little lake promptly sprang out of the Thar Desert, regarded by

A camel struts its stuff in Pushkar

The Pushkar Camel Fair

Over the fortnight leading up to the full moon of Kartika month (late Oct/early Nov), villagers from the desert regions of western India congregate around Pushkar lake for the famous Kartik Purnima festival and camel-trading fair. Decked out in their finest traditional dress, they come to buy and sell livestock, strike marriage deals and meet with relatives. The spectacle, set against a sea of 50,000 dusty camels and rolling dunes, ranks among the most compelling in India.

As accommodation can be scarce over the festival period, the local tourism department and several upscale hotels erect temporary tent compounds on the sand flats around the town. The tents are fitted with fans, electric light, bathrooms and other mod cons. Book in advance through www.rajasthantourism.gov.in.

The City Palace in romantic Udaipur

Hindus as one of India's most sacred sites. During the full moon of Kartika month (usually November), tens of thousands come to bathe in the redemptive waters, and to buy and sell livestock at the huge **Camel Fair** (*mela*) held in the dunes to the south of town (*see opposite* ). The fair has become a major tourist event, for which a whole town of tents is set up.

Even if your visit doesn't coincide with the famous *mela*, Pushkar deserves a detour. Set against a backdrop of sharp-ridged hills, the lake and its entourage of domed temples, bathing ghats and whitewashed *havelis* (merchants' houses) is one of Rajasthan's defining sights. For the ultimate view, climb up the flight of ancient stone steps to the **Savitri Temple**, southwest of town, from whose terrace you can look down the Aravalli mountain range and across the Thar, rippling into the distance.

Udaipur

'The most diversified and most romantic spot on the continent of India' was how the chief annalist and champion of Rajput culture, Col. James Tod, famously described **Udaipur ❽** in 1817. Parts of the fabled lake city have altered beyond recognition since Tod's day, but the palaces where he was so lavishly entertained by the Maharana of Mewar continue to entrance everyone who sets eyes on them. Framed by a distant backdrop of rolling desert hills, they rise from the waters of Lake Pichola like some exquisite orientalist fantasy.

An imposing wall of yellow plaster topped by a crowning layer of domes, golden finials, fluted pillars and whimsical arches, the **City Palace** is part royal residence and part luxury hotel, but the most historic, and vibrantly decorated, portions have been allocated to the **Palace Museum**

⭐ DESERT THREADS

Many explanations have been advanced for the extraordinary richness of the textile traditions of India's desert states. But the very drabness of the Thar itself accounts for the vibrancy of the colours and patterns deployed in clothing, homes and animal liveries throughout rural Rajasthan and Gujarat. Although the rapidly developing economy of modern India has had a generally corrosive effect on village life, these textiles are still very much in demand as tourist souvenirs, which has kept alive many of the skills that might otherwise have disappeared.

Local Skills

An amazing array of different styles and techniques has evolved over the centuries, each particular to a different caste, sub-caste, district or village. The bride's trousseau, which was expected to contain elaborately decorated clothes created over months of labour by female relatives, was an important driving force behind this creativity. Weddings, religious festivals and livestock fairs still provide regular opportunities for women to show off their decorative skills.

Block Printing

Bagru – or 'block printing' – where cotton is patterned using dyes applied with carved wooden blocks, has long been a speciality of the Jaipur region in Rajasthan. You can see artisans at work

Bright colours and intricate design are hallmarks of this region's textiles

in the village of Sanganer, 16km (10 miles) south of the city. Kutch in Gujarat is another centre for this old art form, where it's known as *ajrakh*.

Embroidery, Patchwork, Appliqué

Kutch is also one of the best places in India to shop for embroidered cloth. Some particularly fine specimens are on display at the Kala Raksha Museum north of the capital, Bhuj (www.kala-rak sha.museum.org), where you can watch semi-nomadic Rabari women at work.

Embroidery can take its toll on women's eyesight, which is why in middle age many desert women prefer to sew patches of old cloth together to create 'crazy-patchwork' quilts, cushion covers and bedspreads. In Gujarat, older craft workers also produce beautiful appliqué.

Batik and Tie Dyeing

The technique of resisting dyes by tying fabrics in knots, or by applying impervious gums made from mud, flour and wax, is used throughout Rajasthan and Gujarat, where it's known as *bandhani*. One of the best places to pick up quality examples is the annual Shilpgram Fair, held in December at the Shilpgram artisans' complex on Udaipur's outskirts.

Mirrorwork

Adding tiny mirrors (*shisha*) or fragments of mica to skirts, veils and bodices gives garments a wow factor, and you'll be treated to some splendid displays of such traditional flair at religious gatherings and markets. In tourist shops, mirrorwork is also used to enliven more portable cushion covers and bed linen.

Hard at work embroidering fabric in Kutch

Desert Threads

Drying fabric for *saris* in bulk

(daily 9.30am–4.30pm; charge). Wandering between the various halls you can trace the shift in emphasis from the glorious cusp-arched, onion-domed extravagance of Mughal times to the bohemian-crystal, gilded stucco pomp of the Raj era.

Most of the interest in Udaipur city itself centres on its old quarter, on the eastern shores of the lake. Competing for the best views, several fine *havelis* still stand on the waterside, including the enormous **Bagore-ki-Haveli** (daily 10am–5.30pm; charge), a former prime minister's residence converted into an engaging museum.

A pleasant drive along the banks of Fateh Sagar – the second of Udaipur's lakes – takes you 5km (3 miles) west of the city towards Rana Sajjan Singh's late 19th-century **Monsoon** Palace (Sajjan Garh; daily 9am–6pm; charge). From its eyrie atop a steep-sided mountain summit, this once beautiful royal lodge surveys a vast sweep of the Aravallis.

Mount Abu

Rajasthan's ruling caste, the 'twice-born' Rajputs, trace their mythological origins back to a fire ceremony conducted in the 8th century AD at the top of a huge rocky massif in the southwest corner of the state, near the present-day border with Gujarat. More than a thousand years later, the British founded a sanitarium on the high plateau, centered on circular **Nakki Lake**. **Mount Abu** 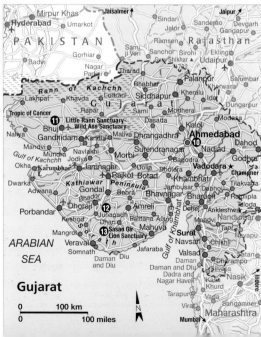 is these days popular mainly with honeymooners, who flock here during the winter wedding season, and middle-class families from the big Gujarati cities.

The Dilwara temples are intricately patterned

Boating on Nakki Lake, a popular retreat

Temperatures at the resort can be noticeably cooler – hardly glacial, but nippy enough. The few foreigners who make the journey up here do so primarily to see the staggeringly intricate **Dilwara temples** (daily noon–6pm; free), a cluster of five white marble Jain shrines situated 3km (2 miles) northeast of town. Dedicated to the first *tirthankara*, Adinath, the oldest of them – the Vimla Vasahi – dates from AD 1031. Every surface inside it has been carved with elaborate patterns and figures.

GUJARAT

Tradition and modernity combine in a vibrant, dynamic fashion in Gujarat. Well-educated and entrepreneurial, the state's inhabitants have made their homeland among the wealthiest and most developed in India. The modern world, however, has made little impact on the region's fringes, where age-old pastoralist and farming ways of life endure. Aside from the wonderfully picturesque traditional dress of its villagers *(see Desert Threads, p.128)*, Gujarat also holds some world-class monuments, India's last wild lion sanctuary and some evocative survivors of Portuguese colonial times. Few of the tourists streaming between Delhi and Mumbai pull off the railway line to experience them, but the state is packed with rewarding sights.

Ahmedabad

Founded by Ahmad Shah I on the site of the ancient city of Karnavati in 1411, **Ahmedabad ⑩**, the capital of the state of Gujarat, is a bustling textile and commercial city straddling the Sabarmati River. Polluted and choked with traffic, its modern centre holds little appeal for visitors, though its densely packed old quarter, sprawling from the river's east bank, is worth a detour for its fine examples of 15th- and 16th-century Indo-Muslim architecture. Particularly well-preserved examples include the **Teen Darwaza**, a chunky, triple-arched gateway carved with a mixture of Islamic calligraphy and typically Hindu ornamentation, the splendid **Jama Masjid** dating from 1424, whose domed prayer hall is supported by 120 ornately sculpted pillars, and the incense-filled **Tomb of Ahmed Shah I**, built in 1442, near Manek Chowk.

One of the city's most splendid old mansions has been converted into the famous **Calico Museum of Textiles at Shahibag** (Thur–Tue, secular textiles 10.30am–12.30pm, religious textiles 2.45–4.45pm; free), whose exceptional collection includes rich brocades and embroideries from Kashmir, Gujarat and the southern states. Ahmedabad's textile industry was the main reason Mahatma Gandhi, who was born in Porbander on Gujarat's southern coast, chose to site his ashram in the city during the Independence struggle. A set of austere buildings nestling amid mango trees, the **Hridey Kunj** (daily 8.30am–6.30pm; free), at the **Sabarmati (Ghandi) Ashram**, now holds a simple museum displaying the great leader's spectacles, sandals, photographs and famous spinning wheel.

Kutch

Cut off behind the salt flats of the Great and Little Ranns, **Kutch** (or Kachchh), in the far northwest of Gujarat, has always been a land apart – a place of refuge for tribes, castes and clans fleeing persecution elsewhere. Over the centuries, a mosaic of cultures evolved under the umbrella of the region's tolerant

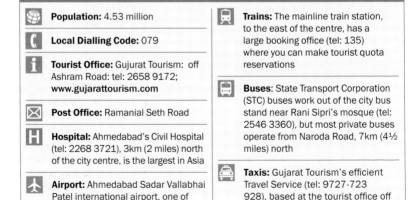

Ahmedabad

Population: 4.53 million

Local Dialling Code: 079

Tourist Office: Gujurat Tourism: off Ashram Road: tel: 2658 9172; **www.gujarattourism.com**

Post Office: Ramanial Seth Road

Hospital: Ahmedabad's Civil Hospital (tel: 2268 3721), 3km (2 miles) north of the city centre, is the largest in Asia

Airport: Ahmedabad Sadar Vallabhai Patel international airport, one of India's ten busiest, lies 8km (5 miles) northeast of the centre

Trains: The mainline train station, to the east of the centre, has a large booking office (tel: 135) where you can make tourist quota reservations

Buses: State Transport Corporation (STC) buses work out of the city bus stand near Rani Sipri's mosque (tel: 2546 3360), but most private buses operate from Naroda Road, 7km (4½ miles) north

Taxis: Gujarat Tourism's efficient Travel Service (tel: 9727-723 928), based at the tourist office off Ashram Road, is the best place to arrange car hire

The Wild Ass Sanctuary protects this unusual animal

rulers, the Maharaos. In spite of depopulation, each has managed to preserve its distinct traditions, making this one of India's most colourful regions.

The survival of so many minority cultures in Kutch is all the more extraordinary given the fact that on the morning of 26 January 2001 (India's Independence Day) the region was devastated by a massive earthquake in which an estimated 25,000 people were killed. One of the worst-hit areas was the medieval walled town of **Bhuj ⑪**, regional capital and site of the Maharaos' medieval palace, whose centrepiece is an opulent pleasure hall, the Aina Mahal. Many of its ceilings collapsed in the earthquake, but the famous **Hall of Mirrors** (Sat–Thur 9am–1pm, 3–6pm; charge) luckily came through intact.

With more time, it's possible to travel out to the fringes of Kutch for a taste of life on the Ranns. In the far southeast, the Little Rann is the site of the isolated **Wild Ass Sanctuary**, part of the Little Rann Sanctuary – a 4,850-sq-km (1,870-sq-mile) reserve set up to protect the rare Indian wild ass.

Rajasthan and Gujarat

Kutchi Handirafts

Kutch is renowned above all for its handicrafts, especially embroidery and block printing. Each of the region's minority groups maintains its own styles and techniques, and the best way to experience them is to visit the villages where the work is carried out. The semi-desert area north of Bhuj harbours a major concentration of these. As a primer, start your tour at the excellent **Kala Raksha Trust** (daily 10am–2pm, 3–6pm; www.kala-raksha.org) in Sumrasar, 25km (15 miles) north of Bhuj, an NGO that is working to help preserve the region's crafts; there's a small museum and shop on site, and workshops where you can watch Rabari and Garasia Jat women at work.

St Paul's in Diu, one of several Portuguese-influenced churches found here

Junagadh

South across the Gulf of Kutch, the spatula-shaped peninsula of Saurashtra (also known as Kathiawar) is dotted with the palatial homes of its former princely rulers. Like neighbouring Rajasthan, the local farmers still retain traditional dress, the men in all-white cotton, and women in colourful *cholis* and pleated skirts.

Junagadh ⑫, in the interior of the peninsula, ranks among the most ancient towns in India. Buddhist caves chiselled between 200BC and AD200 into the rocky hills surrounding it testify to the area's importance as an administrative and religious centre in ancient times, while the squat Maqbara tombs clustered in the centre of town recall the heyday of its 19th-century Muslim rulers. Most visitors who pass through these days do so en route to **Mount Girnar**, an extinct volcano rising out of the plains 4km (2.5 miles) to the east. The massif, which reaches 945m (3,100ft), has five distinct peaks, joined by 8,000 or more stone steps that thread their way between a constellation of small Jain and Hindu shrines, the most revered of them being the temple dedicated to Amba Mata, also known as 'Ambaji', the mother goddess.

The Sasan Gir Lion Sanctuary

In the far south of Saurashtra beyond Junagadh lies the **Sasan Gir Lion Sanctuary** ⑬ (mid-Oct–mid-June, daily 6.30–10.30am, 3–5pm; charge Ⓜ), one of the last places in the world where Asiatic lions can be seen in their natural habitat. Efforts at conservation began in 1900 after the then British viceroy, Lord Curzon, convinced the local nawab that the endangered lions on his land should be protected rather than hunted. After reaching a low point of around a dozen, the population today has reached a more healthy 360. In addition to lions, the reserve hosts leopards, crocodiles, hyenas, *nilgai* (blackbuck) and wild peacocks.

Diu

The Saurashtran coast always played an important role in the maritime trade between northern India and the Persian Gulf, and the first

Portuguese navigators to explore the region were quick to see the strategic potential of a small island called **Diu**, on the southernmost tip of the peninsula. Plenty of Lusitanian character survives in the backstreets of Diu town, with a crop of elegant Indo-Portuguese mansions and churches, and more liberal liquor laws than those prevailing on the mainland. A string of quiet beaches around the island provides further incentive to stop here for a few days ▥.

Palitana

Palitana in the far southeast of Saurashtra near the city of Bhavanagar swarms with Jain pilgrims making their way to **Shatrunjaya Hill**, just to the south. An incredible 863 white marble shrines bristle atop its twin peaks. The walk to the summit involves scaling more than 3,200 steps, an effort for which you'll be rewarded with fabulous views across the Gulf of Cambay.

Daman

In the far south of Gujarat, the one location worth breaking a journey down the coast to visit is the former Portuguese outpost of **Daman**, where a 16th-century fort encloses a collection of grand Lusitanian churches and palacios overlooking the mouth of the Damanganga River. Old Goa is the only other place where you will find Baroque facades so beautifully preserved. Daman's other claim to fame is its Union Territory Status (shared with Diu), which means its liquor licensing laws are more lenient than those of Gujarat – and why the town gets inundated most weekends by Jeep-loads of heavy-drinking Gujarati men.

The peaks of many shrines dot Shatrunjaya Hill, near Palitana

ACCOMMODATION

Since the late 1960s, former royals and nobles in Rajasthan have been compensating for the loss of their privy purses by converting their palaces into so-called 'heritage hotels'. While the majority offer international five-star facilities, or equivalent, some are more modest guesthouses where the accent is on traditional architecture and ambience rather than modern luxuries. At the bottom end of the market, budget hotels and guesthouses around this state frequently give superlative value for money. With less tourist traffic than neighbouring Rajasthan, Gujarat's accommodation also offers exceptionally good value for money, especially at the lower end of the scale, while yet more heritage places abound at the top end of the market.

Jaipur

Alsisar Haveli
Sansar Chandra Road
Tel: 0141-236 8290
www.alsisar.com
A beautiful, quiet, converted mansion with 47 clean, elegant and atmospheric rooms (all a/c). There is a wonderful rooftop swimming pool, surrounded by Rajasthani domed pavilions. **$$$$–$$$$$**

Athiti Guest House
1 Park House Scheme Road

Tel: 0141-237 8679
This family-run hotel-cum-guesthouse is one of the cleanest, brightest, most welcoming places in the state. **$–$$**

Pearl Palace
Hathroi Fort
Tel: 0141-237 3700
www.hotelpearlpalace.com
Probably the best budget hotel in Rajasthan, with spotless and superb-value modern rooms, super-efficient service and a lovely rooftop restaurant. **$**

The rooftop view from the Pearl Palace hotel in Jaipur

Eastern Rajasthan

The Bagh
Agra–Achnera Road, Bharatpur (for Keoladeo Ghana National Park)
Tel: 05644-228 333
www.thebagh.com
Bharatpur's only 'boutique hotel', beautifully situated amid former royal orchards and gardens. The decor combines modern design elements with traditional Rajput style. **$$$$$**

Kiran Guest House
364 Rajendra Nagar (for Keoladeo Ghana National Park)
Tel: 05644-223 845
Has five spacious and immaculate rooms with a lovely terrace-top restaurant serving good food and chilled beer. **$**

Tiger Safari
Ranthambore Road,
Ranthambore National Park
Tel: 07462-221 137
www.tigersafariresort.com
Friendly, comfortable mid-range hotel, whose centrepiece is a well-tended garden. **$$**

Vanyavilas
Ranthambore Road,
Ranthambore National Park
Tel: 07462-223 999
www.oberoivanyavilas.com
The latest Oberoi resort is lavish and luxurious: tent accommodation with colonial-style baths, set in perfectly landscaped gardens. **$$$$$**

Western Rajasthan

Bal Samand Lake Palace
Off the Mandor Road, 8km (5 miles) north of town, Jodhpur
Tel: 0291-257 2321
www.welcomheritagehotels.com
Former royal lakeside summer palace, beautifully converted into one of the most gorgeous heritage hotels in the state, set amid expansive gardens, with a huge pool. **$$$$$**

Bhairon Vilas
Next to Junagadh Fort, Bikaner
Tel: 0151-254 4751
http://hotelbhaironvilas.tripod.com
This eccentric heritage hotel, owned and run by a bohemian cousin of the maharaja, is a real one-off. The family heirlooms and 19th-century Rajasthani architecture are stylishly juxtaposed with funky modern decor. **$–$$**

Fort Rajwada
Jodhpur–Barmer Link Road, Jaisalmer
Tel: 02992-253 233
www.fortrajwada.com
An impressive modern complex on the outskirts, built using filigreed sandstone fragments from old *havelis*; there's also a fabulous pool. **$$$$$**

Hotel Shri Ram
A-228 Sadul Ganj, Bikaner
Tel: 0151-252 2651
www.hotelshriram.com
Impeccable budget accommodation, with very clean attached rooms (some a/c) and cheaper dormitories. **$–$$$**

Shahi
Gandhi Street, opposite Nursingh temple, Old City, Jodhpur
Tel: 0291-262 3802
www.shahiguesthouse.com
Small, intimate guesthouse in a 350-year-old *haveli* deep in the blue city. Its rooms are simply furnished, but the terrace is a superb place to hang out. **$$–$$$**

Shahi Palace
Jaisalmer
Tel: 02992-255 920
www.shahipalacehotel.com
Well-run modern hotel constructed out of traditional sandstone, with glorious fort views and beautifully decorated rooms. **$–$$**

Southern Rajasthan

Amet Haveli
Hanuman Ghat, Udaipur
Tel: 0294-243 1085

http://amethaveliudaipur.com
Exquisite 350-year-old *haveli* with romantic rooms, whose carpeted window seats look through delicate arches across Pichola Lake to the City Palace. Superb value in its bracket. **$$$–$$$$**

Kankarwa Haveli
26 Lal Ghat, Udaipur
Tel: 0294-241 1457
www.kankarwahaveli.com
Old lakeside *haveli* with traditional Rajput rooms straight off the pages of an interiors magazine. Superb value for money.
$$–$$$

Jagat Singh Palace
Ajmer Road, Pushkar
Tel: 0145-277 2402
www.hotelpushkarpalace.com
Assembled from fragments of traditional Rajasthani houses, the Jagat Singh Palace offers Pushkar's most luxurious, elegantly styled accommodation, in a pair of four-storey towers rising from the sandy edges of town. **$$$$–$$$$$**

Lalghat Guest House
33 Lalghat, Udaipur
Tel: 0294-252 5301
A well-known budget travellers' haunt that's showing signs of age but retains its romantic feel thanks to an unrivalled position on the ghats. **$**

Palace Hotel (Bikaner House)
Dilwara Road, Mount Abu
Tel: 02974-238 673
www.palacehotelbikanerhouse.com
Built in 1893 for the Raj of Bikaner, the Palace Hotel has its own private lake and tree-shaded grounds. Each of the 33 rooms is furnished in period style.
$$$$$

Seventh Heaven
Near Mali-ki-Mandir, Chotti Basti, Pushkar
Tel: 0145-510 5455
www.inn-seventh-heaven.com
Beautifully converted 100-year-old *haveli*,

tucked away in the backstreets northeast of the lake, and a real haven for budget travellers. **$–$$$**

Shri Ganesh Hotel
Near Sophia High School, Mount Abu
Tel: 02974-237 292
Clean, efficient, friendly budget travellers' guesthouse situated on the outskirts of Mount Abu. **$**

Gujarat
Gangaram
Behind the Aina Mahal, Bhuj
Tel: 02832-224 231
The best of a generally ropey bunch of hotels in Bhuj, run with great enthusiasm by the amiable Mr Jethi. **$–$$**

Gir Birding Lodge
Bambhafod Naka, Sasan
Tel: 02877-2630 2019
www.girnationalpark.com
Straightforward and attractive accommodation set in a mango orchard close to the entrance to the sanctuary. **$$$$**

The House of Mangaldas Girdhardas
Opposite the Sidi Sayid Mosque, Ahmedabad
Tel: 079-2550 6946
www.houseofmg.com
This heritage boutique hotel in a 20th-century *haveli* has a range of beautifully refurbished room and suites – all very elegant, with four-posters and floaty mosquito nets. **$$$$–$$$$$**

Sao Tomé Retiro
Next to Diu Museum, Firangi Wada, Diu
Tel: 02875-253 137
Laid-back pension housed in a former church (with great panoramic views from the top of the tower). **$**

Volga
Lal Darwaza, off Relief Road, Ahmedabad
Tel: 079-2550 9497
Among the snappiest, brightest mid-range options in the city, in the thick of the action near Siddi Saiyad's mosque. **$–$$**

RESTAURANTS

Combining ingredients from across the subcontinent with centuries of Hindu, Islamic and Jain culinary know-how, Rajasthan's cooking traditions are every bit as sophisticated and refined as the interior decor of Rajput palaces. Wherever you eat – whether in desert villages or royal palaces – you'll be amazed at the variety and complexity of the dishes served. Gujarati cuisine is justly renowned as one of the most sophisticated, refined and healthy in the subcontinent. The influence of the Jain community lies behind the predominance of vegetarian dishes. The high esteem in which Gujarat's most famous son, Mohandas K. Gandhi, is still held, accounts for the continuing prohibition on alcohol.

Jaipur

Anokha Gaon
14 Vishwakarma Road
Definitive Rajasthani cuisine prepared using rustic wood fires and clay ovens and served village-feast-style on long, low tables. Live folk cabaret and camel rides round the evenings off. Avoid at weekends. **$$$**

Om
Best Western Om Tower, Church Road, off M.I. Road
Tel: 0141-236 6683
Revolving restaurant atop Jaipur's newest and glitziest skyscraper, from which you can survey the entire city over delicious Rajasthani and other north Indian specialities. **$$$–$$$$**

Western Rajasthan

Marwar
Taj Hari Mahal, 5 Residency Road, Jodhpur
Tel: 0291-243 9700
Top-drawer local Marwari cuisine, served by black-tie waiters in smart surroundings. Try the spicy, mutton-based Jodhpuri *mas*. **$$$$**

Mishri Lal
Gateway south of the Clock Tower, Jodhpur
A Jodhpuri institution, serving mega-rich makhania *lassis* to a steady flow of silently appreciative, sweet-toothed local aficionados. **$**

Natraj
Opposite Salim Singh ki Haveli, Jaisalmer
A pleasant rooftop restaurant known above all for its Mughlai-style chicken curry. **$–$$**

The Pillars
Hotel Umaid Bhawan, Jodhpur
Tel: 0291-251 0101
Umaid Bhawan has four restaurants, but its tea-garden terrace is the most affordable and atmospheric, with peacocks strutting picturesquely over the grass and grand views of the distant city and desert. **$$–$$$**

Vyas Meals Service
Near the Jain temples, inside the Fort, Jaisalmer
Home-cooked *paratha*-curd and *masala*

In The Pillars' tea garden

chai breakfasts, lunch-time *thalis* and filling traditional *dal batti* suppers served by an endearing elderly couple. **$**

Southern Rajasthan
Ambrai
Hanuman Ghat, Udaipur
Occupying a spit of land that juts into Lake Pichola from Hanuman Ghat, this ranks among Udaipur's best-situated restaurants. The cuisine, mostly rich Mughlai and Rajput specialities, rates as highly as the views. **$$$**

Jodhpur Bhojnalaya
Near the Taxi Stand, Mount Abu
Traditional Rajasthani *thali* joint, renowned above all for its *churma*: crumbly, slightly sweet dumplings spiced with cardamom. **$**

Natraj
New Bapu Bazaar, behind Ashok Cinema, Udaipur
Udaipur's best budget eating option: filling, unlimited north Indian *thalis* served in a grubby dining hall in the north of the city. **$**

Om Shiva
Sadar Bazaar Road, Pushkar
All-you-can-eat buffets are the main attraction of this perennially popular garden café-restaurant, an old hippy hang-out close to the eastern shores of the lake. **$**

Raju Garden
Near Ram Ghat, Main Bazaar, Pushkar
Simple, traveller-oriented place on a rooftop terrace festooned with fairy lights and plants. The food consistently outstrips the

Taste delectable spices in the regional cuisine

competition in this popular end of town, as do the wonderful lake views. **$–$$**

Gujarat
Gopi Dining Hall
Opposite Town Hall, Ellis Bridge, Ashram Road, Ahmedabad
An extremely popular Gujarati vegetarian restaurant renowned for its Kathiawadi *thalis*. **$**

Green Rock
Opposite STC Bus Stand, Bhuj
This air-conditioned first-floor restaurant is the most popular vegetarian place to eat in town, especially on Saturdays and Sundays when they serve a gargantuan 'Special Gujarati Thali'. **$$**

Mirch Masala
7–10 Chadan Complex, Swastik Char Rasta Navrang Pura, Ahmedabad
Quality Punjabi *dhaba* food and Gujarati *chaats* (snacks and nibbles), served in air-conditioned comfort amid displays of puppets and slapstick Hindi film posters. **$$**

O'Coqueiro Music Garden
Near St Thomas' Church, Diu
This place is little more than a few plastic tables set up under a palm tree, but the grilled fish they serve is consistently delicious, the portions generous and the beer chilled. **$$**

São Tomé Retiro
Next to Diu Museum, Firangiwada, Diu
Tel: 02875-253 157
George D'Souza's seafood barbecues are legendary among travellers. Seated around a roaring fire in the family courtyard, you can enjoy skewers of succulent kingfish, pomfret and shark, fresh from the boats. **$$**

Vishalla
On southern edge of the city, opposite Vasana Tol Naka, Ahmedabad
Tel: 079-660 2422
This is the place to sample authentic, village-style Gujarati cooking, against an ersatz-rural setting of mud- and wood-walled compounds. **$$$**

SPORTS AND TOURS

There is no shortage of operators eager to sell visitors packaged tours around Rajasthan and Gujarat; whistle-stop city tours are convenient if you're short on time.

Cricket
Rajasthan Royals
The state grinds to a halt for matches by the local Indian Twenty20 Premier League side, led by Aussie bowling legend, Shane Warne.

Horse Riding
Princess Trails
Tel: 98290-42012
www.horseridingindia.com
Horse riding is a popular leisure activity among the upper classes of Udaipur. Visitors can explore the beautiful countryside around the town on horse safaris.

Polo
Jaipur Polo Club
www.jaipurpolo.com
The region's second sporting passion is polo. The ground alongside the Rambagh Palace in Jaipur is now the game's spiritual home. Matches are held throughout winter.

Tours
CityWise tours
RTDC Central Reservations Office, behind Hotel Swagatam, Station Road
Tel: 0141-220 2586
Runs full- and half-day tours of Jaipur

(9am–6pm, Rs200; 8am–1pm, Rs150). Book tickets at least a day in advance.

House of MG
Ahmedabad
Tel: 079-2550 6946
www.houseofmg.com
This boutique hotel offers synchronised audio heritage tours of the old city, at Rs100.

Jodhpur RTDC City Tour
RTDC travel desk at Hotel Ghoomer on High Court Road
Tours at 9am–1pm or 2–6pm, costing Rs100.

Mt Abu RTDC Sightseeing Tour
Tourist Information counter, bus stand
Tel: 02974-235 434
Tours run 8.30am–1.30pm, costing Rs70.

Rajasthan Tourism Development Corporation
Tel: 1-800-103 3500
www.rtdc.in
Tourism Corporation of Gujarat Ltd
Tel: 0265-242 7489
www.gujurattourism.com
These organisations run city and regional tours in their respective states.

FESTIVALS AND EVENTS

Rarely a day passes when one festival or another doesn't take place here. Listed below are some unique events; enquire about the many others at any tourist office.

January
Makar Sankranti
Ahmedabad
Kite-flying festival.

March
Elephant Festival
Jaipur

Hundreds of decorated elephants process through the streets.

October–November
Pushkar Camel Fair
Pushkar
Hundreds of thousands of villagers converge on Pushkar to buy and sell livestock.

Mumbai and Central India

A journey through India's core takes in the full spectrum of the country's history: from the earliest Buddhist caves and stupas of the Mauryan era, through the splendours of medieval Hinduism at Khajuraho and Orcha, to the Afghan-influenced palaces and tombs of Mandu and, finally, the modern metropolis of Mumbai.

Mumbai

Population: 16.5 million

Local Dialling Code: 022

Tourist Office: Government of India Tourist Office (GITO): Western Railways building, 123 Maharishi Karve Road, Churchgate; tel: 2207 4333; www.incredibleindia.org

Post Office: GPO, behind Chhatrapati

Shivaji Terminus (VT)

Hospitals: Breach Candy Hospital: 60 Bhulabhai Desai Road; tel: 2366 7949; www.breachcandyhospital. org. Bombay Hospital: New Marine Lines; tel: 2206 7676; www.bombay hospital.com

Media: *Time Out Mumbai* (www.timeoutmumbai.net)

Five major river systems flow through this west-central region of India: the Naramada and Tapti in Madhya Pradesh, and the Godavari, Bhima and Krishna in Maharashtra, whose sources lie in the Western Ghats (here known as the Sayadhris) and run eastwards. By trapping the monsoon rains blowing off the Arabian Sea to the west, the mountains form a divide between the lush, densely populated coastal lowlands of the Konkan, and the more arid uplands of the Deccan plateau.

The contiguous states of Maharashtra and Madhya Pradesh cover a vast area of central India. Between them, they hold enough ancient monuments, wildlife reserves, sacred pilgrimage towns and remote forests and mountain ranges to occupy intrepid travellers for several lifetimes. Yet, compared with other parts of the country, India's interior sees comparatively few visitors. Along the way, forays into the central Indian sal forests for a glimpse of wild tigers will bring you into contact with descendants of tribespeople whose presence predates even the oldest stone monuments in the subcontinent.

Meanwhile, the metropolis of Mumbai sets the pace for all western India, its commerce, cinema, energy and global profile instrumental in the rise of the country's ambitions.

MUMBAI

Mumbai  – known until 1996 by its former British name, Bombay – is a city of superlatives. Packed on to a narrow spit of reclaimed land that curls into the Arabian Sea from the Maharashtran coast, it's the world's largest urban sprawl, with a population of 15 million and rising – the most crowded, powerful, corrupt, crime-ridden and compelling metropolis in India. Nowhere else in the country looms as large in the popular imagination, or exerts such far-reaching influence.

From the time the East India Company rented its scattered islets from King Charles II for the princely sum of £10 per month, money making has always been Mumbai's *raison d'être*. And for all the hardship manifest on its streets, there's plenty to go around. Despite holding only 1.5 percent of India's total population, the city

Selling garlands and petals for offerings at Mumba Devi temple

generates one third of its tax revenues and 60 percent of its customs duty.

For visitors, Mumbai isn't so much about unmissable sights as atmosphere. Plenty of wonderful monuments do survive from the city's chequered history, but in many ways travelling between them is where the real interest lies. Immerse yourself in the teeming street life – rubbing shoulders with commuters at rush hour, or jostling with porters in the stations and bazaars – and you'll get a vivid sense of what makes the Maharashtran capital an extraordinary place to live and work.

Colaba and the Gateway of India

The defining monument of **Colaba**, the district at the far southern tip of the peninsula where most foreign tourists congregate, is the grandiloquent **Gateway of India** . A triumphant arch built to commemorate the visit of Britain's George V and Queen Mary for the Delhi Durbar in 1911, it is now – somewhat ironically – better remembered as the place where the last detachment of

On Mumbai's busy streets

British troops marched to their waiting ships in 1947, marking the official end of imperial rule. Surveying the scene imperiously from the background is the **Taj Mahal Palace and Tower** (*see p.159*) – one of India's finest hotels, which hit the headlines in 2008 when it was attacked by terrorists.

Head down Colaba's main street, Shahid Bhagat Singh Marg (S.B.S. Marg, but still better known by its pre-Independence name, 'Colaba Causeway') for 10 minutes and you'll reach the gates of **Sassoon Docks**, where the city's trawler fleet lands its catch each morning. Hundreds of boats tie up here during the day, their flags, masts and rigs forming one of Mumbai's most arresting spectacles.

The Museum and Maidans

Immediately north of Colaba on Mahatma Gandhi Marg (M.G. Road) stands the domed Prince of Wales Museum, now renamed the **Maharaja Chhatrapati Sivaji Museum B**

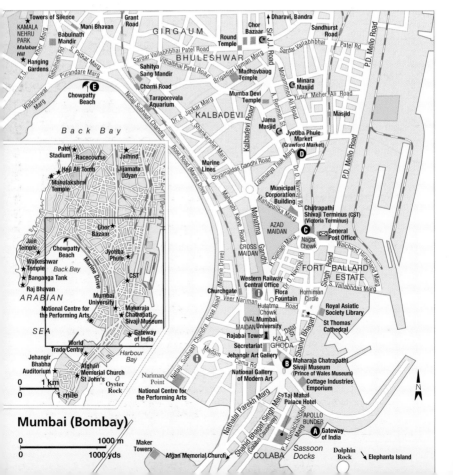

Mumbai (Bombay)

(Wed–Mon 10.15am–6pm; charge). A whimsical fusion of Gujarati, Bijapuri and British municipal architecture, the building is of as much interest as the fine collection of antiquities it houses. Treasures showcased inside include a famous collection of Indian paintings, among which are miniatures and illuminated manuscripts from Akbar's own library, as well as Chola bronzes and a grizzly array of decorated Mughal weaponry.

Bounding the west side of Kala Ghoda are the great maidans – open parks that once formed clear fields of fire for East India Company troops, but which nowadays host cricket matches throughout the day. A phalanx of architectural behemoths dating from the late 19th century forms a suitably imperious backdrop, among them the former **Secretariat**, **Mumbai University** and iconic **Rajabai Tower**.

Victoria Terminus

Opened in 1887, Mumbai principal railway station, Victoria Terminus, was conceived as a symbol of the pride and power of the British Empire. It amalgamated all the stylistic eccentricities of the day – ornate domes, minarets, fancy arched windows and a staggering wealth of sculptural detail – and still forms an imposing spectacle. Renamed **Chhatrapati Shivaji Terminus** , the station remains one of the country's best-loved landmarks, in spite of its imperial past and more recent

Mumbai City Transport

 Airport: Mumbai's Chhatrapati Shivaji Airport (**www.csia.in**), 30km (19 miles) north of downtown, has four terminals – two international and two domestic

 Trains: The city's two busiest railway stations are Chhatrapati Shivaji (aka 'Victoria') Terminus (CST), in the south of the peninsula, and Mumbai Central further north. Reservations are most conveniently made online (see p.31 and p.255), or in the Western Railways booking centre opposite Churchgate Station, next to the Government of India Tourist Office. Always check your point of departure beforehand as many trains leave from stations on the northern outskirts. Churchgate Station, on the north side of the downtown area, is the hub for the city's overloaded suburban train network, run by the Mumbai Railway Vikas Corporation, or MRVC (**http://203.176.113.182/ MRVC/intr.html**). Tourists are advised to avoid the network at all times except on Sundays.

 Buses: Mumbai's city buses are operated by the Brihanmumbai Electric Supply and Transport company (BEST): tel: 2285 6262; **www.best undertaking.com**. The majority of long-distance buses work out of Mumbai Central bus terminus, opposite Mumbai Central railway station. Private buses to Goa leave from just south of the Metro Cinema on Azad Maidan.

Taxis: For nipping between sights, the most comfortable option is to jump in a ubiquitous black-and-yellow cab. Those painted blue are more pricey air-con taxis. Taxis for day trips and local sightseeing are best arranged through the Government of India Tourist Office on Maharishi Karve Road, opposite Churchgate Station (see left).

The ornate facade of Chhatrapati Shivaji Terminus, formerly Victoria Terminus

associations with the bloody terror attacks of 2008, when 50 people were gunned down on its main concourse.

The Markets and Chowpatty Beach

Northwest of the station is the bustling **Crawford Market** (known in post-Independence as Mahatma Jyotiba Phule). Behind the brick facade with bas-relief friezes by Kipling's father over the gate, the stalls retain their original layout: vegetables to the left; fruit and flowers to the right; and fish, mutton and poultry straight ahead.

Beyond Crawford Market lies the heart of Mumbai, where Indians from the entire subcontinent compete in the bazaars. Among the extravagantly coloured Hindu temples, and mosques in the Muslim neighbourhoods, Jain merchants sell gold in the Zaveri Bazaar, while other streets specialise in silver, brass, copper, leather and lace.

Another famous landmark in the city is the promenade of **Marine Drive**, around Back Bay from Nariman Point to the residential area of Malabar Hill. One must-see is **Chowpatty Beach** E, not for swimming or sunbathing, but because it is one of the greatest people-watching spots in western India: fakirs and fakers walk on fire, sleep on nails, climb ropes in midair, or bury their heads in the sand; food vendors hawk *kulfi* ice cream as well as *bhelpuri*, a spicy local speciality.

Elephanta Island

While the city of Mumbai itself has no ancient monuments, an hour's ride away by motor launch from the Gateway of India is the island of **Elephanta** (Gharapuri), site of a magnificent series of rock-cut cave **temples** (Oct–May Tue–Sun 9.30–5pm; charge) with large, sculptured interiors, excavated in the 7th and 8th centuries. 'Elephanta' was the name given to the island by its Portuguese discoverers, after the stone elephant they found on the shoreline. The same mariners inflicted great damage on the devotional sculpture they encountered, although this has miraculously done little to diminish the splendour of the carvings, which continue to exert a powerful spell.

Reached via a flight of 100 stone steps, the pillared cave at the top of the island was dedicated to Shiva. Its centrepiece is the famous Trimurti (or 'Maheshmurti' figure as it's also known), a 6m (20ft) -tall, triple-headed deity set in an alcove at the back of the cave. Although some debate surrounds the exact date the figure was carved, scholars are united in regarding it as the zenith of ancient Hindu art.

MAHARASHTRA

With nearly 100,000,000 inhabitants, **Maharashtra** is India's second most populous state, and its richest. The bulk of economic activity in the region revolves around the capital, Mumbai, to the south of which extends the narrow, humid, palm-fringed coastline of the Konkan. Table-topped mountains

Ganesh Chathurthi Festival

One of Mumbai's defining sights is the **Ganesh Chathurthi festival,** a Hindu celebration held at the height of the monsoon in July and August when, under leaden skies, huge effigies of the god of good beginnings, Ganesh (also known as Ganapati) are paraded through the streets before being immersed in the sea. Crowds of hundreds of thousands gather to watch the event, dancing to the rhythms of the bands that accompany the brightly painted statues as they're carried towards the waves.

The largest mass immersion of Ganesh idols takes place on Chowpatty Beach, at the northern end of Marine Drive. See the Maharashtra Tourism website (www. maharashtratourism.gov.in) for precise dates and other information.

147

Mumbai and Central India

– parched and yellow in summer, and draped in lush vegetation through the monsoon period from June to September – track the shoreline inland all the way to Goa. The Sahyadri spur of the Western Ghat range, these hills form a stepped barrier between the seaboard and Deccan Plateau to the east, and are the source of the innumerable rivers draining across the Konkan into the Arabian Sea.

Tourist attention in Maharashtra focuses mainly on the northeast, where the rock-cut caves of Ellora and Ajanta bear witness to the region's strategic importance in ancient times. Southwest of Mumbai, Pune was the former capital of the Marathas, the warring chieftains who made life

Exploring the carvings of Elephanta Island

★ BOLLYWOOD

India's film industry is the biggest in the world, far outstripping even Hollywood (in terms of ticket sales if not actual box-office receipts). Close on 1,000 films are released in the country annually, half of them from the Bollywood studios of north Mumbai – home of the Pan-Indian, Hindi-language blockbuster.

A Spicy Format

The cipher behind the phenomenal success of Bollywood is the so-called 'masala' (literally 'spice') format. Since its infancy in the late 1960s, directors have realised that to appeal to the masses in villages across the country, films had to include a little (or a lot) of everything: high melodrama, comedy, violence, music, dance, striking outfits and lashings of romance. Plots thus tend to pursue familiar lines, usually involving a maverick 'hero' who battles with injustice and, against all odds, wins through to marry the girl he loves. Religious piety versus moral degeneracy, and the break-up and reunion of a family, are other essential themes.

Romance

At the heart of this colour-saturated maelstrom will, of course, be the love story. In a country where marriages are nearly always brokered by relatives instead of based on sexual attraction, romance is guaranteed to cast a potent spell, which is why your average big-budget Bollywood flick includes at least half-

A classic Bollywood film advertisment

a-dozen love song sequences. Swirling through as many different costume changes as exotic locations, these might switch from a Kashmiri meadow to a Goan beach, before cutting to a Swiss lake or London's Tower Bridge. But because Indian censorship laws forbid touching lips, the lovers never (quite) get to kiss – though they might get to roll around flower-filled Alpine meadows or Nilgiri tea gardens, enjoy plenty of hip-thrusting dances and cavort in skimpy clothes through monsoon rainstorms.

New Horizons

Film costumes have grown noticeably sexier over the past decade. Whereas in the past a well-fed frame was what the under-fed masses in the back country wanted to drool over, nowadays, casting directors also have to please sophisti-cated urban audiences with Western tastes – not to mention their expat cousins in Southall and New Jersey, whose pounds and dollars finance ever-growing film budgets. As a conse-quence, the heroes are leaner, and the heroines more drop-dead gorgeous than ever. You'll see their well-toned abs, glossy locks and shining smiles every-where boredom could possibly need to be alleviated – from giant hoardings at road intersections to endless TV ads.

The vast profits to be made from box-office receipts abroad has not only made Bollywood's current crop of stars unimaginably rich. They've also had an impact on the films themselves, which are nowadays much slicker, and feature more challenging characters and plot lines than the 'masala' format of old.

Inside a Mumbai cinema

Bollywood

Gorgeous stars and passionate romance are de rigueur in Bollywood films

uncomfortable for both the Mughals and, later, the British. Their legacy endures in the proud spirit of independence demonstrated by speakers of the state's principal language, Marathi.

Matheran

On a clear day, after rain has dampened the dust, you can see the outlying skyscrapers of Mumbai from **Matheran**, a genteel British-era hill station situated 108km (67 miles) southeast of the Maharashtran capital. Yet a more stark contrast between two places it is hard to imagine. Spread over a flat-topped, sheer-sided mountain at an altitude of 800m (2,600ft), Matheran is swathed in verdant forest and – thanks to the total absence of motorised traffic (it's closed to all vehicles) – blissfully quiet. Aside from some delightful Raj bungalows, the main reason to visit the resort is the journey to it from the valley floor via a rattling old **narrow-gauge railway** ⚇. Once installed, there's little to do beyond enjoy the cool air, chew blocks of sticky, nut-encrusted local tikki toffee, and savour the panoramas from the various viewpoints that ring the ridgetop.

Aurangabad and Daulatabad

As its name suggests, **Aurangabad**, 370km (230 miles) northeast of Mumbai, has a strong Muslim flavour. The city contains the mausoleum of the Mughal emperor Aurangzeb's wife, the **Bibi ka Maqbara** (8am–sunset; charge), an inferior copy of the Taj Mahal. In addition, amid the arid hills overlooking the city, a dozen Buddhist

The Ajanta Curse

Early efforts by 19th-century artists to document Ajanta's art treasures were bedevilled with disasters, leading to speculation that the site was gripped by a malevolent curse. English painter Robert Gill spent 27 years copying the murals, but lost his entire collection in the fire at London's Crystal Palace in 1866. Exactly the same thing happened to another folio of facsimiles when they were destroyed by fire at the Victoria and Albert Museum in London. A team of Japanese Buddhist artists also lost their copies, crafted on rice paper, after they were buried in an earthquake.

Subsequent attempts to preserve the world-famous wall paintings met with little more success. Restoration work commissioned by the Nizam of Hyderabad in the 1920s nearly destroyed the murals altogether, when the varnish applied began to crack and flake away, taking fragments of paint with it.

caves excavated between the 3rd and 11th centuries AD contain some wonderful carved friezes. The most interesting are nos 3, 6 and 7: carry a torch.

Daulatabad, 15km (9 miles) west of Aurangabad, has a massive hilltop **fort** (daily 6am–6pm; charge). The site dates from the 12th century, but the seven rings of fortifications are from the 15th–16th. A deep moat was also dug to deter invaders, once filled with crocodiles and crossed by a single bridge, after which is a dark labyrinth. The views from the top are spectacular.

Ajanta and Ellora

'The finest gallery of pictures to survive from any ancient civilisation' is how historian John Keay described the Buddhist cave murals at **Ajanta** ❷ (Tue–Sun 9am–5.30pm; charge), 105km (65 miles) northeast of Aurangabad.

Forgotten for nearly 1,000 years, the jungle site was only rediscovered by a party of British tiger-hunters in 1819. Today it is classified as one of Unesco's World Heritage monuments.

The frescoes and sculptures date from around 200BC to AD650, a period when Buddhism was acquiring some of the sensuousness of Hinduism. People used to the idea of Buddhist thought being essentially a negation of the senses will be startled by the voluptuousness of much of the imagery. Highlights include Cave 1 with its superb murals, and the painted ceiling of Cave 2.

Ellora ❸ (Wed–Mon dawn–dusk; charge), 25km (15 miles) northwest of Aurangabad, has 34 rock-cut temples representing the Buddhists (caves 1–12), Brahmanic Hindus (caves 13–29) and Jains (caves 30–34). The

Mumbai and Central India

Buddhist monks exploring the evocative cave sculptures at Ajanta

term 'cave temple' cannot convey the magnitude of the Ellora achievement. These caves were scooped out of the rocks 10 centuries ago, a feat comparable to carving an entire cathedral out of solid rock. The work usually began from the top of the temple and moved downwards to eliminate the need for scaffolding.

The centrepiece at Ellora is the **Kailasa Temple**. Its architects were not modest in their ambitions; Kailasa is, after all, the mythical mountain where the gods dwell. In its galleries are re-created various scenes from Shiva myths. One of them represents the eternal struggle between the forces of evil represented by Ravana, the demon king of Sri Lanka, and the forces of good represented by Shiva and Parvati.

Pune

Pune ❹, 170km (105 miles) from Mumbai, was once the capital of the Maratha Empire. The British captured the city at the Battle of Koregaon in 1818 and developed it along the lines

The incredible rock-cut temples at Ellora

of an archetypal army garrison with the usual uncluttered cantonment areas in distinct contrast to the busy, crowded old quarter. Pune became the centre of many Hindu social reform movements, as well as the epicentre of India's Independence campaign. A metropolis of over 5 million inhabitants, the city today ranks among India's foremost boom centres, with a rapidly expanding IT sector. Shiny new shopping malls, car showrooms, gold emporia and high-end, gated residential 'villages' on the outskirts are just some of the outward signs of this recent prosperity; appalling traffic congestion and air pollution are others.

Well worth a visit is the **Raja Kelkar Museum** (daily 8.30am–6pm; charge), a wonderful showcase for the traditional Indian arts, whose collection includes carved palace and temple doors, 2,000-year-old excavated pottery, traditional Indian lamps and 17th-century miniature

paintings. Of special interest is a collection of brass nutcrackers (some of them explicitly erotic).

The **Agha Khan Palace** (Mon–Fri 9am–5.45pm; charge), with its Italianate arches and spacious, well-tended lawns, was an unlikely place for a prison, but at one time the British interned Mahatma Gandhi and his wife Kasturba here along with other

Pune		
Population: 4.5 million		**Airport:** Pune International (Lohegaon) airport (tel: 2668 3232) is 10km (6 miles) northeast of the city
Local Dialling Code: 020		
Tourist Office: MTDC Tourist Office: tel: 2612 6867; www.mahrashtratourism.gov.in		**Trains:** The main railway station is slap in the centre of the city
Post Office: GPO: Sadhu Vasvani (Connaught) Road		**Buses:** Three separate bus stands are in operation; consult the tourist office to find out the destinations they serve
Hospital: Jehangir Hospital: 32 Sassoon Road; tel: 2622 2551; www.apollohospitals.com		**Taxis:** Cars and drivers for sightseeing should be arranged through the local tourist office (see left)

leaders of the Congress Party. Kasturba died in the palace and a memorial has been erected in the grounds.

Shanivarvada (daily 8am–6.30pm; charge), in the Old City, was the palace of the Peshwa rulers who succeeded Shivaji's empire. It was built in 1736. All that remains from a massive fire in 1827 are its fortified walls, brass-studded gates, 18th-century lotus pools and the elaborate palace foundations.

Unrivalled views over the city and the table-topped mountains surrounding it are to be had from **Sinhagad Fort** (literally 'fortress of the lion') 24km (15 miles) to the southwest, where Shivaji notched up a landmark victory against the Sultan of Bijapur's army in 1670.

The Agha Khan Palace once housed Gandhi and his wife as prisoners

MADHYA PRADESH

In the heart of the subcontinent, the large state of Madhya Pradesh – the name means 'middle land' – is primarily comprised of upland plateaux and hills, interspersed with deep river valleys. A large proportion of India's remaining forest is located here, with some of the finest deciduous hardwoods in the world. Remoter corners are also home to many Adivasi groups such as the Gonds and Bhils. Ancient monuments and sacred sites dominate most tourist itineraries of the region.

Gwalior and Orcha

Established in the 8th century, **Gwalior** ❺ is a city dominated by its hilltop fort, one of the most redoubtable in the world. The best-preserved section is the Rajput palace of Raja Mansingh at the northern end, built 1486–1516 and retaining much of its original blue tiling. At the southern end of the citadel is the wonderful 8th-century **Teli-ka-Mandir** temple, while close by is the modern Sikh gurudwara commemorating Guru Gobind Singh (1595–1644), who was imprisoned here. The view from the battlements near the ornate pair of 11th-century Sas Bahu temples is breathtaking.

Gwalior is a good place from which to visit **Orcha**, a beautiful 16th-century walled town, which looks today much as it must have when it was built. It was founded by the Bundela king, Rudra Pratap, on the banks of the sparkling Betwa River. The countryside undulates gently and the builders of Orcha adorned the landscape with a palace and

Orcha's architecture is a distinctive and delightful hybrid of styles

fortress, plus temples and cenotaphs. The architecture is a synthesis of traditional Hindu and ornate Mughal. One of the finest sights is the view of the architecturally stunning *chatris*, or cenotaphs, from across the blue river with green hills in the background.

Khajuraho

Famed for their eyebrow-raising erotic sculpture, the temples at **Khajuraho** ❻ (daily dawn–dusk; charge) were built under the reign of the Chandellas, who controlled a large area of the northern Deccan between AD950 and 1310. Their facades are fabulously decorated with a myriad deities, nymphs and carvings depicting a mind-boggling variety of sexual acts. Although the Chandellas were a Hindu dynasty, there are both Hindu and Jain temples at the site; the latter are almost all concentrated

Khajuraho's Erotic Sculptures

When the British first encountered the Khajuraho's temples they were shocked (and, no doubt, secretly titillated) by such flagrant displays of what, to their eyes, was pornography. This was, of course, to misunderstand the intention behind the sculpture. To the medieval Hindu mind the unity of the male and female principles bound the universe together; sexual union was not only considered a manifestation of this perfect union but also a homage to the creation of the universe itself. Related to this metaphysical ideal was Tantra, a form of physical devotion, akin to yoga, that sought this unity through sex. Above all, however, these are very humane carvings, celebrating an essential part of human existence and can be, at times, a little tongue-in-cheek: look out for the nymph who part hides her face in either amusement or embarrassment, or the man having sex with a horse.

in a compound at the eastern end of the site and tend to be more modest in size and less highly decorated than the major Hindu shrines.

Many of the surviving 22 temples (there were originally around 85 scattered across the surrounding countryside) are in a remarkable state of preservation. This is due mainly to their relative isolation. When the early Muslim invaders of the Delhi Sultanates arrived in the 10th century they destroyed or defaced many Hindu shrines. Khajuraho was at the time far removed from the centres of conflict, and so was ignored, and the temples were gradually forgotten by the outside world. By the time they were 'rediscovered' by British scholars in the late 19th century, they had been surrounded by thick jungle for centuries.

A good time to visit Khajuraho is in March during the annual 10-day dance festival, when India's leading classical dancers perform on the podium of the largest temple, Kandariya Mahadeva.

Bhopal

Bhopal 7, the capital of Madhya Pradesh, emerged as a princely state during the break-up of the Mughal empire in the 18th century, and the city, ranged around the shores of a sprawling artificial lake, still holds some splendid Islamic monuments – notably India's largest mosque, the **Darol Uloom Tajul Masjid.**

Bhopal is, however, better known these days for being the site of the world's worst industrial disaster. On 2 December 1984, a cloud of toxic gas escaped from a plant on the outskirts owned by US multinational, Union Carbide, and engulfed the downtown area, killing around 1,600 pepole instantly and an estimated 20,000 since. With the issue of com-

One of the erotic sculptures at Khajuraho

The Great Stupa at Sanchi

century BC when Emperor Asoka ordered stupas containing the Buddha's relics to be built across his domains, crowns a 91m (300ft) hill on the Vindhya plateau, overlooking the main Bhopal–Delhi railway line.

The site lay smothered in jungle until it was uncovered by the British in 1818, but delay in restoration work led to the stupas being plundered (the priceless relics looted from here are now on display at the British Museum and Victoria and Albert Museum in London). Built in the 1st century BC, the **Great Stupa** (Stupa I) is the largest surviving monument in a complex comprising more than 50 ruined **burial mounds**, **monasteries** and **temples** (dawn–dusk; charge). It stands on the brow of the hilltop, surrounded by stone railings with four torana gates topped by architraves (crossbars), one placed above the other and decorated with dwarfs or animals.

At the time the structure was built, Buddha himself was not represented in human form, but symbolised by the horse on which he rode away from his palace: the wheel of law, his footprints, and the pipal tree. A small **archaeological museum** (daily 10am–5pm; charge) at the foot of the hill displays antiquities not carried away by British archaeologists.

Mandu

Southwest of Bhopal and approached via a deep wooded ravine, the ruins of **Mandu ❾**, the capital of the Sultanate of Malwa, are scattered over a rocky plateau. The

pensation still unresolved, the gas disaster casts a shadow over the city to this day.

Even so, it makes a worthwhile stopover, with plenty of interest in its old 'Chowk' bazaar area, and a crop of interesting museums, including the **Birla Mandir Museum** (Tue–Sun 9.30am–5pm; charge), which houses some of the finest medieval sculpture in India, and the **Museum of Man** (Tue–Sun 11am–6pm; charge), dedicated to the culture of India's aboriginal (adivasi) peoples.

Sanchi

About one hour northeast of Bhopal, **Sanchi ❽** holds the best-preserved ancient Buddhist monuments in India. The site, dating from the 3rd

The prize sighting in Kanha National Park

complex is today the largest standing walled city in the world, with a total circumference of more than 75km (45 miles). The **Bhangi Gate**, a fearsome defensive bastion, leads to lakes and groves, gardens and palaces. The **Jahaz Mahal**, or ship palace, floats on its own lake, and the **Hindola Mahal**, or swing palace, appears to sway gently in the breeze.

The **Jama Masjid** has acoustics so perfect that a whisper from the pulpit is heard clearly in the furthest corner of the huge courtyard. On the furthest, southern, perimeter of Mandu, Rupmati's Pavilion sits atop a sheer cliff plunging 600m (2,000ft) to the plains of Nimar – a particularly wonderful spot at sunset.

Kanha and Bandhavgarh National Parks

For sheer abundance of wildlife, **Kanha National Park** (www.kanhanationalpark.com; Oct–June dawn–dusk; charge ) and **Bandhavgarh National Park** (www.bandhavgarhnationalpark.com; Oct–June dawn–dusk; charge), in the east of Madhya Pradesh, are the best national parks in India. The journey to them might be a little long, but it's well worth the effort.

The best season is February to May, when you'll be able to see plenty of beautiful cheetal (spotted deer), blackbuck, sloth bear, gaur or bison (largest of the wild cattle), wild boar, *barasingha* ('12-pointer') swamp deer, and also monkeys galore. Enthusiastic birdwatchers might also spot black ibis and the crested serpent-eagle.

The parks, however, are most famous for their tigers; with the big cat population perennially under threat from poaching, sightings are by no means guaranteed, but over the course of a two-night/three-day stay you stand a good chance of seeing India's greatest wildlife symbol.

ACCOMMODATION

Demand for hotel beds is high in Mumbai at all times of the year. Book at least one month in advance to be sure of securing your chosen accommodation. Outside the Maharashtran capital, rates quickly fall and the choice of last-minute options increases.

Mumbai

Bentley's Hotel
17 Oliver Road, Colaba
Tel: 022-2284 1474
www.bentleyshotel.com
An excellent budget option. Large and clean rooms in a convenient location. **$$–$$$**

Grand
17 Shri S.R. Marg, Ballard Estate
Tel: 022-6658 0506
www.grandhotelbombay.com
Recent refurbishment has restored this lovely old colonial-style hotel near the docks to its former grandeur. **$$$$–$$$$$**

Lawrence
3rd Floor, 33 Rope Walk Lane
Tel: 022-2284 3618
Opposite Jehangir Art Gallery, this is a small hotel with clean and great-value rooms. **$**

Moti International
10 Best Marg
Tel: 022-2202 1654
hotelmotiinternational@yahoo.com.in
Small, friendly budget hotel, with inexpensive rooms in a colonial-era building. They're cool, quiet and clean (if showing signs of age) and the management is welcoming. **$$–$$$**

Residency
26 Rustom Sidhwa Marg, D.N. Road
Tel: 022-2262 5525
www.residencyhotel.com
The best-value mid-range place in the city centre, and correspondingly popular. Standard rooms are a steal for this area: be sure to book weeks ahead. **$$$–$$$$**

Strand Hotel
30 P.J. Ramchandani Marg,
Colaba Sea Face
Tel: 022-2288 2222
www.hotelstrand.com
Clean, comfortable rooms on Colaba's seafront. The best have high ceilings, Art Deco features and harbour views. **$$$**

Taj Mahal Palace and Tower
P.J. Ramchandani Marg, Colaba
Tel: 022-6665 3366
www.tajhotels.com
India's most famous hotel, badly damaged in the terror attacks of November 2008, but now restored to its former glory. The old 'Palace' block on the waterfront has more period character, but the views from the high-rise 'Tower' next door are unbeatable. **$$$$$**

YWCA International Guest House
18 Madam Cama Road, Fort
Tel: 022-2202 5053
www.ywcaic.info
A good place to stay for both sexes. Very clean, safe rooms and dormitories. Rates include temporary membership, breakfast and dinner. Reserve with deposit (by international money order) well in advance. **$$–$$$**

Maharashtra

Happy Home
294 Koregaon Park, Pune
Tel: 020-2612 2933
happyhomehostel@yahoo.co.in
Pune's best budget option. The rooms are all clean, have attached bathrooms and balconies, and the neighbourhood (near the Osho ashram) is peaceful. **$$**

Lord's Central

M.G. Road, Matheran
Tel: 02148-230 228
http://matheranhotels.com
Little seems to have changed at Lord's since its 1930s heyday, down to the custard pudding and plaid blankets. Spectacular views extend from the garden (where there's a small pool). 🍴 **$$$–$$$$**

Panchavati

Off Station Road West, Padampura, Aurangabad
Tel: 0240-232 8755
www.hotelpanchavati.com
A well-run place at the western end of Aurangabad's centre. The best option in its bracket as it's cleaner than the competition. **$–$$**

Quality in the Meadows

Off Mumbai–Aurangabad Highway, Aurangabad
Tel: 022-6654 8361
www.themeadowsresort.com
Small luxury resort set in 5 hectares (13 acres) of immaculate gardens on the outskirts. A less formal choice than the bigger five-stars, and the location is handy for early departures to Ellora and Ajanta. 🍴 **$$$$**

The Verandah in the Forest

Above Charlotte Lake, Matheran
Mobile Tel: 02148-230296
www.neemranahotels.com
Sensitively restored 19th-century bungalow filled with gorgeous period decor. Its huge veranda looks through the forest canopy and is a delightful spot for afternoon tea (though beware of thieving monkeys). 🍴 **$$$–$$$$$**

Madhya Pradesh

Bhagira Log Huts & Tourist Hostel

Kisli Gate, Kanha National Park
Tel: 07649-277 227
www.mptourism.com
A range of clean and decent accommodation, from dormitories to double rooms. All of the lodges have restaurants, and offer exceptional value for money given the high tariffs elsewhere in the park. **$–$$$$**

Hotel Chandela

Airport Road, Orcha
Tel: 07686-272 355
www.tajhotels.com
The swankiest address in Khajuraho, with all the class you'd expect from a Taj hotel. **$$$$$**

Hotel DM

Link Road, Gwalior
Tel. 0751-234 2083
Pick of the budget bunch, with cosy rooms opening on to a small lawn to rear. **$**

Hotel Rupmati

Near the SADA barrier, Mandu
Tel: 07292-263 270
A modern hotel with some a/c cottages set around gardens on the edge of the escarpment. Great views from the balconies. **$–$$**

Sheesh Mahal

Jehangir Mahal, Orcha
Tel: 07680-252624
Romantic rooms in a 17th-century palace, with exotic views over the village. Gorgeous interior and restrained tariffs. 🍴 **$$–$$$**

Siddarth

Opposite Western Group, Main Road, Orcha
Tel: 07686-274 627
hotelsiddarth@rediffmail.com
One of the few places that boasts temple views from its balconies – the roof terrace restaurant makes the most of the location. The rooms are a good size for the price. **$–$$**

Tiger's Den

Tala village, Bandhavgarh National Park
Tel: 011-2757 0446
www.tigerdenbandhavgarh.com
Small resort of 20 comfortable, well-maintained cottages ranged around a manicured garden close to the park entrance. **$$$$**

Usha Kiran Palace

Jayendraganj, Lakshar, Gwalior
Tel: 0751-244 4000
www.tajhotels.com
Formerly the maharaja's guesthouse, now a luxury hotel owned by the Taj Group. **$$$$$**

RESTAURANTS

Mumbai is a foodie's paradise. Ranging from vegetarian south Indian to rich, meat-based Mughlai cooking from the north of the country, diverse cuisines have been brought to the city by immigrant communities from all over India. Elsewhere in the region, north Indian-style cooking prevails.

Mumbai

Apoorva
Vasta House, S.A. Brelvi Road
Tel: 022-2287 0335
Sublime Konkan seafood, including an excellent prawn *gassi*, served in a typical 'Mangalorean' with low ceilings and tacky decor, just off Horniman Circle (look for the fairy lights wrapped around the tree). Licensed. **$$–$$$**

Bade Miya
Tullock Road, behind the Taj Mahal Hotel
This kebab-wallah, who's been working from the same sidewalk behind the Taj for three decades, is a Mumbai institution. Try the chicken tikka or shish kebab. Evenings only. **$**

Busaba
4 Mandlik Marg
Tel: 022-2204 3779
One of the city's hippest restaurants, serving sumptuous dishes from across Asia: Tibetan *momos*, Vietnamese fish sizzlers or Korean glass noodle salad. DJs on Fri–Sat. **$$$$**

Indigo
4 Mandlik Marg
Tel: 022-2236 8999
South Mumbai's most fashionable place to eat, with A-list celebs swanning in and out. For all that, a laid-back atmosphere prevails, and both the refined fusion food and sophisticated decor warrant the hype. **$$$$**

Leopold Café
Sahid Bhagat Singh Marg
A legendary travellers' haunt that hit the headlines in the 2008 terrorist attacks. Good, if slightly pricey, Western food and a bar. **$$**

The Sea Lounge
Taj Mahal Hotel
Apollo Bunder
Afternoon tea and cakes, at a window seat overlooking the Gateway of India, is de rigueur for Raj-ophiles. **$$$**

Maharashtra

Food Lovers
Station Road East, opposite MTDC office, Aurangabad
A kitsch concoction of bamboo, waterfalls and fish tanks where the Indian and Manchurian food is consistently good. **$$$**

Hookahs'N'Tikkas
M.G. Road, Matheran
Tasty kebab and tikka dishes, which you can eat alfresco on a terrace overlooking the bazaar or in a more cosy dining room. **$$**

Koyla
Mira Nagar Corner, North Main Road, Koregaon Park, Pune
Tel: 020-2612 0102

In backpackers' favourite, Leopold Café

Extravagantly decorated Hyderabadi restaurant. Rich curries and slow-baked *biryanis* are the mainstay. **$$$**

Shisha Café
ABC Farms, Koregaon Park, Pune
Pune's coolest gastro-bar is a thatched structure on stilts. Irani food dominates the menu, with bebop background music. **$$**

Yogi Tree
Ground floor, Hotel Surya Villa, 284/1 Koregaon Park, Pune
Healthy juices, grilled sandwiches, tofu steaks and delicious koftas. **$**

Madhya Pradesh
Blue Sky
Main Road, Khajuraho

The big plus of this popular tourist restaurant, which specialises in Japanese and Italian dishes, is its tree-house terrace, from where you get a sweeping view over the temple complex below. **$$**

Raja's Café
Main Road, Khajuraho
Tasty north Indian cooking served on a well-shaded courtyard. A spiral staircase leads to a wooden deck with temple views. **$**

Silver Saloon
Usha Kiran Palace Hotel, Gwalior
Tel: 0751-244 4000
Traditional royal banquet fare, as enjoyed by the Maratha and Nepali maharajas, served on tables overlooking a lush courtyard. Meals are accompanied by classical music. **$$$$**

NIGHTLIFE AND ENTERTAINMENT

Mumbai's nightlife is legendary in India. Being seen at the hippest parties in the most fashionable designer clothes is an essential part of being rich and famous in a city that idolises wealth and fame. Attitudes to alcohol have always been more liberal here too, so even women can enjoy a beer without disapproving stares. Elsewhere in this region, nightlife is virtually nonexistent, while entertainment is the usual mix of Indian classical music recitals and cinema-going. All listings below refer to Mumbai.

Bars
Café Mondegar
Colaba Causeway
Draught and bottled beer served against a backdrop of murals by a famous Goan cartoonist. Popular with travellers and locals.

The Dome
Hotel Intercontinental, 135 Marine Drive
Hip rooftop bar with sweeping views of Marine Drive from its white sofas, candlelit tables and chic raised pool.

Olive
4 Union Park Rd, Pali Hill
Favourite haunt of Bollywood A-listers. People come primarily to crowd-watch, but the gourmet Mediterranean food is also terrific.

Entertainment
The Metro
Dhobi Talao Junction
Catch a Bollywood blockbuster at this state-of-the-art multiplex, in an Art Deco cinema.

NCPA
Nariman Point
www.ncpamumbai.com
The prime venue in Mumbai for catching music recitals, dance and drama.

Nightclubs
Enigma
JW Marriott Hotel, Juhu Tara Road
Everyone who's anyone drifts down to Enigma after Olive closes to catch the clingiest outfits, latest film music remixes, lushest decor and heftiest entrance charges.

Polly Esther's
Gordon House Hotel, Battery Street, Colaba
Retro club staging live music as well as
hip-hop and Bollywood nights. Open
Wed–Sun.

Voodoo Lounge
Arthur Bunder Road, Colaba
Slightly edgy bar off Colaba Causeway hosting India's one and only out gay club, open
from 9pm on Sat.

SPORTS AND TOURS

Home to some of the country's most famous grounds, Mumbai is as cricket-
obsessed as anywhere in India. Guided tours are laid on by regional tourist offices.

Cricket
Wankhede Stadium
D Road, Churchgate
Tel: 020-2279 5500
www.mumbaicricket.com
Among Mumbai's most picturesque spec-
tacles are the matches held each day on
Oval and Azad Maidans. For the full-on
Indian cricket experience, however, try to
catch a test game at India's largest sta-
dium. The region's IPL Twenty20 team is
the Mumbai Indians.

Horse Racing
Mahalakshmi Race Course
The home of the Royal Western India
Turf Club is a throwback to British days
that still flourishes as a social venue for
the city's elite. Meetings are held twice
weekly, on Wednesdays and Saturdays,
between November and March. When it's
not hosting races, Mahalakshmi is the
grounds of the Amateur Riders' Club of
Mumbai (www.arcmumbai.com). Temporary
membership entitles you to use the club's
beautiful horses for early-morning hacks
around the course.

River Rafting
Madhya Pradesh Tourism
Runs rafting excursions from Orcha down
the Betwa River; tickets are sold through
their Sheesh Mahal hotel *(see p.160).*

Tours
**Maharashtra Tourism Development
Corporation (MTDC)**
Madam Cama Road, Mumbai
Running half-day tours of Mumbai's high-
lights (Tue–Sun 2–6pm; admission charges
extra). Tickets can be purchased from their
office, also the departure point.

Listings

FESTIVALS AND EVENTS

Rarely a day passes in central India when an exuberant festival doesn't take place.
Below are the main annual events: precise dates are available at tourist offices.

February–March
Festival of Dance
Khajuraho
Classical dancers perform at floodlit temples.

August–September
Ganesh Chaturthi
Mumbai

Millions of worshippers watch giant effigies
of Ganesh get immersed in the sea.

November–December
Tansen Music Festival
Gwalior
One of the founding fathers of Hindustani
music is honoured with four days of recitals.

# Goa

Although only a little over 100km (60 miles) from north to south, Goa, India's smallest state, forms one of the most distinctive pieces in the great cultural mosaic of the subcontinent, thanks to its history of being Portuguese-ruled until 1961. Today, however, the area is best known for its idyllic tropical climate and paradise landscape of white-sand, palm-fringed beaches.

Panaji

Population: 59,000

Local Dialling Code: 0832

Tourist Office: Government of India Tourist Office, Church Square, Panaji; tel: 222 3412; www.incredibleinida.org

Post Office: Avnda Dom Joao Castro, near Pato Bridge

Hospital: Goa Medical College (GMC): Bambolim; tel: 245 8700; www.gmcmec.gov.in

Airport: Goa's Dabolim airport (tel: 254 0788) lies 29km (18 miles) south, near the city of Vasco da Gama

Trains: The nearest train station on the Konkan Railway is at Karmali, 11km (7 miles) east

Buses: Local and long-distance buses work out of the hectic Kadamaba Bus Stand, on the southeast side of town

Taxis: Cars and drivers are best arranged through the local tourist office (see left); there's also a pre-paid taxi booth at the airport listing fixed fares to destinations state-wide

For more than four-and-a-half centuries Goa was run as a Portuguese colony – the lynchpin of a vast trade empire stretching from Japan to Lisbon. As such, its major influences tended to come from across the sea rather than across its borders. Insulated from the rest of coastal India by tidal rivers and mountains, these influences subsequently took root and blossomed into a culture that was neither entirely Indian nor European, but something in between, with its own unique styles of architecture, cuisine and dress.

With a population of around 1.4 million, the modern state is no longer the run-down Lusitanian backwater it had become by the time Jawaharlal Nehru sent in the India army to annexe the colony in 1961. Mass tourism, fast air and rail connections with Mumbai, and mass immigration from neighbouring Maharashtra (to the north) and Karnataka (to the east and south) are blurring its boundaries as never before. Yet much of what has long distinguished it from the rest of the country – its Indo-Portuguese heritage – still survives.

Since the days of the British Raj, travellers have been coming to Goa to relax. Back then, its bars were the main attractions. Nowadays the beaches are what draw the crowds during the winter, and there are plenty of them. The entire 101km (63 mile) coastline is splashed with sand, from vast bays to tiny coves only accessible by boat. The only problem is deciding which one to head for first.

Among the bright buildings of Fontainhas, Panaji's colonial district

CENTRAL GOA

The central part of Goa, between the Mandovi and Zuari rivers, formed the heartland of the former Portuguese colony. Dominated today by the iron ore industry, the area lacks the beaches of the state's extremities, but does hold a scattering of sights worth venturing from the coast to experience.

Panaji

Situated at the mouth of the Mandovi River, the capital **Panaji** (Panjim) ❶ is a pleasant, relaxed kind of a place. It is

Detail on convent of Santa Monica in Old Goa

mainly used by tourists as a transport hub, but there are some sights to see, including the **Church of Our Lady of the Immaculate Conception**, whose whitewashed facade dominates the Main Square. There's also the interesting colonial district of **Fontainhas**, with leafy squares, narrow lanes, red-tiled roofs, shuttered windows, iron balustrades and 19th-century villas painted in pastel shades of blue, green and ochre. Look for old shops with Portuguese names, and little cafés and bars where the locals like to hang out.

Old Goa

At the height of its splendour in the late 16th and 17th centuries, the former Portuguese capital of Goa, 10km (6 miles) upriver from modern Panaji, was a city of extraordinary magnificence. Contemporary engravings delineate a skyline bristling with Baroque cathedrals and church spires, vast paved piazzas and a port heaving with the spoils of empire. Bigger even than Lisbon and London in its day, it was the first great colonial metropolis. Everyone who stepped ashore in the city was dazzled by its grandeur, rising so improbably from the tropical Indian coast.

Goa's decline, however, was as abrupt as its creation. A combination of epidemics, a silted-up harbour and the rise of Portugal's rival powers elsewhere in the Orient strangled its trade and depleted the population beyond recovery. Today, it's almost impossible to imagine the city as it once looked. Jungle has reclaimed its streets, leaving only the domes and towers of the capital's vast churches to soar above the forest like visions of a Lost World.

Even so, **Old Goa ❷** (as the site is nowadays called) fully deserves its status as the state's prime visitor attraction. As well as the surviving cathedral, churches and convents, the tomb of Saint Francis Xavier in the majestic **Basilica of Bom Jesus** attracts

Christians from all over India, while a pair of well-stocked museums showcase historic artefacts from both the Portuguese and pre-colonial periods. (*See walking tour of Old Goa on p.168.*)

Ponda

The town of **Ponda**, in the dead centre of Goa on the main Panaji–Bangalore highway, serves as a hub for the region's iron-ore industry. The only sight to speak of is the compact mosque, **Jama Masjid**, 2km (1¼ miles) west on the outskirts. Erected in 1560, it's among the last surviving vestiges of Muslim Goa, the rest having been systematically dismantled by the Portuguese after the rout of 1510.

The zeal with which the colonisers persecuted native religions and beliefs in the 16th and 17th centuries forced the custodians of Goa's ancient

Old Goa's towers rise from the jungle

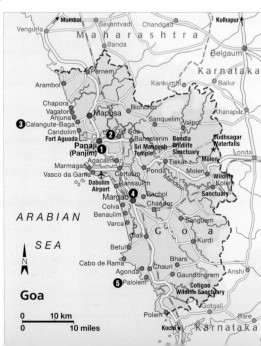

Goa

0   10 km

0   10 miles

Hindu temples to flee inland, beyond the margins of Portuguese territory. A dozen or more of these shrines, built in a distinctive hybrid syle that's unique to the region, nestle in the hidden valleys around Ponda. If you're pushed for time, limit yourself to the **Shri Mangesh temple**, 9km (5½ miles) north on the highway near the village of Priol, and **Shri Mahalsa temple**, a couple of kilometres south near Nardol village. Both feature impressive lamp towers, or *deepmal*, on which hundreds of tiny oil lamps are illuminated during festivals – a magical sight.

Dudhsagar

The waterfalls at **Dudhsagar**, near Goa's eastern border, are the second highest in India. Measuring 600m (3,000ft) from head to foot, they're a spectacular sight at any time of year, but especially just after the monsoon rains in October and November, when water levels are at their highest. Getting to them can be something of an adventure. Although the main Goa–Hyderabad train line slices

The Dudhsagar waterfalls

Goa

straight over the falls, there are no day-return services and no sealed roads to Dudhsagar, so you have instead to drive there in a Jeep from the train station town of Molen via a rutted forest track – a memorable ride through luxuriant teak forest ⛰.

Goan *Palácios*

Nothing encapsulates the hybridity of Goan culture quite as well as the architecture of its colonial-era mansions, or *palácios*. While many fine specimens line the older streets of Panaji, Margao and Mapusa, the most photogenic nestle amid the paddy fields and palm groves inland. They date from the middle phase of Portuguese rule, a time when high-ranking, Goan-born officials and merchants were making profits from trade in opium and gemstones. Many amassed vast fortunes, which they spent converting

their ancestral homes according to the fashionable European styles of the day.

Around traditional Hindu courtyards were sumptuous classical facades with fancy rococo mouldings. Flights of steps would lead to gabled entranceways, where long stone seats were set along deep verandas.

Of the few surviving ancestral Goan homes open to the public, by far the most impressive is the **Braganza-Perreira/ Menezes-Braganza house**, in Chandor, 13km (8 miles) east of Margao.

🚶 OLD GOA

The giant domes and belfries of Old Goa, Portugal's former capital in Asia, are today Unesco-listed and soar above the palm canopy on the banks of the Mandovi River, 10km (6 miles) east of Panaji.

The size and splendour of Old Goa's surviving monuments attest to the wealth amassed by the colony in the 16th and 17th centuries, when it stood at the nexus of a vast trade empire.

Start your tour at the **Viceroy's Arch**, near the river bank, which used to serve as the main entry point to the city. It features a statue of the Portuguese explorer, Vasco da Gama, without whose discovery of the sea route to the Indies via the Cape of Good Hope Goa would never have been founded.

Entering via the Viceroy's Arch

Head up the lane running through the arch (the former 'Rua Direita') and turn left soon after towards the **Church of St Cajetan**, built in the 1600s by the Theatine Order. It was modelled on St Peter's in Rome. On your way to the church, look out on the north side of the road for the carved **door jamb** erected on a stone plinth – the last vestige of the Indo-Muslim city that preceded Goa.

Having looked around St Cajetan, return to the Rua Direita, but turn right off it to admire the splendid facade of the **Sé Cathedral**, the colonial capital's principal place of worship. Dating from 1652, it took 80 years to build and still holds the original bell, whose tolling used to announce the burnings of heretics by the dreaded Inquisition in the square in front.

Walk around the south wall of the Cathedral to reach the **Church of St Francis of Assisi** (1661). Its faded interior features sculpted tombstones of Portuguese *hidalgos*, or nobles, as well as traces of medieval frescoes and

Tips

- Come prepared for the heat: the site gets much hotter and more humid than the coast
- Early morning is the best time to visit
- There is nowhere commendable to eat or drink in Old Goa so bring your own refreshments
- Catch a ferry from the terminal just north of the Viceroy's Arch for a great view of St Cajetan's dome – particularly atmospheric in the late afternoon

The Chapel of St Catherine is on the site of Old Goa's first church

oil-painted wood panels. the **Archaeological Museum** (daily 10am–6pm; free) next door holds temple fragments unearthed in the vicinity, but its most interesting exhibits are the portraits of old Portuguese viceroys displayed in the gallery on the first floor.

Just off the west corner of the museum stands the diminutive **Chapel of St Catherine**, which was consecrated to mark the Portuguese victory over the Sultan of Bijapur's army on St Catherine's Day, 1510. Head south down the lane running past the chapel, cross the main highway and turn right soon after towards the Convent of Santa Monica, where the **Museum of Christian Art** (daily 9.30am–5pm; charge) displays antique ecclesiastical vestments, icons and crosses. At the far west end of the lane running past the museum, you'll fine the Manueline-style **Church of Our Lady of the Rosary** (1549). It was from the natural balcony in front

of the church that Alfonso Albuquerque, founding father of Goa, is said to have directed his forces during the battle of 1510. Inside, look out for the delicately carved marble tomb of Caratrina a Piro, the first European woman ever to have visited Goa.

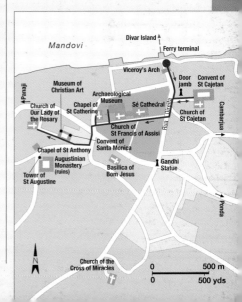

NORTH GOA

North Goa – comprising the districts of Bardez and Pernem – is where beach tourism in the state started out in the 1960s, and it has dominated the coastal strip ever since. Development is densest just across the river from Panaji, along the stretch of beach connecting the resorts of Candolim, Calangute and Baga, but eases off as you press further north.

Mapusa

Mapusa – pronounced '*map*-sa' – is the district headquarters of Bardez *taluka* (district). As the principal source of supplies for north Goa's scattered villages, the town stands in marked contrast to the razzmatazz of the beach resorts, only a short taxi ride west. Heaped up the sides of a low hill, its largely modern centre is unrelentingly hot and drab, and holds little of interest for visitors. You should, however, make time for the colourful **market** that erupts on Fridays in the grid of streets east of the main square. Before you leave, be sure to make a pit stop at F.R. Xavier's famous café, next to the banana section, for a restorative plate of hot prawn patties (flaky pastry puffs served straight from the oven), washed down with spicy ginger *chai*.

Candolim, Calangute and Baga

At the centre of a magnificent 11km (7-mile) beach, **Calangute ❸** forms the hub of north Goa's tourist scene. A cluttered market lined by bars, shops, restaurants, banks and telecom centres, it is these days popular mainly with domestic visitors who travel here by bus on day trips from the capital, Panaji. At the southern limit of the same beach, **Candolim** is a predominantly British package enclave, overlooked by the laterite walls and cannon emplacements of the former Portuguese stronghold, **Fort Aguada**.

The younger charter holiday-makers gravitate to **Baga**, a resort at the opposite (northern) end of Calangute beach, where Tito's nightclub dominates a busy, brightly lit strip. Signs advertising karaoke nights, 'Full English Breakfasts' and 'Happy Hours' jostle for attention with Kashmiri handicraft vendors and restaurants offering authentic Italian cuisine and cocktails. On Saturday evenings, seemingly every taxi in the state turns out for the **Night Market** at nearby **Arpora**, where foreigners sell designer wear and stallholders from across the country tout souvenirs ▥.

Coconuts

Along with fishing and rice cultivation, coconuts (*Cocos nucifera*) have always formed the backbone of Goa's economy. Around 40 million are consumed in the state every year (that's one per day per family), most often mixed with fish curry. One-sixth of the local population are engaged in tending the trees, which not only form a cornerstone of the Goan diet but also provide coir for making seawater resistant rope, thatch for shade and huts, wood for construction and for sale to the cosmetic and cooking-oil industries.

Palm trees are also 'tapped' two or three times daily for their sugar-rich sap – watching 'toddy tappers' shimmy up the notches in slender palm trunks to reach the thicket of stems at the top is one of Goa's defining sights.

Boats on the beach at Baga, one of the major tourist resorts

Anjuna to Arambol

The night market evolved out of the older-established **Flea Market** , still held on Wednesdays at the next village up the coast – **Anjuna**. This has long been a bastion of a harder-edged, more hedonistic hippy tourism, with its drug-fuelled full-moon parties and techno dance music, which you can sample at the famous Nine Bar in nearby **Vagator** after the Flea Market.

North of Anjuna, development thins out after the Siolim River, only rearing its head again at **Arambol**, Goa's northernmost village. Beyond the reach of package tourism, this remains essentially a hang-out for long-staying 'alternative' visitors. If you've come to India to learn yoga, have ayurvedic massages or space out on the beach doing t'ai chi, Arambol will be the place for you.

SOUTH GOA

A magnificent stretch of sand spreads south virtually from the foot of the Dabolim Plateau, site of Goa's civil airport. Arriving in the state by plane, it's possible to clear customs and be swimming from this wonderful beach within an hour. Dotted through the dense palm forest behind it is a string of mainly Christian fishing villages, together with a chain of ultra-luxurious resort hotels that between them hold accommodation to suit most pockets. Further south still, a much more indented coastline backed by low hills shelters a succession of beaches, among them Agonda and Palolem, the jewels in the crown of Goa's coastline.

Margao

With a population of over 100,000, **Margao** ❹ (also known as 'Madgaon') is Goa's second-largest town. It can feel frenetic compared with the resorts just 10 minutes' drive west, but does hold a wonderful crop of elegant 18th- and 19th-century Portuguese houses. The centrepiece of the old colonial enclave on the north side of Margao is the splendid **Church of the Holy Spirit**, built in 1675 and a textbook late Baroque edifice, with a grand white-washed facade, fronted by a monumental cross whose base is carved with episodes from the Easter story.

Colva and Benaulim

South Goa is on the whole much more sedate than the north, with most visitors corralled inside one or other of the five-star resorts backing **Colva Beach**. Extending for 25km (15.5 miles), this stretch remains comparatively uncrowded even in peak season. While the rather run-down resort of **Colva** soaks up most of the domestic tourist traffic, independent travellers congregate more in neighbouring **Benaulim**, a predominantly Catholic fishing village that has retained plenty of traditional Goan charm. It also offers the best selection of budget guesthouses in the area. For more luxury, head south of Benaulim to the **Taj Exotica**, the flagship among the rank of glamorous five-star hotels built behind the beach over the past decade.

Palolem and Agonda

In the far south of the state, a couple of hours' ride across the Sayadhri hills, **Palolem** ❺ is undeniably Goa's most picturesque beach – a gently curving bay of golden sand set against a curtain of coconut palms. Remote and unfrequented until as recently as the early 1990s, it has since become the first-choice destination for backpackers. Thankfully, however, building has been held in check by the local municipality's ban on concrete construction, and accommodation is mainly in the form of eco-friendly palm-leaf 'huts' 🏨.

Just to the north, **Agonda** is starting to soak up the overspill from Palolem. Lacking the palm trees, it's not quite as pretty, but does hold plenty of good-value accommodation, restaurants and cafés. Moreover, since the 2004 Boxing Day tsunami reshaped its beach, swimming is safe and – thanks to the picturesque backdrop of forested hills – inspirational, especially at sunset.

The curved beach at Palolem, one of Goa's most idyllic resorts

ACCOMMODATION

Most of Goa's plentiful hotel and guesthouse accommodation consists of simple rooms with small balconies or verandas, overhead fans and en suite bathrooms. What you end up paying will depend on a range of factors: location, time of year and proximity to the beach. Advance booking is essential, especially over the New Year peak period.

Central Goa

Panjim Inn
E-212, 31 Janeiro Road, Fontainhas, Panaji
Tel: 0832-243 5628
www.panjiminn.com
Delightful heritage hotel in the heart of Panaji's picturesque colonial quarter, with three differently priced wings. **$–$$$**

North Goa

Alidia
Saunta Vaddo, Baga Road, Baga
Tel: 0832-227 6835
alidia@rediffmail.com
A wide range of lovely rooms with verandas ranged around a curving pool, in the dunes right behind the beach. **$$–$$$**

Casa Seashell
Fort Aguada Road, Candolim
Tel: 0832-247 9879
www.seashellgoa.com
A conveniently located, well-run guesthouse with larger-than-average rooms and a small pool. Excellent value. **$$**

Elsewhere/Otter Creek
Mandrem, 8km (5 miles) south of Arambol
Tel: 0832-253 8451 or 9820-037 387
www.aseascape.com
Arguably the most beautifully situated and elegantly restored period property in Goa, Elsewhere is a 19th-century bolthole with gorgeous pillared veranda looking across empty dunes to a stretch of undeveloped beach. A less pricey alternative on the same site are the Otter Creek architectural tents. **$$$$–$$$$$**

Grandpa's Inn
Gaun Waddo, Anjuna
Tel: 0832-227 3270
www.granpasinn.com
The pleasant rooms of this hotel are set around the bougainvillea-filled courtyard of an old Portuguese mansion. Good restaurant and large pool. **$$$**

Ivon's
Girkar Waddo, Arambol
Tel: 0832-224 2672
Immaculately clean, en suite budget rooms fronted by tiled balconies facing the beach. Best-value budget option in the village. **$**

Nilaya Hermitage
Near Baga
Tel: 0832-227 6793
www.nilayahermitage.com
Ultra-exclusive boutique hotel, on a hillside 3km (2 miles) inland. The new-agey interiors have lots of organic curves, and there is a wonderful pool out front. **$$$$$**

Peaceland
Soronto Waddo, Anjuna
Tel: 0832-227 3700
Anjuna's best-value budget place, with clean, well-aired rooms fitted with mosquito nets – a 15-minute walk to the seafront. **$**

Pousada Tauma
Porba Vaddo, Calangute
Tel: 0832-227 9061
www.pousada-tauma.com
Ultra-stylish boutique hotel constructed

entirely from local red laterite. The decor's low-key and the pool magical, plus there's an ayurvedic spa. **$$$$$**

South Goa
Bioveda
Doval Kazan, Agonda
Tel: 9422-388982
www.bioveda.in
Luxury huts with en suite bathrooms, right behind the beach. **$–$$$**

Oceanic
Tembi Waddo, Colom, Palolem
Tel: 0834-264 3059
www.hotel-oceanic.com
Pleasantly furnished guesthouse on the wooded fringes of Palolem, boasting a small pool and terrace restaurant. 🍴 **$$$**

Ordo Sounsar
Far northern end of Palolem beach
Tel: 9822-488769
www.ordosounsar.com
Palolem's grooviest hut camp, tucked away on the tranquil side of the river at the far north side of the beach. **$**

Palm Grove
Tamdi Marti, Vas Vaddo, Benaulim
Tel: 0834-272 2533
www.palmgrovegoa.com
Surrounded by a lovely garden, this is a clean and pleasant place to stay. The decent restaurant serves Goan dishes and seafood. 🍴 **$$–$$$**

Xavier's
Sernabatim, Benaulim
Tel: 832-277 1489
jovek@sanchar.net
Spacious rooms grouped around a leafy garden, only a stone's throw from the beach. **$$**

RESTAURANTS

Standards of cooking in Goa are extraordinarily high and it's rare indeed to be presented with a duff meal, even in a modest roadside fish-curry-rice joint. In order to keep clients for their own restaurants, hotels routinely warn guests against eating on the beaches, but shacks offer much less expensive meals and are often more enjoyable places to hang out. After a period of experimentation, you'll soon settle on one or two favourites which you'll probably patronise for the rest of your holiday.

Restaurant Price Categories
Prices are for a standard meal for one, excluding alcoholic drinks

$ = up to Rs200
$$ = Rs200–500
$$$ = Rs500–1000
$$$$ = over Rs1000

Central Goa
Viva Panjim
178 Rua 31 de Janeiro, Fontainhas, Panaji
Hidden down a narrow alleyway in the old quarter, this is just the place to try traditional Indo-Portuguese and Goan food. **$$**

North Goa
Double Dutch
Main Street, Arambol
Lounge under the palm canopy enjoying delights such as the famous 'mixed stuff' (stuffed mushrooms and capsicums with sesame potato), sublime Dutch apple pie, delicious cakes and fragrant south Indian coffee. **$$**

Fellini's
Glastonbury Street, Arambol
Fabulous, authentic wood-fired pizzas and tasty pastas at this local institution, beloved of Arambol's long-term residents. 🍴 **$**

Make the most of your setting and eat on the beach, as here in Benaulim

Fiesta
Tito's Road, above the beach, Baga
Twinkling with fairy lights and lanterns, Fiesta is Baga's most extravagantly dressed (and highly rated) restaurant. The Mediterranean-Portuguese menu has stood the test of time: house specialities include carpaccio of beef and juicy wood-baked pizzas. **$$$$**

German Bakery
South Anjuna
www.german-bakery.org
Famous hippy wholefood café-restaurant, serving tasty, healthy meals to health-conscious travellers. Live music, dance and circus cabarets in season. **$**

Pete's Shack
Escrivao Waddo, Candolim
Sumptuous, hygienic salads, dressed with real olive oil and balsamic vinegar, or main dishes of seafood sizzlers and tandoori specialities. One of the best beach shacks in Goa. **$$**

Plantain Leaf
Calangute Market, Calangute
Housed in a grand laterite dining hall with marble tables, this popular vegetarian restaurant serves the standard range of south Indian fast food – *dosas*, *idlys*, *wadas*, *samosas* and *uttapams* – in addition to good-value *thalis*. **$**

South Goa
Café Inn
Pundalik Gaitondi Road, Palolem
The best coffee and breakfast joint in Palolem, and they do a range of meals and snacks during the rest of the day until 11pm. **$**

Madhus
North side of beach, Agonda
Mouth-watering tandoori meat and fish, served alfresco under the palms. Always packed out in the evenings, so get there early. **$**

Palmira's
Beach Road, Benaulim
Homely roadside shack restaurant run by a delightful local family who serve up delicious all-day breakfasts. Palmira's creamy curd, dolloped on mounds of fresh papaya, pineapple and grated coconut, is a legend. **$**

NIGHTLIFE

Since the government's ban in 2000 on amplified music after 10pm, Goa's legendary full-moon party scene has become a thing of the past. That said, a handful of above-board clubs still pump out trance and techno – the definitive soundtrack to the north Goan beach scene – although they usually have to shut down by 10pm. As for bars, you're spoilt for choice: the state boasts more than 5,000 premises licensed to sell liquor, at all hours.

Nine Bar
Ozran, Vagator

Large crowds gather at this walled club each day for sunset, accompanied by a thumping trance sound system. Drink prices are high but the views serene. Admission is free.

Silent Noise
Neptune's Point, Palolem
www.silentnoise.in

This expat collective has dreamed up a novel way to circumvent the 10pm ban: headphone parties, where the music is broadcast digitally to individual headsets instead of through PAs. Held on Saturday nights at an idyllic cove on the south side of Palolem beach (9pm–4am). Admission charge.

Tito's
Tito's Lane, Baga
www.titosgoa.com

Goa's most famous nightspot plays in the dunes above Baga beach, lounge grooves till 11pm, and hip-hop, house and salsa

Nine Bar's stunning setting

thereafter. Open 8pm–late from Nov–Dec. Admission charge.

Westend
Mollem Bhat Valley, Sangolda (4km/2½ miles inland from Calangute/Candolim)
Tel: 0832/324 6727

Hilltop dance floor surrounded by jungle, with a rooftop pool and chillout areas. One of the few venues to ignore the 10pm ban; held 2–3 times weekly 9pm–4.30am. Frequented mainly by young Russians. Admission charge.

SPORTS, ACTIVITIES AND TOURS

The closest most visitors get to a sporting event in Goa is a game of volleyball or cricket on the beach. But there are plenty of more adventurous alternatives on offer in and around the resorts should you feel like broadening your horizons.

Boat Trips
John's Boats
Candolim
Tel: 0832-562 0910
www.johnsboatrips.com

Dolphin-spotting excursions run off most of the beaches in season: look for signs posted around the shacks. This is one of the

oldest-established operators, who also offer overnight cruises through local backwaters on a Keralan rice boat.

Diving
Dreamz Diving
Palolem
Tel: 9326-113466

www.dreamzdiving.com
This outfit offers reputable scuba diving, including guided dives in the region.

Sailing
Goa Sailing
Palolem
Tel: 9850-458 865
www.goasailing.com
Rents out 4.5m (15ft) Prindle Catamarans, complete with a fully qualified, British instructor – ideal for explorations of hidden coves in the area.

Tours
Daytripper
www.daytrippergoa.com
Pitched at British charter tourists, several private firms operate all-in tours (including meals, guides and transport). This is one of the largest.

GTDC
www.goa-tourism.com
The Goa state tourism development corporation runs bus tours to various locations. Ranging from half-day excursions to longer trips taking in the sights of the interior,

they're inexpensive but extremely rushed. Full details are posted at GTDC's tourist offices in Panjim, Mapusa and Margao.

Yoga
Goa is rapidly becoming one of the world's most desirable yoga venues, attracting teachers and practitioners from all over the world. The following, open from October to April, are the state's best centres.

Ashiyana Tropical Retreat Centre
Junasa Waddo, Mandrem, north Goa
www.ashiyana-yoga-goa.com

Brahmani Centre
Grandpa's Inn *(see p.173)*, Anjuna, north Goa
www.brahmaniyoga.com

Harmonic Healing and Eco Retreat Centre
Patnem, south Goa
www.harmonicingoa.com

Purple Valley Centre
Assagao, north Goa
www.yogagoa.com

FESTIVALS AND EVENTS
Festivals are a way of life in Goa, as elsewhere in India; the principal ones are noted below, but visit any tourist office for a complete list of what's on locally.

January–March
Shantadurga Temple
near Ponda
A solid silver image of the goddess Shantadurga is carried from Fatorpa to Cuncolim.

Carnival
Panaji
Three days of mayhem in the run up to Lent.

Shigmo
State-wide
Goa's version of the Hindu Holi festival features processions, music and dance.

November–December
International Film Festival of India
Panaji
India's answer to Cannes brings the capital to a virtual standstill for a week each year.

Feast of St Francis Xavier
Old Goa
Most important date in the calendar for Goan Catholics, featuring a huge open-air Mass.

Christmas/New Year
The Christian festive season is marked with parties, with the 10pm music curfew ignored.

Kolkata and Northeast India

Bordering the Bay of Bengal, India's eastern corner is a distinctive, naturally bountiful and colourful part of the country, anchored by the vibrant city of Kolkata and encompassing the states of Orissa and West Bengal, while almost cut off from the rest of India are the physically and culturally remote northeastern states.

Kolkata

Population: 15.6 million

Local Dialling Code: 033

Tourist Office: Government of India Tourist Office: 4 Shakespeare Sarani, Chowringhee; tel: 2282 5813; www.incredibleindia.org

Post Office: GPO: BBD Marg

Hospital: Apollo Gleneagles: 48/iF Lila Roy Sarani, Gariahat Road; tel: 2461 8028; www.apolloglenegles.in

Media: *Cal Calling* (Rs45) and *CityInfo* (free)

Because of its long history of political unrest, the northeast of India is the least-visited corner of the country, yet it holds both extraordinary scenic variety and a wealth of traditional cultures. The region's principal centre of gravity is the metropolis of Kolkata (formerly Calcutta), whose charismatic Raj-era architecture, endlessly fascinating street life and rich intellectual and artisitic traditions can come as a surprise to visitors expecting only to find deprivation and poverty.

On the Ganges delta further south lies one of India's great wilderness areas: the Sunderbans swamps, where honey-gatherers and fishermen still wear masks on the backs of their heads to fool predatory swimming tigers. Jungles inhabited by numerous indigenous Adivasi groups spread through the interior of neighbouring Orissa, whose main attractions are its gigantic, ornately decorated medieval temples. To the north of Kolkata, the plains give way suddenly to the foothills of the Himalaya. Reached by an 88km (55-mile) journey on a 'toy' train, the hill station of Darjeeling is justly famed for its tea gardens and views of the distant mountains. Sikkim, further north still, adds orchids, Buddhist monasteries and close-up vistas of the mighty ice peaks to this compelling list of attractions.

Few foreign travellers venture far in the troubled northeastern hill states, which are almost cut off from the rest of the country by Bangladesh, and remote in other ways, too. Away from the rain-soaked Brahmaputra lowlands dominating Assam and Meghalaya, permits are required to penetrate the isolated valleys and forests of Arunachal Pradesh and Nagaland, inhabited by tribal groups who have, despite centuries of attention from colonial rulers and missionaries, retained their traditional ways of life.

KOLKATA

Until 1999, when it took on the local Bengali name of **Kolkata** ❶, the capital of West Bengal was known to the world as Calcutta. Its history dates back to 1686, when the East India Company selected the site for its new headquarters. A factory

A shopkeeper in Kolkata's old town

The Howrah Bridge is a symbol of Kolkata

was established soon after which, by 1773, had gained a European population of more than 100,000, swollen by the arrival of new writers, traders, soldiers and what the administration called 'cargoes of females'. Two further massive influxes followed Independence, forcing Calcutta's infrastructure to the verge of collapse. Since then, however, the overcrowding situation has gradually improved. With a population of around 8 million (the figure for the metropolitan area is more than 15 million), Kolkata is less a byword for third-world poverty than it used to be. A Soviet-designed metro and efficient one-way system give the impression of a well-run city, and its long-standing reputation as a centre for intellectuals, left-wing activists and artists endures.

The West Bank

Even if you're not arriving by train, start your visit at **Howrah Station**,

Kolkata and Northeast India

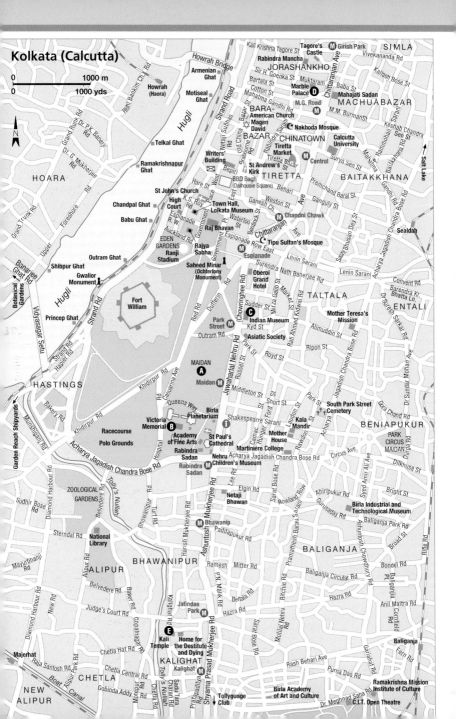

The Raj-era Victoria Memorial *(see p.182)*

one of India's great Raj-era railway hubs, and a hive of activity, day and night. The nearby **Howrah Bridge**, another national monument regarded with considerable affection despite its constant crowds, conveys you across the river. Built during World War II to transport military traffic, this massive steel suspension bridge is 705m (2,350ft) long. It carries an eight-lane highway used by an estimated 80,000 vehicles and more than 1 million pedestrians every day – as well as countless cows and bullocks. The traffic jams can reach epic proportions; photography on, and of, the bridge is strictly prohibited.

The Maidan

Kolkata's heart is the broad, open playing field known as the **Maidan** . Originally laid out to create a

Kolkata and Northeast India

Kolkata City Transport

 Airport: Netaji Subhash Bose International Airport, or NSCBI (tel: 2511 8787), lies 20km (12 miles) north of the city

 Trains: Kolkata has three major train stations, with a fourth under construction; the largest of them is Howrah, on the west side of the river, close to the iconic bridge

 Buses: Long-distance buses terminate at Babu Ghat Bus Stand, while most others arrive at Esplanade Bus Stand, just north of Sudder Street

 Metro: Kolkata's justly famous Metro (www.kolmetro.com) is the cleanest and least stressful way to get around

 Ferries: To reach Howrah station, you can cross the river by ferry; catch them from the Eden Gardens ghats

 Trams: Trams are useful for reaching Sealdah station and Gariahat

 Rickshaws: The city is the last in India where human-pulled rickshaws are still operating

 Taxis: Yellow Ambassador taxis are ubiquitous, with pre-paid booths at Howrah station and the airport. Alternatively, book through the government tourist office *(see p.178)* or West Bengal Tourism at 3/2 BBD Bagh: tel: 2243 7260, **www.wbtourism.com**.

The Indian Museum in Kolkata houses several fascinating antiquities

clear line of fire from the East India Company's fort, it attracts joggers, soapbox orators, charlatans peddling cure-alls, and droves of office workers with their lunch boxes. At the end of the day, football and cricket matches take over. On the maidan's northern side, the 48m (157ft) -high **Ochterlony Monument** (Saheed Minar) was built in 1828 in honour of the British general Sir David Ochterlony, whose outflanking of the Gurkhas near Kathmandu decided the Anglo-Nepalese War of 1814–15. **Eden Gardens**, Kolkata's legendary test cricket ground, lies nearby.

Victoria Memorial

Set amid well tended grounds on the south side of the Maidan, the white-marble **Victoria Memorial ❸** (Tue–Sun 10am–5pm; charge) epitomises perhaps better than any other building in India the pride and pomposity of the British Raj at its zenith. Commissioned by Viceroy Lord Curzon and completed in 1921, it was paid for by 'voluntary contributions' from maharajas and nawabs. More recently, historians of the British India have reminded us that its construction

corresponded precisely with the third and most lethal of a series of devastating famines in which an estimated 20–30 million peasants starved to death.

Chowringhee Road and the Indian Museum

Running along the eastern edge of the Maidan, **Chowringhee Road** (Nehru Road) marks the limits of the old European neighbourhood whose mansions, rather misleadingly, once won Kolkata the epithet of 'City of Palaces'. These days, it is a busy shopping street with big hotels and cinemas, gigantic film billboards and a roadway choked with traffic.

The run-down **Indian Museum ⓒ** (www.indianmuseumkolkata.org; Tue–Sun, Mar–Nov 10am–5pm, Dec–Feb 10am–4.30pm; charge) by Chowringhee Road and Sudder Street is a storehouse for ancient Mauryan and Gupta treasures, with a collection regarded by many as India's finest. Prize items include a beautifully preserved 3rd-century BC Mauryan lion capital and fragments of the 2nd-century BC stupa at Barhut in Madhya Pradesh.

BBD Bagh (Dalhousie Square)

Centred on a palm-lined water tank, **BBD Bagh,** still widely referred to by its former colonial name, Dalhousie Square, lies on the site of the original Fort William, immediately north of the Maidan. Some of the city's finest colonial buildings survive in the streets flanking it, among them the **Writers' Building** – once the centre of Britain's imperial bureaucracy, where legions of young East India Company clerks duplicated everything they could lay their hands on. Today, it houses government offices with even greater numbers of pen-pushing beaurocrats.

Kali Temple is very holy to Hindus (see p.184)

The Marble Palace

Erected by the wealthy family of Raja Majendra Mullick Bahadur, the opulent **Marble Palace** 🅓 (Tue–Wed, Fri–Sun 10am–4pm; arrange visit in advance with Deputy Director of Tourism, 3/2 BBD Bagh, tel: 033-2248 8271) on tiny Muktaram Babu Street, northeast of Dalhousie Square, is a grandiose Palladian villa-turned-museum, set in a park filled with exotic birds and packed with an imaginative juxtaposition of ancient Roman and Chinese sculpture, fine Venetian glass chandeliers, old Flemish masters and naughty French erotica. The elderly resident, a descendant of the original owners, still regales visitors with Chopin in the ballroom.

Satyajit Ray

One of Kolkata's most famous sons is the film director **Satyajit Ray** (1921–92). So far the only Indian director to win an Oscar, which he received in 1991 for Lifetime Achievement, Ray was a visionary, almost single-handedly responsible for developing an Indian 'new wave' of arthouse cinema.

Although he had almost no cinematic experience, he was encouraged by visiting French film-maker Jean Renoir to go ahead on a shoestring budget to shoot his first feature *Pather Panchali* (1955). Although this is considered his greatest work, Ray went on to make many other films, including *Charulata* (1964), the *Calcutta Trilogy* (1970–5) and his first Hindi/Urdu film *Shatranj ke Khilai* ('The Chess Players', 1977). For detailed information on the great director's life and individual films, see www.satyajitray.org.

Crowds in Darjeeling market

The Kali Temple

Built in 1809 on the site of a much more ancient structure, Kolkata's famous **Kali Temple** ❺ (daily 5am–2pm, 4–10pm; free), on the south side of the city near Kalighat Metro station, is the holiest site in the city for local Hindus. It is said to stand on the spot where Sati's little toe landed after her dead body had been dismembered by Vishnu. Pilgrims queue to make offerings of milk mixed with Ganges water and *bhang* (cannabis). Goats are also sacrificed to assuage the goddess' insatiable thirst for blood.

WEST BENGAL

Visited by Greeks, Chinese and Persians, Bengal was long ago a seafaring nation, sending traders to Sri Lanka, Sumatra and Java. From the end of the 19th century onwards it became one of the most prosperous territories of the British Empire. Temples were built, the Bengali language was enriched by poets and writers such as Bankim Chandra Chatterjee and Rabindranath Tagore, and major religious philosophers such as Ramakrishna and Vivekananda emerged.

The Sunderbans

Formed by the Ganges-Brahmaputra delta, the **Sunderbans** ❷, to the south of Kolkata, encompass the largest estuarine forest mangrove marshland in the world. A Unesco World Heritage Site, the region is also a stronghold of the Royal Bengal Tiger, which swims and has been known to attack fishermen. Due to

The Mountain Railway

Classed as a Unesco World Heritage Monument, the Darjeeling Himalayan Railway (www.dhrs.org 🅜) – better known as the 'Toy Train' – was built between 1879 and 1881 to transport the European inhabitants of Calcutta to their summer capital. The line climbs 1,500m (5,000ft) over 88km (54 miles) through lush hillsides and tea gardens, reaching its highest point at the station of Ghoom (2,225m/7,300ft), before rounding the spectacular Batasia Loop with its amazing views; Darjeeling is its final terminus.

The steep ride takes around seven hours. Oil-fired engines, converted from the original coal-burning rolling stock, and a dozen working vintage steam locomotives haul the picturesque Victorian carriages. During the monsoon the service may be disrupted by landslides. Strikes (a prominent feature of this notoriously militant region) also cause sporadic disruptions.

the enveloping cover of long grass, the chances of seeing one are slim, but crocodiles are usually seen sleeping on mudflats along the river.

Shantiniketan

Shantiniketan, 136km (85 miles) northwest of Kolkata, is where Rabindranath Tagore's father founded an ashram in 1861. The poet spent most of his Nobel Prize money to make it an educational institution. Then, with the help of the Maharaja of Tripura, he upgraded it to the level of a university in 1921. This is where the poet revived the traditional Indian way of teaching in the open air, under a tree, in close contact with nature. Shantiniketan soon became one of the hubs of intellectual life. One of the university's most famous alumni is the late Indira Gandhi.

Darjeeling

Astride a high ridge in the Himalayan foothills, with tea plantations wrapped around its terraced flanks and mesmeric views of distant Kanchenjunga on the horizon, **Darjeeling** ❸ is the quintessential Indian hill station – cluttered and ramshackle, but full of charisma. Its incarnation as a retreat for heat-weary Brits dates from the 1830s, when the raja of the then-independent kingdom of Sikkim was pressured into ceding the territory to the East India Company. With tea from seeds smuggled out of China and an influx of plantation labour from Nepal, the 100-strong village quickly grew to a community of 10,000. Nepali remains the official language and most residents are of either Nepalese or Tibetan origin.

West Bengal and Orissa

0   100 km
0   100 miles

Among the few surviving relics of the British Raj are the stalwart **Darjeeling Club**, and a couple of tea rooms and Edwardian hotels such as the **Windamere**. The real British legacy, however, lies in the tea gardens spread around town. **Happy Valley** (Mon–Sat 8am–4pm) is one that welcomes visitors without obligation to buy.

A drive out to **Tiger Hill** before dawn has long been a popular excursion for visitors wanting to see the famous sunrise over Kanchenjunga. The summit, 11km (7 miles) south of town in nearby Sikkim, is 8,598m (28,660ft) above sea level; from the observation platform there's a superb view to the northeast as the sun first lights up the twin peaks of the great mountain.

ORISSA

A trio of spectacular shrines forms the backbone of tours around the state of Orissa, on the northeast coast of India. Evolved from the ancient kingdom of Kalinga, whose merchants were responsible for spreading Hinduism across the Bay of Bengal to southeast Asia, it remains a staunchly religious part of the country, attracting millions of pilgrims each year to its most revered shrine, the mighty Jagannath temple in Puri. The greatest of this region's architectural treasures, however, is a shrine that's no longer an active place of worship; the Sun Temple at Konark, just up the coast from Puri, lay beneath a giant sand heap until it was excavated in the 19th century,

The Sun Temple in Konark is one of Orissa's major sights

revealing intricate carvings from the golden age of the Ganga dynasty.

Bhubaneshwar

The remains of an astonishing 500 temples may be traced in and around Orissa's state capital, **Bhubaneshwar** ❹. Dating from the 7th and 8th centuries, the oldest are grouped around the sacred 'Ocean Drop' lake of Bindu Sagar, the focus for bathing and purification ceremonies.

East of the water tank, the 10th-century **Muktesvara** (daily 24 hours; free) is a rust-coloured stone shrine dedicated to Shiva, with a small bathing pond and gracefully arched *torana* gate. The **Rajarani** (dawn–dusk; charge), standing on a platform at the end of a pleasant garden nearby, is a more robust structure than that of the Muktesvara, with a pronounced pyramid over the worship hall, and a powerful *sikhara* behind it.

The greatest of the city's monuments is without doubt the 11th-century **Lingaraja**, south of the Bindu Sagar. Although off limits to non-Hindus, it can be viewed from an observation platform specially erected for the purpose by Lord Curzon. It is dedicated to the Lord of the Three Worlds, Tribhuvanesvara, who gave the town of Bhubaneshwar its modern-day name.

Puri

Even if you cannot be in **Puri** ❺ for the awesome **Rath Yatra Festival** in June/July *(see box, above)*, the town is worth a visit to experience a community whose lives are devoted almost entirely to a single building: the great **Jagannath temple**. Some 6,000 priests, artisans and other workers are employed within its walled precincts and many thousands more depend on the constant flow of pilgrims through the surrounding streets.

Non-Hindus are not permitted to enter, but you can get a good view from the roof of the **Raghunandan Library** (Mon–Sat 10am–noon, 4–6pm; free) near the temple wall. Puri also has a large **beach**, southwest of town, which is ideal for a breezy stroll. Jagannath devotees come here for a propitiatory dip, leaving behind miniature sand temples, for this is the **Swarga Dwara** (Heaven's Gateway) – one of the principal stops on the town's ritual circuit.

> ### Rath Yatra
>
> One of India's major religious gatherings, **Rath Yatra**, is held in Puri amid the stifling heat of late June/early July. Hundreds of thousands of onlookers descend on the town to watch the spectacular procession of the temple's presiding deity, Lord Jagannath, his brother, Balabhadra, and sister, Subhadra, down the main street. The gods are carried on colossal chariots, or *rathas*, 12m (40ft) in height, with wheels 2m (7ft) in diameter. They are preceded by four wooden horses, but actually drawn by hundreds of devotees to Gundicha Mandir (Garden House), 8km (5 miles) away, where they stay for seven days. The rituals completed, the deities ride back to their shrine.
>
> In previous centuries, fervent devotees of Jagannath considered it auspicious to be killed by the mighty chariots, and it is said that many used to commit suicide by throwing themselves under the wheels – the origin of the term 'juggernaut'.

⭐ DURGA PUJA

A fierce, ten-armed deity brandishing an armoury of spears, tridents, maces and other lethal weapons while sitting astride a lion would seem a peculiar focus for a family-oriented festival. But for millions of Hindus across West Bengal, Orissa and the Northeast Hill States, veneration of the goddess Durga during her annual Puja is the social and religious high point of the year – Christmas, Day of the Dead and Carnival all rolled into one.

A Major Celebration

Nowhere is the celebration more fervently marked than in Kolkata. For 10 days in the month of Aswim (September –October), the streets of the Bengali capital are inundated with extravagantly decorated stages showcasing effigies of the goddess and her mythical family. The statues are the object of intense religious rituals, drumming and dancing displays, and the wide-eyed admiration of droves of dressed-up families 🏃.

Origins

Since the 1950s, the start of Durga Puja has traditionally been heralded by a much-loved two-hour programme on All India Radio featuring special festival songs, or *chalisa*, invoking strength to overcome adversity. Hindus believe it was the deity's power that Rama invoked before his epic battle with the evil demon Ravana, as recounted in the *Ramayana*; her Puja commemorates this auspicious occasion.

Crowds swarm around a *pandal* at the Durga Puja celebrations

Durga Puja has been upheld with great enthusiasm in Bengal since at least the 16th century, but it was in the twilight years of the Raj – when the goddess became a symbol of Mother India and the Independence struggle – that the event gained mass popularity.

Preparing to carry a deity to the water on Dashami, the final day of celebrations

The Deities

A caste of specialist effigy makers works for months ahead of the festival. In Kolkata, the artisans ply their trade in rows of backstreet workshops lining the Kumartuli district of the city. Sacred clay extracted from the Ganges is used for the modelling. Every stage of the process is accompanied by precise rituals to ensure the purity of the statues.

Pandal Hopping

When the deities are finished, they're dressed and installed on exuberantly decorated stages called *pandals*, made from bamboo, wood and paper. Thousands of neon lights and metres of shimmering polyester are used on the structures, which have grown increasingly sophisticated, often reaching several storeys in height. The money to build them is raised by neighbourhood committees or corporate sponsorship.

Festival-goers in their hundreds of thousands turn out to admire the temporary shrines, 'pandal hopping' their way between them. On the festival's final day, or 'Dashami', the deitics are dismounted from their *pandals* and carried amid more wild drumming and dancing to the Hoogly, where they're ritually immersed in the water – one of the region's great photo opportunities.

A deity in all her splendour

Konark

The **Sun Temple** (daily 9am–6pm; charge) of **Konark** ❻ was conceived as a gigantic horse-drawn chariot (*rath*) for the sun-god, Surya. The *sikhara* that once towered 60m (200ft) above it has gone, but the grandiose pyramid of the main Jagmohan (Hall of Audience) still soars above 12 pairs of huge stone wheels sculpted into its huge platform, pulled by galloping horses. As you clamber over the remains, look out for the profusely carved green chlorite statues of *parsvadevatas* (sun-deities) set in niches facing the four points of the compass.

The wheels of the chariot themselves, symbols of the Hindu cycle of rebirth, have beautifully carved spokes decorated with kings and gods. Beneath them are lively carved friezes of elephants playing with children. The masterpieces among the freestanding statuary, though, are the war-horses trampling the king's enemies and the splendid elephants crushing demons.

NORTHEAST HILL STATES

India's northeastern states, largely isolated from the rest of the country, form one of its most beautiful, spectacular and least visited areas. The landscape ranges from the steamy valley of the mighty Brahmaputra river with its World Heritage Site national parks, to the high mountains of Sikkim and the forested hills of the Adivasi states that border Burma (Myanmar) and Bangladesh.

Over the last few decades it has been difficult to gain access to the 'seven sisters' of Assam, Tripura, Meghalaya, Arunachal Pradesh, Nagaland, Manipur and Mizoram, but more recently the situation has

Sikkim is home to stunning landscapes

A tea picker in Assam

Sikkim are mostly made up of Nepalese and Lepchas – the country's original settlers known also as Rongpan, the people of the ravines – and Bhutias from Tibet.

The colourful Tibetan Buddhist monasteries, clinging to the hillsides around Gangtok, remain an attractive feature of the region. The most easily accessible of them is **Rumtek**, built in 1968 after China drove the maroon-robed Tibetan monks of the Karmapa sect into exile. Other, older monasteries from the 18th century, based 150km (92 miles) west of Gangtok at **Pemayangtse** and **Tashiding**, are also well worth visiting, though you'll need to arrange a permit to do so.

Assam

Assam means 'undulating', which best describes this state of rolling plains dissected by the Brahmaputra and its many tributaries. The river often floods during the July monsoon, and in successive years recently the state has experienced terrible deluges, due largely to excessive deforestation.

Long a melting pot of Buddhist and Hindu peoples, the region was dominated by the Ahom dynasty until the 17th century, when it was invaded by the Burmese. The Assamese ruler, King Gaurinath Singh, had to request the East India Company for help expelling the intruders, but the ensuing Anglo-Burmese War of 1824–6 resulted in loss of his kingdom to the British; the most visible legacy of colonial rule can be seen in the region's 300 manicured tea estates.

improved. Although there are still the rumblings of insurgencies in Assam, Nagaland and, especially, Tripura and Manipur (the latter are excluded from the following account on the strength of official travel advice), much of the region is free from trouble and more than repays the effort required to reach it, though visitor permits are required for many areas.

Sikkim

As with Darjeeling, a great incentive to visit **Sikkim** is the journey itself. The road to the capital, **Gangtok** ❼ (1,768m/5,800ft), leads through some of the most spectacular scenery in India: rivers gushing through sheer gorges and deep valleys outlined by terraced rice paddies. The people of

The gradual fragmentation of the territory since Independence has resulted in a growing imbalance between ethnic Assamese and immigrant Bengali Hindus displaced by Partition in 1947, and Muslim immigrants fleeing poverty in Bangladesh. Local fears of being swamped sparked a full-scale revolt in the 1980s, which snowballed into violent secessionist movements. Militants now have a powerful presence in the region and, as a result, Assam was shut to foreign tourists until the 1990s. The state is now open, but visitors should keep an eye on the political situation.

Former seat of the Kamrup kings, the state capital is **Guwahati** ❽, which, despite its dramatic location on the south bank of the Brahmaputra, is not the prettiest of cities. However, the **State Museum** (Tue–Sat 10am–4pm, closed alternate Sats; charge), is well worth a visit for its rare stone sculptures, while to the southwest of the centre the **Kamakhya Mandir** on Nilachal Hill ranks among India's main Tantric centres.

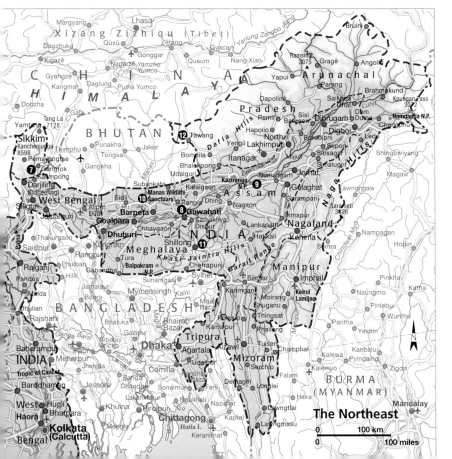

The Northeast

0   100 km

0   100 miles

See the one-horned Indian rhino at Kaziranga National Park

Assam's big tourist attractions, however, are the two famous wildlife reserves northeast of the capital. **Kaziranga National Park** ❾ (Nov–Apr; charge) 230km (145 miles) from Guwahati, is the principal sanctuary for the Indian one-horned rhinoceros. Nearing extinction at the turn of the 20th century, this powerful beast is now being rehabilitated. Despite stringent protective measures, a number are still poached every year, and their horns are smuggled to traditional medicine markets in East Asia.

The less well-known **Manas Wildlife Sanctuary** ❿ (Oct–Mar; charge) is set around a thickly forested bend in the river along the Bhutan border. Protecting several endangered species, including tigers, leopards and elephants as well as rhinos, the park is also an angler's paradise thanks to the presence of mahaseer, a local variety of carp.

Meghalaya

Meghalaya, 'the abode of clouds', was previously part of Assam but became a separate state in 1972. A hilly region, it is dominated by three Adivasi groups: the Garos in the west, the Khasis in the centre, and the Jaintias in the east. The capital, **Shillong** ⓫, lies 100km (60 miles) south of Guwahati, a three-hour drive through hills covered with pineapple and betel plantations. It has been called the 'Scotland of the East' because of its climate and its location at an altitude of 1,500m (4,900ft). English-style country houses spill across the surrounding hillsides; the bazaars specialise in Nepali silver and Khasi gold jewellery, spices and textiles.

Fog and rain are an all but permanent feature of the state's unforgiving climate. **Cherrapunji**, 56km (35 miles) to the south, is said to be the world's wettest location, with 11,500mm (450ins) of rainfall each year.

Kolkata and Northeast India

Arunachal Pradesh

North of Assam lies Arunachal Pradesh, isolated for years by its strategic location on the frontier between India and China. The area has 600,000 inhabitants divided into 82 different peoples. Most are Buddhists.

Itanagar, the state capital, has a couple of interesting sights, including **Itar Fort**, a brick-built citadel said to have been constructed by the Ahoms, and the **Jawaharlal Nehru Museum**, which has good coverage of the state's customs and peoples. At **Tawang** **⓬**, over the Sela Pass (4,215m/13,820ft), lies India's largest Buddhist monastery, founded in 1642. Set amid breathtaking scenery, it is very similar to those in Tibet, with colourfully painted windows and murals.

In the southeast of the state, the **Namdapha National Park** (Oct–Apr; charge) has retained much of its pristine state due to its inaccessibility. It covers a wide variety of environments, ranging from around 200m (650ft) to 4,500m (14,750ft) above sea level. The remote sanctuary is home to the very rare Hoolock gibbon, and four cat species – tigers, leopards, clouded leopards and snow leopards – as well as a population of elusive red pandas.

Nagaland

Remote Nagaland is inhabited by a variety of Tibeto-Burmese peoples, speaking more than 20 different dialects, the largest groups being the Aos, Angamis and Konyaks.

The British encountered the fearsome, head-hunting Naga tribes for the first time in 1832, and made attempts to beat them back into the hills, but suffered several bloody noses before a permanent truce was finally reached in 1889. During World War II the Japanese (aided by the maverick Indian National Army) launched an attack on the capital, **Kohima**, taking half of the city in 1943 – the furthest point west reached by the Japanese. The Nagas were of great help to the Allied forces, carrying supplies to the front and spying behind enemy lines.

Following Independence, some tribes demanded autonomy, but soon seccessionist elements were asking for full independence. In November 1975, at Shillong, an agreement was reached whereby the Nagas accepted

A village in Arunachal Pradesh

A traditional celebration of Republic Day in Nagaland

the Indian Constitution, but there are still occasional outbreaks of violence, and visitors may encounter army checkpoints. Naga villages are usually perched on hills and are surrounded by a stone wall. One, **Barra Basti**, is a suburb of Kohima. To the west of Kohima, at the railhead of **Dimapur**, are the remains of the former capital of the Cachar Hills razed by the Ahoms in 1536.

Mizoram

The former Lushai Hills District, Mizoram is bordered by Bangladesh on one side and Burma on the other. The region has deep river gorges, the sides of which are densely forested with bamboo. Related to the Shan, Mizos are a group of peoples (Lushais, Hmars, Pawis) that came relatively recently to India. They started raiding tea plantations in 1871. The British retaliated and established control over the area in 1872, but could not establish peace until a decade later. Thereafter, only missionaries were allowed through. As a result, 95 percent of the population is now Christian,

The capital, **Aizawl**, is built along a ridge. In town is Bara Bazaar, the central shopping area where local people in traditional costume sell their produce, including river crabs in small wicker baskets. The small **Mizoram State Museum** (Mon–Fri 9am–5pm, Sat 9am–1pm; charge) has an interesting collection of local artefacts. Other places of interest include the **Dampha Wildlife Sanctuary** on the Bangladesh border, and the busy town of **Champhai**, from where you can visit the traditional Mizo village of **Ruantlang**.

ACCOMMODATION

Among backpackers, Kolkata is legendary for the grim, bed-bug-infested state of its cheaper lodges, grouped mainly in the Sudder Street area. So if you're travelling on a budget, never book anywhere without checking it out first. Bear in mind that in summer air conditioning is all but essential. Pressure on beds is especially acute during Durga Puja.

Kolkata

The Astor
15 Shakespeare Sarani
Tel: 033-2282 9950
www.astorkolkata.com
A very popular Victorian house with comfortable and characterful rooms. With a garden and a couple of decent restaurants, this is a good option for the centre of town.
$$$$–$$$$$

Fairlawn Hotel
13a Sudder Street
Tel: 033-2252 1510
www.fairlawnhotel.com
A legendary hotel, dating from 1783, which seeks to maintain a Raj-era ambience (for example, the full English breakfast). Well run and not without a certain eccentric charm, it has comfortable rooms and a pleasant garden. 🍴 **$$$**

ITC Sonar
1 JBS Halden Avenue, opposite Science City
Tel: 033-2345 4545
www.itcwelcomgroup.in
A very comfortable hotel set in a striking block that ensures each room has a great view. Attractive rooms, good restaurants and some of the most extensive gardens in the city – with a wonderful pool. **$$$$$**

Lytton Hotel
14–14/1 Sudder Street
Tel: 033-2249 1872
www.lyttonhotelindia.com
A well-established decent hotel with comfortable, if slightly old-fashioned, rooms. As

The Oberoi Grand is a top-notch choice

well as being clean and safe, the staff are friendly and efficient, and it is good value for its central location. **$$$–$$$$**

The Oberoi Grand
15 Jawaharlal Nehru Road
Tel: 033-2249 2323
www.oberoihotels.com
A Kolkata landmark. A very elegant hotel with extremely luxurious rooms and palm-edged pool. **$$$$$**

The Park Hotel
17 Park Street
Tel: 033-2249 9000
www.theparkhotels.com
A central five-star, flagship of the swish design hotel group, with very chic rooms and public areas. **$$$$$**

Tollygunge Club
120 Deshapran Sasmal Road
Tel: 033-2473 4539
www.tollygungeclub.org

The accommodation at Kolkata's most famous club, dating back to 1895, is a bizarre cross of Butlins and Fawlty Towers. It does, however, have beautiful grounds and excellent sports facilities. **$$$$**

YWCA
1 Middleton Row
Tel: 033-2229 7033
www.ywcaindia.org
A quiet and pleasant option; very clean rooms and a dormitory; admits both men and women. Tariffs include all meals. **$$**

West Bengal
Camelia Hotel
Prantik, Shantiniketan
Tel: 03463-262 042
Congenial, pleasantly furnished mid-range place set amid greenery within walking distance of the university. **$$**

Dekeling Hotel
51 Gandhi Road, Darjeeling
Tel: 0354-225 4159
www.dekeling.com
A friendly and attractive Tibetan-run hotel with pleasant rooms (the ones in the attic are best), some with views; all have an attached bath and hot water. **$$**

Dekeling Resort at Hawk's Nest
2 A.J.C. Bose Road, Darjeeling
Tel: 0354-225 3092
www.dekeling.com
Late 19th-century building in a fabulous position. Lovely wood-panelled rooms – open fires are set in the rooms during the evening – with great views. Friendly staff and good food. **$$$**

The Planters' Club
7 Nehru Road, Darjeeling
Tel: 0354-225 4348
Set in an atmospheric, Raj-laden building, with 20 suites. There is a billiards room, naturally, and a great bar as well as superb views over the mountains. **$$–$$$**

Sunderban Tiger Camp
The Sunderbans

Tel: 033-3293 5749
www.sunderbantigercamp.com
Upscale wildlife resort offering all-in rates that cover comfortable accommodation (in tents, huts or a/c cottages), quality food and tiger-spotting trips in boats. **$$$$**

Tower View
Dr Zakir Hussain Road, Darjeeling
Tel: 0354-225 4452
Pick of the budget bunch: cosy place run by a welcoming Tibetan family, with a homely dining room and great views. **$**

Windamere Hotel
Observatory Hill, Darjeeling
Tel: 0354-225 4041
www.windamerehotel.com
A legendary heritage hotel with no phones or TVs in the rooms, but oodles of old-fashioned grandeur, and stupendous panoramic views of the world's 20 highest peaks. 🍴 **$$$$$**

Orissa
The Ginger
Jayadev Vihar, Nayapalli, Bhubaneshwar
Tel: 0674-230 933
www.gingerhotels.com
Located in a quiet suburb, this modern, business-oriented place is part of a national chain and is the best value of any midscale hotel here, with immaculate rooms. **$$$**

Railway Hotel
Puri
Tel: 06752-222 063
www.irctc.co.in
An excellent option. A well-kept heritage hotel, run by Indian Railways, in a pleasant old building. Clean rooms (some a/c) and a good restaurant. **$$$**

Z Hotel
C.T. Road, Puri
Tel: 06752-222 554
www.zhotelindia.com
The rooms in this former royal palace house, now an atmospheric budget hotel set in a leafy garden, are large and clean; some have sea views. **$**

Northeast Hill States

Aranya Tourist Lodge
Book through: Tourist Information Officer,
Kaziranga National Park, Golaghat, Assam
Tel: 03776-266 2423
www.assamtourism.org
Clean and simple rooms, all with en suite.
Helpful staff and a good restaurant. **$–$$**

Dynasty
S.S. Road, Lakhtokia, Guwahati, Assam
Tel: 0361-2251 0496
www.hoteldynastyindia.com
The town's top hotel, situated in the main
bazaar and boasting four-star facilities. **$$$**

Hidden Forest
Middle Sichey, Gangtok, Sikkim
Tel: 03592-205 197
www.hiddenforestretreat.org
Wonderful eco-friendly Tibetan guesthouse
on the edge of town, set in orchards and
flower gardens, with relaxing wood-floored
rooms.  **$$**

Hotel Sonam Delek
Tibet Road, Gangtok, Sikkim
Tel: 03592-202 566
www.hotelsonamdelek.com

At the attractive Wild Grass Resort

Well located, dependable and great value,
with a pleasant garden and decent restau-
rant serving good local food. **$$**

Wild Grass Resort
Kaziranga National Park, Golaghat, Assam
Tel: 03776-266 2085
www.oldassam.com
Simple but attractive huts and comfortable
tents set in beautiful surroundings. Excellent
food and activities centred on local music
and dance. **$$**

RESTAURANTS

Eastern India has a wide range of
food. In the mountains some of the
most popular dishes are Tibetan,
such as noodle soups *(thukpa)* or
the ubiquitous *momos* (steamed
dumplings). While many of the best
places to eat are, as ever, in the more
expensive hotels, local stalls serving simple rice- and *dal*-based meals or Tibetan
food can produce delicious and safe food at a very reasonable price. Be warned
that outside Kolkata, many places shut by 8.30pm.

Restaurant Price Categories

Prices are for a standard meal for one,
excluding alcoholic drinks

$ = up to Rs200
$$ = Rs200–500
$$$ = Rs500–1000
$$$$ = over Rs1000

Kolkata

Aheli's
Peerless Inn, 12 Jawaharlal Nehru Road,
Chowringhee
Tel: 033-2228 0301

Top-notch, traditional Bengali cuisine –
including a sumptuous *maha* ('great') *thali*
– served in one of Kolkata's oldest and
most authentic restaurants by waiters in
traditional dress. **$$$**

Baitakkhana

The Indian Coffee House, 15 Bankim Chatterjee Street

This famous coffee shop near the university has long been a meeting place for Bengali intellectuals. Snacks available, open all day. **$**

Bojohari Manna (Ekdalia)

9/18 Ekdali Rd
Tel: 033-2440 1933
http://bhojohorimanna.com

Home branch of an expanding chain that made its name serving inexpensive, fresh, seasonal Bengali cooking, with a strong accent on local seafood. Specials are posted daily on a white board. **$–$$**

Fire & Ice

Middleton St
Tel: 033-2288 4057
www.fireandicepizzeria.com

Trendy offshoot of the acclaimed Neapolitan restaurant of the same name in Kathmandu, where waiters in black bandanas serve proper pizza, pasta, risottos, oven-baked lasagne and imported Italian ice cream for dessert. **$$**

Mainland China

Uniworth House, 3a Gurusaday Road
Tel: 033-2283 7964

The finest Chinese cuisine in the city, featuring the tastiest lobster in black bean sauce you'll probably ever eat. **$$$**

Oh! Calcutta

Lala Lajpat Rai Sarani
Tel: 033-2283 7161

Excellent Bengali-fusion food, one of the first restaurants to raise the profile of the cuisine on a country-wide basis. All extremely tasty – plus they serve chilled beers. **$$$–$$$$**

Zen

The Park, 17 Park Street
Tel: 033-2249 9000

The über-trendy Zen at The Park is a Conran-designed restaurant serving up pan-East Asian food in a very cool interior. **$$$$**

West Bengal

Big Bite

Laden La Road, Darjeeling

The best of Darjeeling's numerous south Indian places. You can tuck into piping hot *idly-wada* and crunchy *masala dosas*, or order a full-on *thali* for less than Rs100. **$**

Deveka's

52 Gandhi Road, Darjeeling

Just below the Dekeling, this Tibetan-run place is popular with both locals and backpackers for its gorgeous Himalayan decor and simple, filling mountain cooking, as well as a mean banana custard for desert. No smoking. **$**

Glenary's

Nehru Road, Darjeeling
Tel: 0354-225 7554

A well-established restaurant, bar and café with a good bakery and sweet shop. A good place for breakfast or a snack, as well as more filling mains such as sizzlers, Chinese dishes and tandoori items. They also offer Wi-fi internet access. **$$–$$$**

Orissa

Dalma

157 Madhusudan Nagar, Sachivalaya Marg, Bhubaneshwar
http://dalmahotels.com

Taking its name from one of the region's best-loved dishes (a potato and aubergine curry), this small restaurant is among the few serving authentic Orissan food, drawing crowds from across the city for its good-value *thali*. **$$**

Wildgrass

VIP Road, Puri
Tel: 9437-023 656

A well-known restaurant, popular mainly with travellers. Their Indian, Continental and Orissan specialities are first rate, but the jungly garden setting, with its terracotta lanterns, temple sculpture and ramshackle tree house, is the big draw here. **$**

Follow the signs to a choice of eateries

Northeast Hill States
Delicacy
G.S. Road, 2km (1¼ miles) south of town,
near Gangeshguri Flyover, Guwahati, Assam
Definitive Northeastern cooking: a dozen
different kinds of rice, smoked duck and
pigeon, and freshwater fish in coconut and
mustard gravy, served in traditional bell-
metal bowls. **$$–$$$**

Paradise
G.N.B. Road, Chandmari, Guwahati, Assam
The best place in the town centre to
sample Assam's refreshingly un-spicy
style of cooking: order one of their popular
lunchtime *thalis*. **$**

Tangerine
Ground Floor, Chumbi Residency,
Tibet Road, Gangtok,
Sikkim
Smart, fashionable bar-restaurant whose
stylish decor and cocktail menu contrasts
sharply with the traditional Sikkimese cuisine: try their delicious *churpi* (yak cheese
with green nettles). **$**

NIGHTLIFE

The Bengali capital's nightlife is by far the most sophisticated in the region,
though it's still not a city you'd come to in order to party. Bars tend to be dingy and
male dominated. In Darjeeling, a popular travellers' stop, tea is consumed in far
greater quantities than alcohol, but there are a few good meeting places dotted
around the hill station.

Kolkata
Tantra
Park Hotel
www.theparkhotels.com
'Glide, circulate and discover' is the
mantra of the city's most glamorous
club, spread over split levels with a single
dance floor. Visiting DJs and theme nights
hosted on weekends, but there's a stiff
entrance charge.

West Bengal
Joey's Pub
SM Das Road, Darjeeling
The liveliest pub in town, boasting a
wide-screen TV broadcasting sports, and
chilled draught Kingfisher – although as
with all watering holes hereabouts it's
not recommended for solo women travellers, who may experience unwanted
attention.

SPORTS AND TOURS

Kolkata is home to the spiritual home of Indian cricket, the Eden Gardens, in this most British-influenced of regions. Tours are offered by all regional tourist offices.

Cricket

Eden Gardens
Established in 1864, the Bengali capital's stadium is legendary as the home of the state's trophy-winning team, and the IPL Twenty20 league's Kolkata Knight Riders. Impromptu matches are also held during evenings and at weekends on Kolkata's iconic Maidan.

Golf

The Royal Calcutta Golf Club
8 Golf Club Road, Tollygunge
Tel: 033-2473 1352
www.rcgc.in
The second oldest club in the world after St Andrew's, founded in 1829.

Swimming

The Kolkata Swimming Club
1 Strand Road, Kolkata
Tel: 033-2248 2894
Entitling you to use the club pool, temporary membership is open to non-members.

Tours

Orissa Tourism
Paryatan Bhawan, Lewis Road,
Bhubaneshwar
Tel: 0674-243 2177
The state tourism corporation has introduced a handy hop-on-hop-off bus connecting Bhubaneshwar's highlights (8am–8.30pm).

Sikkim Tourist Information Centre
MG Marg, Gangtok
Tel: 03592-221 634
www.sikkimtourism.travel
Offers heli-tours and can direct you to accredited trekking agencies.

West Bengal Tourism
67A Kali Temple Road, Kalighat
Tel: 033-2243 7260
www.westbengaltourism.gov.in
Offers five set package tours of Kolkata and surrounding region.

Listings

FESTIVALS AND EVENTS

Kolkata and the surrounding area is known for its exuberant festivals, especially the famed Durga Puja. See any tourist office for a full list of events in the region.

January–March

Gangasagar Mela
Sagar Island; January
Vast crowds gather where the Ganges flows into the sea for a sin-cleansing dip.

Losar
Sikkim; March
Tibetan New Year is marked with masked *cham* dances in the Buddhist monasteries.

June–July

Rath Yatra
Puri

The hauling of the Jagannath temple's three deities down Puri's main street on wooden chariots is an unforgettable spectacle.

October–December

Durga Puja
Throughout the region; October
Statues of the 10-armed goddess are the subject of intense devotion and merrymaking.

Kolkata Film Festival
November
www.kff.in
A week of films from Bengal and the world.

Karnataka and Andhra Pradesh

The states of Karnataka and Andhra Pradesh lie on the threshold of India's deep south, straddling the subcontinent from the lush Konkan and Coromandel coasts via the largely inhospitable Deccan plateau. Draws include the regions' beautiful boulder scenery and evocative ruined cities, impressive ancient temples, palaces and ruined forts.

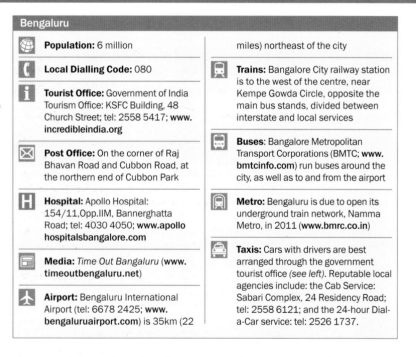

Bengaluru

Population: 6 million

Local Dialling Code: 080

Tourist Office: Government of India Tourism Office: KSFC Building, 48 Church Street; tel: 2558 5417; **www.incredibleindia.org**

Post Office: On the corner of Raj Bhavan Road and Cubbon Road, at the northern end of Cubbon Park

Hospital: Apollo Hospital: 154/11,Opp.IIM, Bannerghatta Road; tel: 4030 4050; **www.apollohospitalsbangalore.com**

Media: *Time Out Bangaluru* (**www.timeoutbengaluru.net**)

Airport: Bengaluru International Airport (tel: 6678 2425; **www.bengaluruairport.com**) is 35km (22 miles) northeast of the city

Trains: Bangalore City railway station is to the west of the centre, near Kempe Gowda Circle, opposite the main bus stands, divided between interstate and local services

Buses: Bangalore Metropolitan Transport Corporations (BMTC; **www.bmtcinfo.com**) run buses around the city, as well as to and from the airport

Metro: Bengaluru is due to open its underground train network, Namma Metro, in 2011 (**www.bmrc.co.in**)

Taxis: Cars with drivers are best arranged through the government tourist office *(see left)*. Reputable local agencies include: the Cab Service: Sabari Complex, 24 Residency Road; tel: 2558 6121; and the 24-hour Dial-a-Car service: tel: 2526 1737.

The states of Karnataka and Andhra Pradesh occupy the buffer zone between north and south India – the region historically referred to as 'the Deccan'. A high tableland whose dark, volcanic soils and temperate, dry climate provide perfect growing conditions for cotton, the plateau and its rich agriculture for centuries supported India's richest and most powerful dynasties, including the Chalukyas, the Rashtrakutas and Hoysalas.

The greatest of all the Deccani kingdoms, however, was one which rose to prominence in the 15th and 16th centuries. From their resplendent capital at Hampi, on the Tungabhardra River, the Vijayanagar kings ruled an empire stretching from coast to coast, and south as far as the tip of India. But in 1565, a confederacy of Muslim princedoms laid waste to the city, ushering in a period of Islamic rule that would endure across the Deccan until the British victory over Tipu Sultan at the Battle of Srirangapatnam in 1799.

An extraordinary wealth of Indo-Islamic monuments lies scattered over modern Karnataka and Andhra Pradesh, which today number among the most prosperous states in India. A major factor in the boom has been the success of the IT sector, which

The Maharaja's Palace at Mysore *(see p.205)*

dominates the economies of Bengaluru (Bangalore) and Hyderabad.

KARNATAKA

Created in 1956 from the former state of Mysore, Karnataka is one of India's most varied states, with a series of distinct regional landscapes. A narrow fertile coastal strip to the west – the so-called Konkan coast – is flanked by the hills of the Western Ghats, their well-watered slopes sustaining dense tropical forests famed for their teak, rosewood and bamboo. With much of the moisture from the rain-bearing monsoon expended on the ghats, the Deccan plateau to the east is a much drier region. Karnataka has a population of around 55 million, the majority of whom speak Kanad, the state's offical language.

Bengaluru (Bangalore)

Modern and efficient, the capital of Karnataka, **Bengaluru** ❶ (which changed its official name from Bangalore in November 2006) is a convenient gateway to the western half of the peninsula. Situated 930m (3,000ft) above sea level, it boasts a temperate,

Relaxing in Bengaluru's Lalbagh gardens *(see p.205)*

Karnataka and Andhra Pradesh

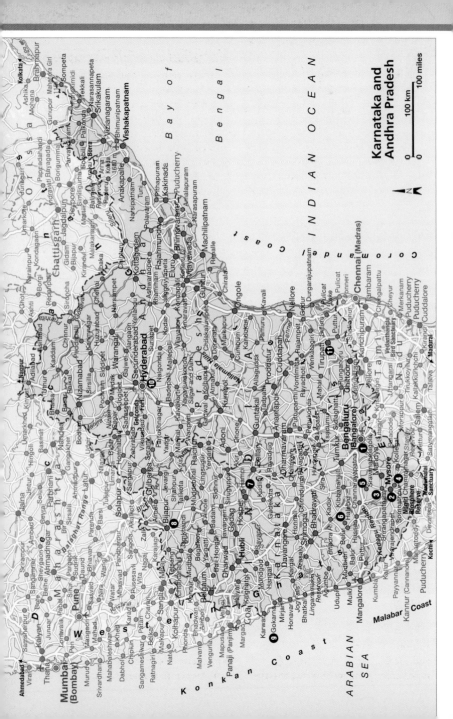

Karnataka and Andhra Pradesh

In Srirangapatnam's palace *(see p.206)*

The Art of Living

Bengaluru is the headquarters of the **Art of Living Foundation**, the spiritual and humanitarian organisation founded by New Age guru and Hindu evangelist Sri Sri Ravi Shankar (not to be confused with the classical sitar player). The focal point of the state-of-the-art Ved Vignan Mahahvidyapeeth, or VVM campus, is a massive meditation hall, built entirely of marble in the shape of a lotus, with 1,008 stone petals encrusting its exterior. Inside, adoring audiences, drawn mostly from the city's English-speaking elite, gather on the marble floor to listen to the teachings of their long-haired, bearded guruji, who sits on a stage in flowing silk robes – British journalist Edward Luce once remarked that the scene 'looked as if Jesus were shooting a shampoo advertisement'.

mild climate that's noticeably cooler than that of the coast – which is why the British made it summer capital of the Madras Presidency. The spectacular growth of India's boom town in electronics, software, telecommunications, back-office and call-centre support has not only greatly increased the population (to well over 6 million) but has also transformed the healthy climate; it is now several degrees hotter here now than it was 30 years ago. However, there are still pleasant walks to be had in **Cubbon Park** and in the terraced greenery of the botanical gardens of **Lalbagh** (sunrise–sunset; charge).

Mysore

Famous for its sandalwood carving and incense factories, **Mysore ➋** ranks among the most pleasant cities in India. Chief among the visitor attractions here is the **Maharaja's Palace** (www.mysorepalace.in; daily 10am–5pm; charge 🅜), constructed in 1897 after its predecessor was burnt down. The architecture and interior design epitomise the excesses of Mughal nostalgia and Victorian pomp: doors of solid silver open onto the multicoloured marble, mahogany and ivory. The highlight is an art gallery featuring portraits of the maharajas in very British, landed-gentry poses, and a glass case containing a 'rolled gold replica of the British crown' set next to a tea pot. The palace is illuminated each night, but the most striking decoration is reserved for the annual Diwali celebration, when tens of thousands of electric bulbs festoon its outer surfaces.

On the summit of the **Chamundi Hill**, the **Sri Chamundeswari Temple** offers a fine view of Mysore. On your way back down, take a look at the massive black Nandi bull, Shiva's sacred vehicle (*vahana*), with chains and bells that are a mixture of both real and sculpted items hung around its neck.

Srirangapatnam

Situated southeast of Mysore, **Srirangapatnam ❸** was the former capital of Hyder Ali and his son and successor, Tipu Sultan – perennial thorns in the side of British trade and territorial ambitions in southern India. By assuring the East India Company control of the peninsula, the bloody battles that took place here in the 1790s shaped the future of the entire subcontinent.

Srirangapatnam's fort, stormed by Lord Cornwallis and Colonel Arthur Wellesley (the future Duke of Wellington of Waterloo fame), no longer stands, but the sultan's summer palace, **Darya Daulat Bagh** (daily 9am–5pm; charge), has been preserved and made into a museum honouring the brave resistance of Tipu and his father.

Somnathpur

Dating from 1268, the **Kesava Temple** at **Somnathpur ❹** (daily 9am–5.30pm; charge) is considered one of the greatest examples of the so-called Hoysala style, renowned above all for its breathtakingly intricate decoration. The structure is small – no more than 10m (33ft) high – and its *vimanas* (shrines) are set on a low, modest platform, but the temple achieves a distinct grandeur – a tiny, shining jewel in the crown of medieval Indian architecture.

The Kesava Temple at Somnathpur

Every square centimetre of the shrine's surface is elaborately sculpted. The carvings were intended to be read like a book by those who had no access to the Hindu scriptures. They tell the stories of the mischievous tricks of Krishna, as a child stealing butter from his mother and later as a young man stealing saris from girls bathing in the river – and of the adventures of the epic *Mahabharata*.

Sravanabelgola

Three hours by road west of Bengaluru, **Vindhyagiri Hill** rises 140m (463ft) above the flat Deccan landscape, with one of the most dramatic monuments in all India rising from its domed summit. Erected in AD983, the colossal statue of **Gommatesvara** crowns a sanctuary erected in the village of **Sravanabelagola** ❺ 1,400 years earlier by the Digambara sect of Jains. Jains regard nakedness as a necessary sacrifice to achieve true enlightenment, and in the 4th century BC, the Mauryan Emperor Chandragupta, a convert to Jainism, fasted to death on the hilltop.

Approaching the statue barefoot, via the 644 rock-cut steps leading up Vindhyagiri Hill, is an awe-inspiring experience. The colossus looms 17.5m (57ft) tall, carved from a granite monolith polished by centuries of libations with milk. Gommatesvara, the son of the prophet Adinath, is entirely naked except for a single vine-creeper winding itself around his legs and arms. The creeper symbolises the impassiveness he is said to have observed in this upright position of *pratimayoga*, which he adopted for one whole year in response to his brother's lust for worldly power. An ant hill and serpents at his feet symbolise the mental agony that his smile shows he had conquered.

Belur and Halebid

The most comfortable way to see these important Hoysala temples is to visit them on either side of an overnight stay at **Hassan**, 120km (75 miles) northwest of Mysore.

The **Chenna Kesava Temple** in **Belur** was built in 1117, 150 years before the Kesava Temple at Somnathpur. Its silhouette makes for an unfinished look, but it is not certain that towers or domes were ever planned. Here too, the sculpture rather than the overall shape gives the shrine its impact. The bracket figures, in particular, are regarded as masterpieces, showing a huntress, girls dancing or singing, and a woman about to spray her lover with rose-water.

Dedicated to Shiva and his wife Parvati, the Hoysalesvara Temple in **Halebid** ❻, 16km (10 miles) from Belur, is the biggest of the Hoysala shrines. It suffered some destruction at the hands of Muslim iconoclasts, so it's worth visiting the adjacent **Archaeological Museum** (Halebid

Karnatakan Entertainment

One of the most memorable experiences that Karnataka has to offer is an evening spent outdoors, sitting on a straw mat watching a *bayalata* (field play). These traditional dramas, which depict the exploits of heroes and heroines from India's epics, may run from early evening until sunrise. The performances are an amalgam of music, dance and drama, and there is the easy camaraderie of people who are willing to explain it to you.

When the fields are flush with water, there is another sight popular in

Karnataka and not to be missed: the annual *kambala* (buffalo race). Held in a paddy field, the race is contested by pairs of specially trained racing buffaloes, egged on by men riding behind them. To start the race the driver jumps up, his hand cocked, his whip held high, and the huge animals lunge forward, bellowing, their hooves churning the muddy waters and sending their wet spray into the hot air, their eyes wide, wild and white. The races are a good excuse for some serious gambling, and a highly charged atmosphere is guaranteed.

🚶 HAMPI

Set over 26 sq km (10 sq miles) of boulder hills and banana groves, Hampi's atmospheric ruins are concentrated into two areas. This walking tour covers the northern group's highlights, beginning at the western end of Hampi Bazaar.

Start at the spectacular **Virupaksa temple** (daily 8am–12.30pm and 3–9pm; charge), the greatest surviving shrine of the Vijayanagars' former city. Once you've admired its colonnaded courtyards and raised central shrine, whose ceilings retain their original medieval paintings, head beneath the main entrance tower *(gopura)* and once outside the main gateway turn sharply right. Follow the paved walkway along the foot of the temple wall, then bear right towards the top of **Hemakuta Hill**, where a scattering of ruined shrines affords impressive views over the Virupaksa complex and its environs – an especially beautiful spot at sunset.

To return to the main bazaar, you can either drop down the far, east flank of the hill, turning left when you reach the tarmac road, or else retrace your steps northwards back along the side of the Virupaksa temple. Either way, turn right when you reach the village's broad main street and follow it to its far end, from where a grand flight of steps leads to a saddle between two boulder hills. Keep to the narrow, rocky, stepped path as it drops down the far side to the wonderful **Achyutharaya temple** (open dawn–dusk; free), whose ruined towers are encrusted with erotic sculpture.

Pilgrims bathing in Tungabhadra River, Hampi

Looking out over the Virupaksa complex at Hampi as the sun goes down

If you're feeling energetic, climb the steep granite steps winding through the rocks around the foot of **Matanga Hill**, just to the south of Achyutharaya, to reach the flat-roofed temple crowning the summit. Looking east across a huge expanse of banana plantations, giant boulders and hills, this is a superb place to be at sunrise.

Another wide, dead-straight bazaar – now deserted and in ruins – slices due north from the Achyutharaya temple to rejoin a well-worn track running along the south bank of the Tungabhadra River. Turn right when you reach it and follow it for 15 or 20 minutes until you arrive at the famous **King's Balance**, a ceremonial archway beneath which the Vijayanagar kings were formerly weighed in gold (which would be distributed among the city's needy afterwards).

Nearby, high walls enclose the **Vittala temple** (daily 6am–6pm; charge). Administered by the Archaeological

Survey of India, the shrine is no longer a place of active worship, but its exquisitely carved pillars, adorned with the forms of rampant horses and mythical beasts, have earned it Unesco World Heritage Monument status.

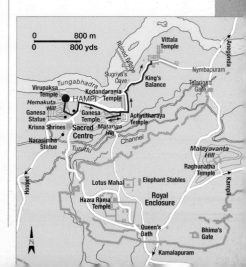

archaeological museum Sat–Thur 10am–5pm, temple sunrise–sunset), too, where some of the best of its statues are now kept. Look at the surprisingly fine carving of the bracket figures in the dancing hall, achieved by the craftsmen working with soft soapstone which subsequently hardened to the texture of granite.

Hampi

It was among the huge boulder-strewn landscape of the Deccan plateau that a pair of brothers, Harihara and Bukka, escaped the clutches of the tyrannical Delhi Tuqhluq sultans sometime in the first half of the 14th century and carved out for themselves an independent kingdom, **Hampi** ❼ . Within 150 years, the rule of the dynasty they founded extended from coast to coast and to the tip of India. Vast riches poured in from the trade in horses and spices across the Arabian Sea, which successive rulers lavished on carved temples, palaces

The Kali shrine at Hampi

and a glorious city spread around the bend in the sacred Tungabhadra River.

The empire's unifying force was its rulers' fear of attack from the north by the Deccani sultans. With its vast standing army, Hindu **Vijayanagar** proved a major obstacle to the Muslim kingdom's expansion plans, so it was inevitable that sooner or later the two would come into conflict. The decisive battle took place in 1565 at Talikota, in the no-man's-land buffering the warring kingdoms which ended with the destruction of the Vijayanagaran forces.

The ensuing sack of Vijayanagar lasted six months. By the end of it, the city lay entirely in ruins, its inhabitants slaughtered, its temples, palaces and gardens burnt to the ground. Hindu pilgrims still come here to bathe in the river and worship at the **Virupaksa** shrine (daily dawn–9pm; free), whose gateway gopuras somehow survived the Muslim onslaught and still tower over the surrounding banana groves. For foreign visitors, the chief attractions of Hampi, aside from the wonderful archaeological remains, are the magical riverine landscape and surreal beauty of the boulder hills, which provide an exotic backdrop for bicycle rides and sunset walks around the ruins.

A walking tour of Hampi's monuments features on p.208.

Bijapur

The powerful Bahmani dynasty formed the backbone of the Muslim confederacy that ultimately defeated Vijayanagar. This victory provided the funds to endow their capital at **Bijapur** ❽, a day's journey northeast

The Golgumbaz mausoleum at Bijapur

of Hampi, with a glittering crop of mosques, palaces and fortifications – collectively the finest display of Islamic architecture south of Agra.

Rising from the eastern fringes of town, Bijapur's pièce de résistance is the gigantic **Golgumbaz** mausoleum (daily 6am–5.45pm; charge). The tomb dates from the twilight years of Bahmani rule and perfectly captures the spirit of a regime in decline: conceived on a ruinously grand scale, it exudes more self-importance than grace. All the same, it is an undeniably impressive spectacle. Capping the building, the vast free-standing dome is said to be the largest in the world after St Peter's in Rome.

At the opposite end of town – and architectural spectrum – is the **Ibrahim Rauza** (daily dawn–dusk; free),

a gem of a walled tomb built on an altogether more human scale. Its appeal lies in its ornate decor, notably the famous pierced stone *jali* windows cut in the form of Koranic inscriptions, and slender minarets and cupolas, which provide cover for flocks of screeching parakeets.

The Konkan Coast: Gokarna

The narrow coastal strip dividing the Western Ghats from the Arabian Sea, known as the Konkan or Dakshini Kannada, is in many ways a region apart from the rest of Karnataka, boasting its own language (Konkani), seafood-rich cuisine and a long history of contact with foreign traders and invaders.

The most appealing base in the region is **Gokarna** ❾ 🏨, an ancient Hindu temple town near Goa. Top of most pilgrims' hit list, after they've taken a purificatory dip in the step-lined Kooti Theerta tank on the east side of town, is the **Mahabaleshwar Temple** on the western side of Gokarna's main street. Within its smoke-blackened core resides one of India's most revered Shivalinga, said to have been dropped here by the arch-demon Ravana during his epic struggle with Rama.

Gokarna is also a place of refuge for long-staying hippie travellers from Western countries, thanks to the presence over the headland from town of a string of delightful sandy coves, reachable on foot or by fishing boat. In recent years, a handful of luxury hotels has started to mushroom on the bare laterite hillsides overlooking **Om Beach**, the most picturesque of the

Karnataka and Andhra Pradesh

Half Moon beach at Gokana, one of several lovely sandy coves in the area

string (its name derives from the shape of its twin bays, thought to replicate the auspicious Hindu Om symbol).

ANDHRA PRADESH

Geologically one of the oldest parts of South Asia, Andhra Pradesh has stunning landscapes of hilly, rock-strewn plateaux, fertile river valleys, and a long coastline to its east. Yet it can be difficult to explore. The harsh climate – hot and dry for most of the year, interrupted by the flooding of rivers during the monsoon months – can make life very difficult. Cyclones frequently hit coastal areas during May, October and November, paralysing transportation; the pre-monsoon period from April to June is baking hot, with temperatures regularly topping 45°C (113°F).

Hyderabad
Hyderabad ⑩, capital of Andhra Pradesh, is India's fifth-largest city. It dates from 1591, when Mohammed Quli of the Qutb Shahis moved his capital here from nearby Golconda. In 1687 the Mughal Emperor Aurangzeb overthrew the dynasty and appointed a viceroy, whose descendants ruled as the Nizams of Hyderabad until 1949.

The city's most famous landmark is the **Charminar** (daily 9am–5.30pm; charge), dating from 1591, a magnificent square archway supported by a quartet of 56m (184ft) towers. Nearby stands one of the largest mosques in India, the black granite **Mecca Masjid** (9am–5pm; free), said to have bricks made of red clay from Mecca over the central archway. Surrounding the Charminar are bazaars with narrow cobbled lanes lined with rows of shops selling spices, tobacco, grain, perfume oils and Hyderabadi specialities.

The **Salar Jung Museum** (www.salarjungmuseum.in; Sat–Thur 10am–5pm; charge), on the southern bank of the Musi River, is the largest single-person collection of art and artefacts in the world. Salar Jung was a minister at the court of the Nizams, and his collection of over 43,000 objects and 50,000 rare books and manuscripts includes a good selection of European artworks and some wonderful decorated manuscripts from all over the Islamic world. The large Mughal jade collection in the museum is equally outstanding.

Golconda Fort

A visit to the former capital of the Qutb Shahi dynasty, **Golconda Fort**, 11km (7 miles) west of Hyderabad, makes an easy day trip via local bus, auto-rickshaw or taxi. It was used by the last of the Qutb kings in the 17th century as a bastion against Mughal attack. Situated on a steep hill, the fort was encircled by immense walls sporting 87 semicircular bastions and eight gates with elephant-proof spikes. The remains of its once splendid palaces and gardens give an idea of its former grandeur.

A little over 1km (½ mile) northwest of the fort stand the remains of the Qutb Shahis' **tombs** (daily 9am–5pm; charge), a splendid assortment of onion-domed, cusparched mausoleums set amid neatly cropped lawns.

Tirupati

In the far south of the state, one of the busiest pilgrimage sites in the world, **Tirupati ⓫**, is famous as the site of the **Lord Venkatesvara Temple**, which stands on nearby Tirumala Hill. The efficient temple administration handles around 60,000–70,000 pilgrims daily, and operates an 18-hour-a-day *darshan* (ritual viewing of the deity) regulated by a token system. Many pilgrims shave their heads as a pledge, or to thank the deity. The hair is used to make wigs, which are sold locally and exported. The steep road up the hill has 57 hairpin bends and affords lovely views.

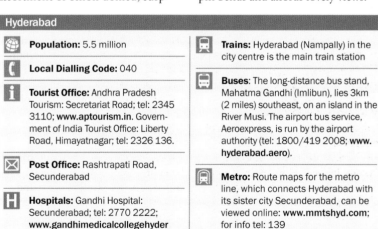

Hyderabad

Population: 5.5 million

Local Dialling Code: 040

Tourist Office: Andhra Pradesh Tourism: Secretariat Road; tel: 2345 3110; www.aptourism.in. Government of India Tourist Office: Liberty Road, Himayatnagar; tel: 2326 136.

Post Office: Rashtrapati Road, Secunderabad

Hospitals: Gandhi Hospital: Secunderabad; tel: 2770 2222; www.gandhimedicalcollegehyder abad.org; CDR Hospital: Nizam Shahi Road, Gawlhigudea; tel: 2322 1221

Media: *Channel 6*, at most bookstalls

Airport: Rajiv Gandhi International Airport (tel: 6654 6370) is 20km (12 miles) south of central Hyderabad

Trains: Hyderabad (Nampally) in the city centre is the main train station

Buses: The long-distance bus stand, Mahatma Gandhi (Imlibun), lies 3km (2 miles) southeast, on an island in the River Musi. The airport bus service, Aeroexpress, is run by the airport authority (tel: 1800/419 2008; www.hyderabad.aero).

Metro: Route maps for the metro line, which connects Hyderabad with its sister city Secunderabad, can be viewed online: www.mmtshyd.com; for info tel: 139

Taxis: hire a car and driver at the APTDC on Secretariat Road, next door to the Andhra Pradesh Tourism Office (tel: 2345 3036; www.tourism inap.com). Alternatively, try the Meru Cab Company: tel: 4422 4422; or Easy Cabs: tel: 4343 4343.

ACCOMMODATION

Accommodation of the highest standards is to be found in the region's cities, but grows increasingly basic the further towards the states' margins you travel. Karnataka and Andhra Pradesh possess the range of choice you'd expect of some of the country's most developed states, though resultantly, tariffs at the top end can be steep.

Karnataka

Casa Piccola
2 Clapham Road, Richmond Town, Bengaluru
Tel: 080-2229 0337
www.casapiccola.com
A British-era bungalow, restored in period style and fitted with modern comforts, including a/c and Wi-fi connections. Meals are served under a gazebo in the garden. More of a homestay than a five-star, though at comparable rates. **$$$$$**

Green Hotel
Chittaranjan Palace, 2270 Vinoba Road, Jayalakshmipuram, Mysore
Tel: 0821-425 5000
www.greenhotelindia.com
A charming palace conversion in its own gardens a little way out of town. A project in sustainable tourism through energy-saving and equal-opportunity employment, with profits funding local charities and environmental groups. Good-value, attractive rooms and superb food. 🍽 **$$$–$$$$$**

The delightful Villa Pottipati

Hampi Boulders
Narayanpet, Bandi Harlur, Hampi
Tel: 08539-265 939
On a bend in the Tungabhadra River, this small hotel is the best high-end choice in the area. You get there via coracle and 6km (4 mile) walk, or else by a 30-min (20km/12 mile) car ride from Hampi bazaar. Accommodation is in cottages around the boulders, and there's a lovely pool. 🍽 **$$$$–$$$$$**

Hotel Malligi
6/143 Jambunath Road, Hospet
Tel: 08394-228 101
www.malligihotels.com
The best-value option in the area, offering a choice of 160 differently priced rooms (from basic economy to a/c suites) a bar, multi-cuisine restaurant and decent-sized pool. **$–$$$**

Hotel Ritz
5 Regency Theatre Complex, Mysore
Tel: 0821-242 9082
Pleasant little budget hotel near the zoo, only 10 minutes' walk from the palace. The rooms have mosquito nets and attached bathroom and there's a bar-restaurant downstairs. **$**

Hotel Suvarna Regency
97 B.M. Road, Hassan
Tel: 08172-264 006
An excellent-value modern hotel with comfortable a/c rooms. There is also a restaurant serving Indian food. **$$**

Shashinag Residency
Sholapur–Chitradurga Bypass Road, Bijapur
Tel: 08352-260 344

www.hotelshashinagresidency.com
The smartest place to stay in town, with a small pool. **$$–$$$**

Tourist
Ananda Rao Circle, Race Course Road, Bengaluru
Tel: 080-2226 2381
One of Bengaluru's few appealing budget lodges. Its rooms aren't large, but they're well aired and open onto a long pillared veranda. No advance reservations, so get there early. **$**

Villa Pottipati
142 4th Main, 8th Cross, Malleswaram, Bengaluru
Tel: 080-2336 0777
www.neemranahotels.com
A heavenly heritage hotel, out in the sub-urbs, ensconced amid a fragrant garden of jacaranda trees and aromatic shrubs. Its rooms, decorated and furnished in period style, ooze old-world elegance, with private verandas, deep baths and direct access to an outdoor swimming pool. **$$$$–$$$$$**

Andhra Pradesh
Amrutha Castle
5/9–16, Saifabad, Opposite Secretariat, Hyderabad
Tel: 040-5563 3888
www.amruthacastle.com
Kitsch rules at this fantasy Bavarian castle, part of the Best Western chain. Good rooms and amenities, including a 5th-floor open-air swimming pool. **$$$$**

Bhimas Deluxe
34–38 G. Car Street, Tirupati
Tel: 0877-222 2252
www.thirupathibhimashotels.com
A well-run hotel just around the corner from the railway station. Friendly, helpful staff. **$$**

Taj Banjara
Road No.1, Banjara Hills, Hyderabad
Tel: 040-6666 2323
www.tajhotels.com
Gorgeous five-star featuring a superb sunken swimming pool in the gardens, and several top-notch restaurants. **$$$$**

RESTAURANTS

Karnatakan cuisine includes the usual south Indian *dosas*, *idlis* and the staple *thali*, but also offers such specialities as *bisi bele bath*, a delicacy of rice seasoned with lentils, spices and tamarind, and *hoalige*, a flat pancake-like wafer filled with molasses, coconut

Restaurant Price Categories
Prices are for a standard meal for one, excluding alcoholic drinks
$** = up to Rs200 **$$** = Rs200–500 **$$$** = Rs500–1000 **$$$$ = over Rs1000

and lentils. The cuisine of Andhra Pradesh is known for its fiery curries served with rice or *parathas*. Hyderabad has its own distinct nawabi cuisine, essentially Mughal but adapted to the tastes of the local royalty. Aromatic *biryanis*, *halim* (a spiced mixture of wheat and mutton) and *mirch ka salan* (green chilli curry) are some typical Hyderabadi specialities.

Karnataka
Casa Piccola
A-14 Devatha Plaza, 131 Residency Road, Bengaluru
Tel: 080-221 2907
Continental snacks and meals – from tapas to pasta and steak – snappily served

at sensible prices, amid bright, modern decor. **$$**

Karavalli
Taj Gateway Hotel, 66 Residency Road, Bengaluru
Tel: 080-58 4545

Award-winning gourmet coastal cuisine, from Mangalorean pomfret to grilled seer fish, tiger prawns, butter-garlic crab, and pearlspot fresh from the Keralan backwaters, all served alfresco under a giant rain tree. **$$$–$$$$**

Koshy's
39 St Mark's Road, Bengaluru
An old-fashioned, relaxed café that's a Bengaluru institution, with split-cane blinds and drinks served in pewter tumblers and teapots. **$$**

Lalitha Mahal Palace Hotel
Siddhartha Nagar, Mysore
Superb *biryanis* and other Deccani speci-alities served amid opulent surroundings, and accompanied by live Hindustani music. **$$$–$$$$**

Mavalli Tiffin Rooms
Lalbagh Road, Bengaluru
Open since 1924, MTR serves definitive Udupi-Brahmin food – notably *masala dosas*, for which queues regularly stretch out of the door (the management boasts that the Chief Minister of Karnataka even stood in line for one once). **$**

Naivedyam/Manasa
Hotel Priyadarshini, V-45 Station Road, Hospet
Garden restaurant looking out on sugar-cane and banana plantations. Good vegetarian and non-vegetarian food; also serves beer. **$$**

RRR
Gandhi Square, Mysore
Andhra-style *thalis* dished up to hungry local workers in busy, no-frills canteen on banana leaves. One of the most enduringly popu-lar cheap places to eat in the city, and it's handy for the shops and palace. **$**

The Waves
Hotel Malligi, 10-90 Jambunath Road, Hampi
Pleasant terrace restaurant serving tasty tandoori, south Indian and Chinese dishes, along with chilled beers (the last from

7–11pm only). Bring plenty of mosquito repellent. **$$**

ANDHRA PRADESH
Hotel Ista
Road 2 I.T. Park, Nanakramguda Gachi Bowli, Hyderabad
Tel: 040-4450 8888
One of the best places in town for foodies: the Deori serves excellent Andhran food and the Collage international dishes. **$$$$**

Pickles
Baseraa Hotel, 9/1–167/8 Sarojini Devi Road, Secunderabad
The 24-hour coffee shop at the Baseraa Hotel is one of the most popular late-night eateries in town; their midnight *biryani* is particularly highly rated. **$$–$$$**

Taj Krishna
Road No.1 Banjara Hills, Hyderabad
Tel: 040-5566 2323
Perhaps the best place in town to get real Hyderabadi food, with some of the more unusual Muslim dishes. **$$$$**

Udipi Anand Bhavan
Machli Kaman, Pathar Gatti, Hyderabad
A good vegetarian 'meals' and *dosa* place right in the heart of the Old Town. Very popular and clean, with an air-conditioned section if you are desperate to escape the heat. **$**

In the smart Lalitha Mahal Palace Hotel

NIGHTLIFE AND ENTERTAINMENT

In common with the rest of the country, Bollywood reigns supreme when it comes to popular entertainment, though classical Indian music and dance also enjoy enthusiastic followings. Bengaluru may be subject to a strict 11.30pm ban on boozing, but its nightlife – centred on the trendy Church Street–Brigade Road area – is the most consistently full-on and sophisticated in the south. Things tend to be more subdued in Muslim-influenced Hyderabad, where a midnight curfew is enforced, but the scene is evolving fast with the influx of hip young IT graduates.

Bars

Coconut Grove Bar
86 Church Street, Bengaluru
A relaxed outdoor bar next to the restaurant of the same name, perfect for a quiet beer.

Liquids Again
Bhaskar Plaza, Road No. 1 Banjara Hills, Hyderabad
Tel: 040-66259907
Cool lounge bar patronised by the city's well-heeled, young IT crowd. Open 6pm–midnight.

NASA
1–4 Church Street, Bengaluru
Space Shuttle-themed pub – lots of metal – with very loud music. Open 11am–11pm.

Peco's
Rest House Road, off Brigade Road, Bengaluru
A long-standing slightly 'alternative' bar, less in-your-face than some. Open 11am–11pm.

Entertainment

Nrityagram Dance Village
30km (20 miles) west of Bengaluru
www.nrityagram.org
Model village and cultural centre, hosting regular performances of Indian dance.

Ranga Shankara
36/2 8th Cross, JP Nagar, Bengaluru
www.rangashankara.org
The city's premier theatre stages plays as well as regular classical and folk dance recitals.

Ravindra Bharati Theatre
Public Gardens Road, Hyderabad
http://ravindrabharathi.org/
Top venue in the city for classical music, dance and drama.

FESTIVALS AND EVENTS

A fascinating dimension to this region's festival calendar is the extent to which both religious and arts events fuse Hindu and Muslim influences.

January–February

Makar Sankranti
Across the region
Cattle are painted bright colours and rice-flour *rangoli* patterns made on doorsteps to mark the conclusion of the annual harvest.

Deccan Festival
Hyderabad
Celebration of Deccani poetry and music, featuring Sufi-inspired Qawwali.

Bangalore Habba
Bengaluru
Music, dance, film, theatre and sports take centre stage in this week-long cultural bash.

September

Batakamma
Hyderabad
To honour the goddess Batakamma, the city's female population make flower arrangements and set them ablaze on rivers and ponds.

Tamil Nadu and the Andaman Islands

For many Indians, Tamil Nadu *is* the south. The mighty Chola temples rising from the state's central rice flats are considered to be the principal highlights of the region. A two-hour flight across the Bay of Bengal, the brilliant turquoise bays of the Andaman Islands provide the perfect antidote to the fierce heat of the deep south.

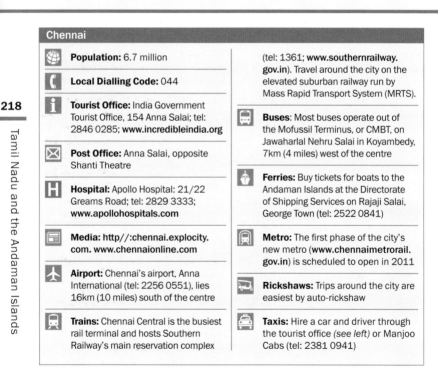

Chennai

Population: 6.7 million

Local Dialling Code: 044

Tourist Office: India Government Tourist Office, 154 Anna Salai; tel: 2846 0285; www.incredibleindia.org

Post Office: Anna Salai, opposite Shanti Theatre

Hospital: Apollo Hospital: 21/22 Greams Road; tel: 2829 3333; www.apollohospitals.com

Media: http//:chennai.explocity. com. www.chennaionline.com

Airport: Chennai's airport, Anna International (tel: 2256 0551), lies 16km (10 miles) south of the centre

Trains: Chennai Central is the busiest rail terminal and hosts Southern Railway's main reservation complex (tel: 1361; www.southernrailway. gov.in). Travel around the city on the elevated suburban railway run by Mass Rapid Transport System (MRTS).

Buses: Most buses operate out of the Mofussil Terminus, or CMBT, on Jawaharlal Nehru Salai in Koyambedy, 7km (4 miles) west of the centre

Ferries: Buy tickets for boats to the Andaman Islands at the Directorate of Shipping Services on Rajaji Salai, George Town (tel: 2522 0841)

Metro: The first phase of the city's new metro (www.chennaimetrorail. gov.in) is scheduled to open in 2011

Rickshaws: Trips around the city are easiest by auto-rickshaw

Taxis: Hire a car and driver through the tourist office *(see left)* or Manjoo Cabs (tel: 2381 0941)

Sprawling from the Western Ghats to the Coromandel Coast, the former heartland of the Chola dynasty is a repository of the world's oldest-surviving classical culture. Ancient gopura temple towers still dominate the skyline of its towns and cities, and the devotional songs blaring from the sound systems of pilgrims' buses in the region would have been familiar to Hindus 1,500 years ago. Yet for all the tenacity with which they have retained the traditions of the past, the 62 million inhabitants of this vast state have enthusiastically embraced the modern era.

Car manufacturing and the IT sector are booming in the dynamic capital of Tamil Nadu, Chennai (Madras), which is also the hub of a thriving film industry whose stars monopolise the region's political scene as well as its cinema screens. Chennai also serves as the springboard for the remote archipelago of islands lying 1,000km (600 miles) east in the Bay of Bengal. For visitors, the Andaman Islands offer a tempting tropical getaway, where jungles tumble on to empty whitesand beaches and turquoise bays ringed by coral reefs.

A Tamil man in Chennai

Chennai has varied architecture

TAMIL NADU

Historic monuments and temples tend to loom large on most visitor itineraries in Tamil Nadu. Top of your list should be the ancient city of Madurai, in the far south of the state, and the seaside capital of the Pallavas, Mamallapuram, in the north. Take your time travelling between the two: the region's distinctiveness reveals itself as much in its markets, fishing villages and festivals as its famous temples, busy year-round with pilgrims from across southern India.

Chennai (Madras)

The major metropolis of the south, **Chennai ❶** – known as Madras until 1996 – is India's fourth-largest city, home to over 6 million inhabitants. The city today is a curious mixture. While it retains the legacy of the British Raj, and is, in some ways, a conservative bastion in social and religious matters, it is also the Bollywood of south India. Church towers and staid Victorian piles stand cheek by jowl with giant-size cut-outs of cinema heroes and heroines, painted in bright colours and dotted with

Tamil Nadu and the Andaman Islands

flashing sequins. Now one of the south's booming software and call-centre hubs (rivalling Bengaluru and Hyderabad), the centre is sprouting glossy new high-rise buildings and shopping malls, patronised by the city's middle classes.

The British East India Company established one of its earliest seats of power in India in the former Madras, and the construction of **Fort St George** Ⓐ was begun around 1640 – making it the oldest colonial structure in the country. Today its whitewashed buildings – famous as the place where Robert Clive, future victor of the Battle of Plassey, and founding father of the British Raj, lived and worked – house the Tamil Nadu Government Secretariat and the Legislative Assembly. Within the fort, a number of other early structures still stand,

among them **St Mary's Church** (daily 9.30am–5pm; free), consecrated in 1680 and the earliest English building surviving intact in India. The **Fort St George Museum** (Sat–Thur 10am–5pm; charge), housed in what was built as the Public Exchange, gives a good overview of the early British colonial lifestyle.

Across town on Pantheon Road, the **Government Museum** Ⓑ (www.chennaimuseum.org; Sat–Thur 9.30am–5pm; charge), displays excellent Chola bronzes and a detailed collection of Dravidian sculpture and architecture. From 9th-century Pallavas and Cholas to the rich style of the Vijayanagar kingdom, the exhibits make a fascinating demonstration of the glory of south India. Foremost among its treasures are the Amaravati Marbles, fragments from the stupa which was all but destroyed

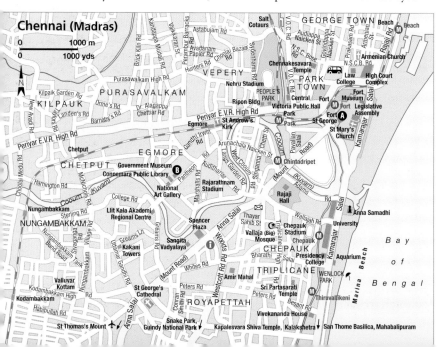

Touring the fascinating monuments at Mamallapuram

by excavators in the early 19th century (and whose principal treasures nowadays reside in the British Museum in London). The bas-reliefs, which outshine even those of Sanchi *(see p.157)*, are widely regarded as the high watermark of ancient Buddhist art in India.

Mamallapuram

The ancient port of the Pallava kings, **Mamallapuram** ❷ (charge for single ticket covers entry to Mammallapuram's main monuments; the rest are free) is a high point in any tour of south Indian monuments. It lies only 60km (36 miles) south of Chennai, but stay there overnight, rather than making a day trip from the capital, if possible. It has accommodation on the sandy beach, enabling you to see the carvings, *ratha* shrines and Shore Temple by the sea in the early morning and at night.

The town is named after King Narasimha Mamalla (630–68), 'the great wrestler', in whose reign its many extraordinary temples and shrines

were begun. Like the cave temples of Ellora, most monuments are carved, rather than built, from solid rock.

South of the village stands a set of **rathas** (daily 6.30am–6pm; charge), monolithic shrines hewn from one table of rock. Imitating elements of the region's wood-and-brick construction, some have the same arched and domed roofs as the inner *vimana* sanctuaries that you can see at Thanjavur *(see p.224)* and at Srirangam *(see p.225)*. The largest shrine, the three-storey pyramidal Dharmaraja, at the southern end, has 50 figures, including gods, heroes and, fascinatingly, modest subjects such as temple servants.

Of the rock carvings north of the *rathas*, the most celebrated is **Arjuna's Penance** (also known as Descent of the Ganges). The narrative sculpture panels cover an entire rock face, in which a natural fissure has been assimilated as the Ganges River as it descends through the hair of Shiva. The **Shore Temple** (daily 6.30am–6pm; charge), which has withstood

French India

Puducherry came under French rule in the mid-18th century and was finally returned to India in 1954. The town was originally divided by a canal. On one side was the **Ville Blanche** for the French inhabitants and on the other the **Ville Noire** for the Indian population. **Government Park** formed the heart of the city, around which the **Raj Nivas** (residence of the lieutenant governor) and other official buildings are now located. Near the railway station is the Gothic-style **Sacred Heart Church**. The streets of the old French area are cobbled, and the waterfront is designed to resemble Nice.

the wind and waves for 12 centuries, has two shrines, now walled off from the corrosive breezes by a line of fir trees. The temple, which would have served as a good orientation point for Pallava sailors, is clearly inspired by the styling of the monolithic Dharmaraja shrine, though more tapered.

Worth a visit amid the sandy backstreets on the fringes of the village are dozens of small stone carvers' workshops where craftsmen chisel Hindu deities and other, secular, statues for sale to visitors, and for export.

Kanchipuram

Kanchipuram ('Golden City') ❸, an easy trip of 70km (43 miles) northwest from Mamallapuram, holds scores of medieval temples, and it is highly revered as one of the seven holy cities of ancient India. The town's largest and most important temple, the **Ekambareshvara** (daily 6am–12.30pm and 4–8.30pm; free), is topped by a towering sequence of *gopuras* (towered gateways) and contains an extensive array of shrines and other buildings, including a magnificent 'thousand-pillared hall'. **Kailasanatha** (daily 6am–12.30pm and 4–8.30pm; free) is one of the most important Shiva sanctuaries, dating from the 8th century. Other monuments in town worth extending your trip to visit include the medieval **Devarajaswami temple** (daily 6am–12.30pm and 4–8.30pm; charge), whose famous 1,000-pillared hall features chains carved from single blocks of stone, and the ancient **Vaikunta**

Kanchipuram is the site of many magnificent temples

Perumal temple (daily 6am–12.30pm and 4–8.30pm; free), built shortly after the Kailasanatha.

Puducherry (Pondicherry)

The most visible Gallic vestige in the former French colony of **Puducherry** ❹ (previously known as 'Pondicherry') is the scarlet *képi* worn by the town's white-uniformed traffic police. Many of the street names are still French. However, only few people speak the former colonial mother tongue today. Apart from the pleasant

white sandy beach, for nostalgics of the 1960s there's a pilgrimage to be made to the **Auroville**. This utopian settlement, 10km (6 miles) north, was started in 1968 by a Mira Alfassa, a Parisian painter of Egyptian-Turkish descent who was the spiritual partner of the Bengali mystic-philosopher, Sri Aurobindo Ghose. Auroville lost some of its dynamism because of squabbles following the death of Alfassa, known to Aurobindo's acolytes as simply 'The Mother.' But the organic forms of the buildings still have an impact on the

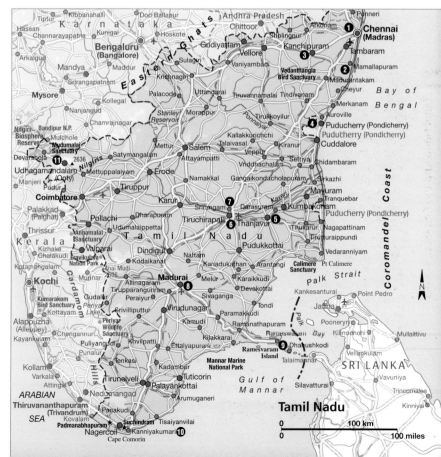

Tamil Nadu

0   100 km
0   100 miles

The horses on the Sesharayar Mandapa

landscape. Visitors are welcome to look around the formal **gardens** (Mon–Sat 10am–1pm and 2–4.30pm; free), but the site's spiritual nerve centre, the futuristic Matri Mandir complex, where the world's largest solid crystal ball is enshrined inside a marble-lined dome building, is off limits.

Thanjavur (Tanjore)

Thanjavur ❺ was the historic capital of the great Chola kingdom that spread Tamil culture to Southeast Asia. The extent of the influence of its artful sculpture and architecture can be seen to this day in the temples of Cambodia, Thailand and Java. More than the divinity of Shiva, the architecture of the 11th-century **Brihadisvara temple** (6am–1pm and 3–8pm; free) celebrates the victory of the great Chola kingdom over the Pallavas of Kanchipuram and the Cheras of Kerala. The accent is on the grandiose: the temple's main *vimana* shrine consisting of a massive, 13-tiered pyramid some 61m (200ft) high. Shiva's sacred bull, Nandi, is built on a similarly colossal scale, as is the phallic lingam, believed to be the biggest in India.

Close by, to the northeast of town, is the **Royal Palace** (daily 9am–6pm; charge). The Maharaja of Thanjavur's family continue to occupy some apartments here, but the palace is now used mainly as a **museum** (daily 9am–1pm and 3–6pm; charge), home to a magnificent collection of Chola bronzes, including some unique representations of Shiva Nataraja.

Tiruchirapalli (Trichy)

The official, Indianised name of this town is **Tiruchirapalli** ❻, literally 'City of the Sacred Rock', but the place is still identified by its colonial name, Trichy, a short form of the equally European name Trichinopoly. Today it is a base for pilgrims visiting Tamil Nadu's great temple complexes, but every schoolchild once knew Trichy for the British defeats of the French here in the 1750s.

The **Rock Fort** (daily 6am–8pm; charge) looms over the city from atop the great solid granite hill that gave the town its name. From early days, the impregnable rock served as a sanctuary, graced by temples and cave-shrines. Steep steps bring you up to the Hall of a Thousand Pillars, as well as the shrine of Shiva and the Temple of Ganesh, from which there is a fine view over the Kaveri (Cauvery) River, the towers of Srirangam and the plains beyond. On the way up, look for the 7th-century, stout-pillared Pallava cave-shrines.

Srirangam

The numerous temple precincts of **Sri Ranganathaswami** (daily 6am–1pm and 3–9pm; free), set on an island formed by two arms of the Cauvery River at **Srirangam** ❼, 5km (3 miles) from Trichy, enclose a complete township of busy shops, booths and dwellings. Beyond the town's outside wall are the temple's farmland and the coconut plantations, and a large, square, lotus-covered bathing tank. The temple itself, dedicated to Vishnu and already a theological centre by the 11th century, was founded a couple of thousand years ago – tradition takes it back to the time of the Flood. Its present form comprises a total of seven concentric enclosures, culminating in an inner sanctum, and dates from the 15th and 16th centuries, after it had been liberated from Muslim invaders who had previously used it as a fortress. However, many of the sanctuaries are in fact much older than this.

Enter on the south side and proceed through an ornamented *gopura* gate-tower characteristic of south Indian architecture. The streets inside are crammed with vendors selling shrine offerings. Elsewhere, men are cleaning the stables for the temple elephants and the storehouses for the chariot-shrines that carry the deities through the streets during the festivals.

On the south side of the fourth courtyard stands the **Temple of Venugopala Krishnan**, with its charmingly sculpted figures in the famous Hoysala style. Non-Hindus can proceed as far as the sixth wall, but not into the golden-topped *vimana*, the inner sanctum, and its arched roof with the god Vishnu portrayed on each side.

Most spectacular of all, though, set in the eastern courtyard of the fourth enclosure, is the famous **Sesharayar Mandapa** (worship hall), with eight carved pillars of rearing horses bearing proud warriors. These minutely detailed sculptures from the 16th century, which honour the military prowess of the then-great Vijayanagar kingdom, rank among the high achievements of south Indian art.

Madurai

The ancient capital of the Pandya kings and one of the world's oldest cities, **Madurai** ❽ is still an important repository of Tamil culture. Today it is a bustling university town, Tamil Nadu's second largest after Chennai.

The feverish religious activity around the nine towering *gopuras* of the **Sri Meenakshi Temple** (daily

Tamil Nadu and the Andaman Islands

Sri Meenakshi Temple in Madurai

On the beach at Kanniyakumari, an important site of pilgrimage for Hindus

6am–12.30pm and 4–9pm; free) gives a vivid sense of the intensity of Hinduism. It is dedicated to a pre-Hindu 'fish-eyed goddess' taken into the pantheon with her husband, Shiva, whose Sundaresvara Shrine stands next door.

The busiest place in the entire complex is the **Kambattadi Mandapa**, the ambulatory to the Sundaresvara shrine. Worshippers in procession prostrate themselves, bringing offerings of coconut and fruit, and toss tiny balls of butter onto blackened statues of Shiva. The Hall of 1,000 Pillars is in the northeast corner of the complex, filled with carved, bizarre lion-elephants. Outside the eastern wall is the **Pudhu Mandapa**, Tirumalai Nayak's, the temple's builder, Hall of Audience– now a bustling artisans' bazaar.

Stop off at the **Tirumalai Nayak Palace** (daily 9am–1pm and 2–5pm; charge), about 1km (½ mile) southeast of the Great Temple. An elegant relic of former splendour, the 17th-century palace boasts cusped arches and massive pillars modelled on the style of the great Rajput palaces of Rajasthan, but also some tubby Dravidian gods on a frieze running around the courtyard.

Rameswaram

The Ramalingesvara Temple (daily 4am–1pm and 3–8.30pm; free) on **Ramesvaram Island ❾**, 150km (93 miles) southeast of Madurai, severed from the mainland by a cyclone in the 15th century, is one of the holiest spots in India. This is believed to be the place where Rama stopped to worship Shiva after his conquest of Lanka: the two lingams in the sanctum of the magnificently sculpted **Ramanatasvami Temple** are said to have been installed on this spot by Rama himself. The temple took 350 years to complete; its crowning glory is a magnificent 1,220m (4,000ft) -long pillared corridor that surrounds the main quadrangle.

Kanniyakumari

At the southernmost tip of India, **Kanniyakumari** ❿ occupies a unique position in the mythology, as well as the geography, of the subcontinent. Close to 2 million Hindu pilgrims travel here each year to worship at the temple dedicated to the Virgin Goddess, Kanya Devi, whose weathered stone walls overlook the place where the waters of the Bay of Bengal, Indian Ocean and Arabian Sea merge. It's considered particularly auspicious to bathe at the ghats extending into the waves below the shrine during the full-moon phase of April, when you can watch the sun set and moon rise on the same horizon.

Standing offshore, their bases lashed by surf, is a pair of rocky islets, one of which sports a giant 29m (92ft) image of the Tamil poet-saint Thiruvalluvar. The colossus, inaugurated in 2000, took 150 workmen more than a decade to build, at a cost of more than US$1 million. On the other island rests a memorial to the 19th-century spiritual leader Swami Vivekananda, one of the figures responsible for introducing yoga and Vedic philosophy to the West. Four hundred people were stranded on the islet after the 2004 Boxing Day tsunami laid waste to much of the coast hereabouts.

Udhagamandalam

When John Sullivan, Collector of Coimbatore, and his detachment of Indian sepoys hacked their way to the head of the Hulikal Ravine in 1819, they discovered a huge, saucer-shaped depression ringed by high ridges and fed by rivers crashing through virgin forest. Sullivan was quick to see the potential of this lost Eden and, after purchasing land from the local Toda tribals for Rs1 per acre, moved there with his family in 1822 to establish a tea estate.

Within a couple of decades, Ootacamund had mushroomed into a prosperous settlement, to which increasing numbers of colonials started to flee to escape the heat and humidity of the plains. By the 1880s it had acquired all the trappings of a Home Counties Victorian town, most infamously, a Members' Club whose verandas and lawns became synonymous with the Raj at its snobbiest. 'Snooty Ooty', now known as **Udhagamandalam** ⓫, survived Independence and, thanks to its cool climate, continues to thrive as a hill resort.

Lakshmipur
North Andaman
Diglipur
Middle Andaman
Mayabunder
Bharatpur
Amkunj
South Andaman
Havelock Island
Mahatma Gandhi
Marine National Park
Neil Island
Port Blair
Sentinel Island
Chiriya Tapu
Rutland Island
Cinque Island
Duncan Passage
Nachuge
Tambeibui
Little Andaman
Toibalewe

Ten Degree Channel

Bay of Bengal

Car Nicobar Island
Malacca

Andaman and Nicobar Islands

Tarasa Dwip Island
Bongala
Koihoa
Camorta Island
Koimekeah

Andaman Islands

Nicobar Islands

0   50 km
0   50 miles

> ### The 2004 Tsunami
>
> On 26 December 2004 the islands were hit by the enormous tsunami that also devastated parts of Southeast Asia. The damage was overwhelming, particularly in Little Andaman, at the far southern end of the archipelago. More than 3,000 were officially listed as having been killed, with many more missing, presumed dead, and thousands more displaced. Much of the infrastructure is still being repaired.

THE ANDAMAN ISLANDS

The Andaman and Nicobar islands lie 1,220km (760 miles) southeast of Kolkata across the Bay of Bengal, or 'Kala Pani' (Black Water), as this cyclone-prone sea was traditionally known. Their existence was reported in the 9th century AD by Arab merchants sailing towards the Straits of Sumatra, but with dense forests, mangrove swamps and shark-infested seas, the 572 islands were considered fit only for political prisoners and Malay pirates. Their development as a tourist destination, attracting scuba divers, birdwatchers and honeymooners, has happened only in the past three decades. Most of the islands, however, are Adivasi (tribal) reserves and only a limited number are open to visitors – while the Nicobar group remains completely off-limits. The best time to visit is from December to April.

Port Blair, on the island of **South Andaman**, is the capital and only sizeable town in the chain. It was named after Lt Reginald Blair, who conducted a survey of the area in 1789. The **Cellular Jail**, where 400 freedom fighters were held during the struggle for Independence, is now a museum (Tue–Sun 9am–noon and 2–5pm; charge).

Havelock Island, around 2½ hours by boat to the northeast of Port Blair, is the main focus of tourism in the archipelago, with an abundance of fabulous beaches . There is a range of accommodation available to independent travellers, with the attendant hustle from commission-driven vendors. To the south, Neil Island is quieter and has fewer facilities, but is just as beautiful.

A pristine beach on Havelock Island

ACCOMMODATION

Hotels in Tamil Nadu offer some of the best value in India, with high standards of cleanliness and efficiency, and reasonable tariffs. Seasonal fluctuations only apply to the resort of Mamallapuram, where pressure on beds peaks during the Christmas–New Year period; room prices also rise by up to 50 percent across the Andamans at this time – advance booking is essential.

TAMIL NADU

Anandha Inn
154 S.V. Patel Road, Puducherry
Tel: 0413-233 0711
www.anandhainn.com
A comfortable and good-value modern hotel with two restaurants serving Indian and Continental food. **$$$**

Femina Hotel
Williams Road, Tiruchirapalli
Tel: 0431-241 4501
Business-oriented place in a central location offering a wide choice of differently priced rooms, and a pool. **$–$$$**

Fernhills Palace
High Level Road, Udhagamandalam
Tel: 0423-244 3097
www.welcomheritagehotels.com
This sumptuous heritage hotel is set in the expansive grounds of the former British Country Club. Accommodation is in richly furnished suites. **$$$$$**

GRT Regency
Gandhi Road, Kanchipuram
Tel: 044-2722 5250
www.grthotels.com
Best of the mid-range places in the town centre, within walking distance of the temples. A/C available. **$$$**

Hotel de l'Orient
17 rue Romain Rolland, Puducherry
Tel: 0413-234 3067
www.neemranahotels.com
An 18th-century neoclassical mansion, now an elegant heritage hotel. It has lovely rooms and a Creole restaurant. **$$$$**

Hotel Mamalla Heritage
104 East Raja Street, Mamallapuram
Tel: 044-2744 2060
www.hotelmamallaheritage.com
Lacking the heritage feel promised by its name, but with large, comfortable rooms and a good-sized outdoor pool. **$$–$$$**

Hotel New Woodlands
72–5 Dr Radhakrishnan Road, Mylapore, Chennai
Tel: 044-2811 3111
www.newwoodlands.com
A large hotel with large, clean rooms and a popular vegetarian restaurant. **$$**

Reflections
North Lake Road, Udhagamandalam
Tel: 0423-244 3834
Simple, but clean and relaxing budget accommodation in Ooty's friendliest guesthouse, situated on the lakeside. Home-cooked meals by arrangement. Good value. **$**

Puducherry's Hotel de l'Orient

Savoy Hotel
77 Sylks Road, Udhagamandalam
Tel: 0423-244 4142
www.tajhotels.com
Forty rooms, some in cottages evocative of
the Raj. Fires are lit in the guest rooms. Lovely
gardens, restaurant and coffee shop. **$$$$$**

Taj Connemara
2 Binny Road, Chennai
Tel: 044-5500 0000
www.tajhotels.com
One of the great hotels of India, in an Art
Deco building. It has a lovely pool and good
restaurants, as well as a chic cocktail bar.
$$$$$

West Tower
42/60 West Tower Street, Madurai
Tel: 0452-234 6098
This clean, well-run mid-scale place enjoys
a prime position close to the temple. **$–$$**

YWCA International Guest House
1086 E.V.R. Periyar High Road, Chennai
Tel: 044-2532 4234
ywcaigh@indiainfo.com

Rooms with attached baths and also camping
facilities. Rates include breakfast. **$–$$**

The Andaman Islands
Barefoot At Havelock
Radhnagar, Havelock
Tel: 03192-220 191
www.barefootindia.com
Boutique resort offering luxury cottages a
stone's throw from the beach – and morning
swims with a local elephant. **ⓜ $$$$**

Fortune Resort Bay Island
Marine Hill, Port Blair
Tel: 03192-234 101
www.fortuneparkhotels.com
Port Blair's top hotel, 1km (2/3 mile) south of
town, enjoys fine views over the bay. **$$$$$**

Sun Sea Resort
M.G. Road, Middle Point, Port Blair
Tel: 03192-238 330
www.sunsearesortandamans.com
Easily the best-value option, with a/c and
modern furnishings. More comfortable than
most of the upscale competition, at a fraction
of the price, though on a busy road. **$$–$$$**

RESTAURANTS

The vegetarian food of Tamil Nadu
is one of the world's great cuisines.
Dishes such as the *dosa*, a crisp thin
pancake made with fermented lentil
dough, and the dry curries known as
poriyals, are popular all over India.
Visit a busy 'meals' place, where at

Restaurant Price Categories
Prices are for a standard meal for one, excluding alcoholic drinks
$ = up to Rs200
$$ = Rs200–500
$$$ = Rs500–1000
$$$$ = over Rs1000

lunch time a banana leaf is used as a plate and the huge pile of rice deposited
in the middle is surrounded with *poriyals*, *sambar*, *rasam* (lentil-based soups)
and *chatni*. Eating options in the Andamans are mainly rough-and-ready cafés –
recommended for cheap breakfasts or *thali* lunches. In the evenings you'll find
better food and a more relaxed atmosphere in hotel restaurants.

Tamil Nadu
Ananda Bhavan
Gandhiji Road, Thanjavur
Clean, with extremely cheap and very tasty
vegetarian meals. **$**

Annalakshmi
804 Anna Salai, Chennai
Quality Southeast Asian vegetarian food
prepared by volunteers (all profits go to
charity). **$$**

Bell Jumbo
Kochadai, Madurai
The largest eating hall in the city, spotlessly clean and serving an array of tasty and well-cooked north and south Indian food. **$$**

Coffee Palace
Eliamman Kovil Street, Thanjavur
The best place in Thanjavur for real south Indian coffee and snacks. **$**

Luna Magica
On the beach, Mamallapuram
Fresh, succulent tiger prawns and lobster served in a buzzing beachside eatery, where diners lounge after hours over jugs of sangria. **$$**

Only Appam
Town Hall Road, Madurai
A tiny place serving some of the best local dishes in Madurai. **$**

Rendez Vous
30 Suffren Street, Puducherry
Proper croissants and fresh coffee for breakfast, and delicious Continental specialities (including scrumptious pizzas) served until late evening, indoors or up on a delightful rooftop terrace. **$–$$**

Saravana Bhavan
Many branches in Chennai including:
Shanti Theatre Complex, 44 Anna Salai; Central Railway Station; 77–9 Usman Road, Theagaraya Nagar; 209 N.S.C. Bose Road, George Town
An excellent chain of clean, cheap and tasty south Indian vegetarian meal halls. Open all day. **$**

Sidewalk Café
Nahar Hotel, Commercial Road, Udhagamandalam
Wood-fired pizzas, toasties, veggie burgers and crunchy salads are the specialities of this snazzy, Mumbai-style fast-food joint. It's also a good spot for a pit stop, serving cool shakes, fresh fruit juices and proper cappuccinos. **$–$$**

Dosas and *chatnis* at Ananda Bhavan

Velu's Military Hotel
Valluvar Kottam High Road
You can't get much better than this long-standing institution for superb Chettinad non-veg food. **$$**

The Andaman Islands

Annapurna Café
Aberdeen Bazaar, Port Blair
The best Indian food in town, including the usual Udipi snacks, and some tasty Chinese and north Indian alternatives. Resident Tamils stream in at breakfast for hot *pongal*, a rice dish made with *moong dal* (split beans) and coconut. **$**

Mandalay
Fortune Resort, Marine Hill, Port Blair
This is about as swanky as Port Blair gets: a breezy alfresco deck restaurant with fine views over the bay and good-value buffets at lunch time. The Nico bar next door serves alcohol. **$$–$$$**

New Lighthouse
Marina Park, near Aberdeen Jetty, Port Blair
A choice selection of local seafood (including affordable lobsters and tiger prawns), fresh off the boats, served on an airy terrace overlooking the harbour. The building has seen better days, but the cooking is dependable and they also serve chilled beers. **$$**

NIGHTLIFE AND ENTERTAINMENT

The only place with anything resembling a nightlife in Tamil Nadu is the capital, Chennai, where hotel bars provide the focus for late-night drinking. Devotees of south Indian music and dance come from all over the country every year to attend Chennai's three-week 'season' of concerts, held in December and early January. Among the festival's highlights are the annual dance-dramas at the Kalakshetra Institute, a college of traditional arts. Carnatic music recitals and performances of Bharatanatyam dance are also staged in various venues year-round; consult the local press for details.

Bars

Distil
Taj Connemara Hotel, Binny Road, Chennai
Tel: 044-6600 0000
One of the nicer – and quieter – bars in Chennai but still with a contemporary edge. Good for cocktails. Open 6pm–midnight.

Geoffrey's
Radha Park Inn, Chennai
Hip pub-style bar, hosting live music every night from 6–11pm and popular mainly with the city's trendy young things.

The Leather Bar
The Park, 601 Anna Salai, Chennai
Tel: 044-4214 4000
Immensely popular with Chennai's young and fashionable set, who come here to be seen. The outside decking area is a bit of a relief after the crush inside. The Park's nightclub, Pasha, on the side of the building is also worth checking out.

Entertainment

The Music Academy
TTK Road/Dr Radhakrishnan Salai, Chennai
Tel: 044-2811 2231
www.musicacademymadras.in
Leading venue for Carnatic classical music and Bharatanatyam dance. Founded in 1936 with the intention of reviving traditional Indian music, dance and crafts, and hosting regular performances.

SPORTS AND ACTIVITIES

Sporting life in Tamil Nadu is dominated squarely by cricket. One escape from the wall-to-wall coverage is to take to the crystal-clear waters of the Andamans, where scuba diving is an increasingly popular pastime.

Cricket

MA Chidambaram Stadium
Tamil Nadu's cricket team, based in Chennai, is one of the top three sides in India, regularly winning the coveted Ranjit Trophy. The state also has an IPL Twenty20 side, the Chennai Super Kings (www.chennaisuperkings.com).

Diving

Barefoot Scuba
Café del Mar, No.3 village, Havelock
Tel: 282 181
www.barefootindia.com

Blue Lagoon Divers
Eco Villa, No.2 village, Havelock
Tel: 99332-01327
www.divingandaman.com
Surrounded by crystal-clear waters and dazzling coral reefs to explore, the Andaman Islands are a world-class scuba-diving location, and a handful of accredited dive schools, including the two recommended operators above, have opened in and around the resort of Havelock, offering guided dives and longer PADI course training.

TOURS

Guided tours of varying lengths are run by most regional tourist offices.

Tamil Nadu

Hi! Tours
123 East Raja Street, Mamallapuram
Tel: 044-2744 3360
www.hi-tours.com
Runs popular guided cycling trips to sights around the village, as well as minibus tours to Kanchipuram. Full details online.

Madurai Tourist Office
180 West Veli Street, Madurai
Tel: 0452-233 4757
Tick off the area's numerous sights on the tours offered here.

Puducherry Tourist Office
40 Gubert Avenue, Puducherry
Tel: 0413-233 9497
Operates full- and half-day trips taking in the area's highlights, including Auroville.

Tamil Nadu Tourism Development Corporation (TTDC)
Tourism Complex on Wallajah Road, Triplicane, Chennai
Tel: 2536 7850
www.tamilnadutourism.org
This government-run organisation offers inexpensive half-day group tours of Chennai, and full-day trips to Mamallapuram.

The Andaman Islands

Andaman and Nicobar Islands Tourist Office
Kamaraj Road, Port Blair
Tel: 03192-232747
www.tourism.andaman.nic.in
Snorkelling trips, boat excursions and guided tours of the Cellular Jail are three among many sightseeing tour options here. Tickets may be booked in advance at their office.

FESTIVALS AND EVENTS

The festivals and events punctuating Tamil Nadu's calendar reflect the state's cosmopolitan make-up. For a full list of events, visit any tourist office.

January
Pongal
State-wide
A three-day festival celebrating the prosperity associated with the harvest.

January Island Tourism Festival
Port Blair
Ten days of recitals by dance groups, plus other events celebrating Andaman culture.

April–May
Chitrai
Madurai
The marriage of Meenakshi is among the pivotal points of the city's religious calendar.

July
Bastille Day
Puducherry, 14th July
Festival drawing on the town's Gallic heritage, with street parades and music.

December
Mamallapuram Dance Festival
The cream of the country's dancers comes to perform on an open-air stage set.

Cricket is an obsession in Chennai

Kerala and Lakshadweep

Glorious beaches, jungles filled with wildlife, teeming backwaters and exotic costumed temple dramas – Kerala ticks just about every box as an exotic holiday destination. Its lush beauty is simply a complement to its rich traditions, legends and culture. Off the west coast is the stunning, remote island chain of Lakshadweep, complete with perfect, white-sand beaches.

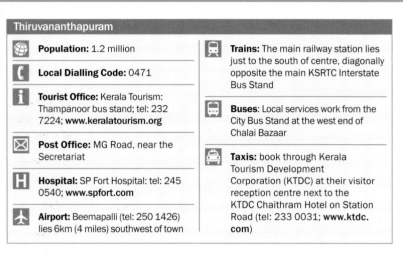

Thiruvananthapuram

Population: 1.2 million

Local Dialling Code: 0471

Tourist Office: Kerala Tourism: Thampanoor bus stand; tel: 232 7224; www.keralatourism.org

Post Office: MG Road, near the Secretariat

Hospital: SP Fort Hospital: tel: 245 0540; www.spfort.com

Airport: Beemapalli (tel: 250 1426) lies 6km (4 miles) southwest of town

Trains: The main railway station lies just to the south of centre, diagonally opposite the main KSRTC Interstate Bus Stand

Buses: Local services work from the City Bus Stand at the west end of Chalai Bazaar

Taxis: book through Kerala Tourism Development Corporation (KTDC) at their visitor reception centre next to the KTDC Chaithram Hotel on Station Road (tel: 233 0031; www.ktdc.com)

'India-lite' is how the state, in the far southwest of India, is often billed in tourist literature. Visibly more prosperous and better organised than most of the rest of the country, it boasts the highest rates of literacy and standards of living in the nation, with among the top GDP – a consequence of the remittance cheques sent home each month by emigrant workers in the Gulf states.

The appealing thing about Kerala from a visitor's point of view is that it offers an enticing combination of beaches, backwaters and hills. When you tire of lounging on soft, surf-lashed sand, you can head off on backwater cruises in converted wooden rice barges, venture up into the cooler climes of the Western Ghat mountains for a stay on a tea plantation, or go elephant and tiger spotting in any number of remote national parks. Kerala's rich tradition of elaborately costumed ritual theatre – notably the masked drama form, Kathakali – adds yet another dimension to travelling in the state, as do its vibrant temple festivals, featuring spectacular processions of caparisoned elephants, drum orchestras and firework displays.

Finally, travellers with a flexible budget looking for a paradise break may consider the remote archipelago of Lakshadweep, an hour's flight west of Kochi-Ernakulam, where coral reefs encircle tiny, palm-fringed islets of dazzling beauty.

SOUTHERN KERALA

The roots of Kerala's economic success lie in the philanthropic policies pursued by its former Maharajas who, under protection from the British, did much to promote education, health care and the arts among their subjects. Nowhere is this legacy more apparent that in the far south, where the Maharajas of Travancore instigated a particularly tolerant and liberal regime.

Thiruvananthapuram

Thiruvananthapuram (Trivandrum) ❶, the capital of modern Kerala, is set around seven low, wooded hills

Keralan people in Thiruvananthapuram

The Napier Museum in Thiruvananthapuram

in the far south of the state. Seat of the Maharajas of Travancore, its old city, bounded by high granite walls, is dominated by the **temple of Sri Padmanabhasvama** (closed to non-Hindus), which the region's rulers built to honour Lord Vishnu. Its majestic, Tamil-style gateway towers are reflected to stunning effect in the waters of the adjacent ablutions tank, on whose southern side stands the **Puttan Malika Palace** (Tue–Sun 8.30am–12.30pm and 3–5.30pm; charge). With its elegant gables, elaborately carved pillars and enclosed courtyards, the complex is a wonderful example of regal Keralan architecture.

North of the city centre, in a park popular with picnickers and strollers, stands Thiruvananthapuram's **Napier Museum** (Tue–Sun 10am–5pm; charge), housed in an extraordinary Indo-Saracenic building, whose collection of jewellery, ivorywork, Chola bronzes and Keralan woodcarving is somewhat upstaged by the showy Rajera architecture. Also worth a visit, in the northern corner of the park, is the **Shri Chitra Art Gallery** (Tue–Sun

Kerala and Lakshadweep

10am–5pm; charge), featuring canvases by Raja Ravi Varma – a minor Keralan royal who became hugely popular across India in the late 19th century for his realist depictions of curvy, sari-clad women and mythological scenes.

Kovalam

Kovalam ❷, 16km (10 miles) south of Thiruvananthapuram, has been Kerala's principal beach resort since the late 1980s. A ramshackle agglomeration of hastily erected hotels, the village extends across paddy fields and palm groves inland from a trio of separate coves, each with its own distinct character. Most foreign tourists congregate on Lighthouse beach where, at night, the revolving lamp of the eponymous lighthouse casts its beam across a strip of brightly lit café-restaurants.

Get up early enough in the morning and walk around the low, rocky promontory dividing Lighthouse beach from its neighbour, Hawa beach, and you'll be treated to one of the quintessential spectacles of the Keralan coast: teams of local fishermen, dressed in cotton turbans and Madras-chequed *mundus* (lunghis), hauling huge nets ashore with ropes.

Varkala

Varkala ❸, 54km (32 miles) north of Thiruvananthapuram, is an attractive village with a less commercialised, fine sandy beach at the base of dramatic red cliffs. Though tourists come primarily to swim and sunbathe, it is also one of Kerala's major Hindu pilgrimage centres, where families immerse the ashes of recently deceased relatives in the waves. Flights of rock-cut steps

Cruising on the backwaters

Cruising the Keralan Backwaters

A network of narrow canals and wide lakes, the backwater region, known as Kuttanad, offers visitors the chance to see a uniquely Keralan landscape at close quarters. Boats of all descriptions are punted or sailed along the shallow green waterways with palms arching overhead. The best way to explore this fascinating area is to hire a converted rice barge, or *kettu vallam*. Made of oiled jackwood and mounted by canopies of plaited palm leaves, these used to transport rice between farms and market towns. Now more than 400 carry tourists around the waterways near Alappuzha, along with fleets of diesel-powered excursion boats and smaller, more environmentally friendly, dugout canoes.

lead from the beach to the cafés, guest-houses and souvenir shops lining North Cliff, where the sea views are sensational, especially at sunset.

Alappuzha

Alappuzha ❹ is a bustling, typically Keralan market town, set on a grid plan formed by intersecting canals. In colonial times, these formed an important link between the interior and the sea. Coir, cashews, spices, rubber, tea and coffee were transported to the go-down warehouses lining the town's waterways and shipped to Europe from a long pier, whose rusting remnants still preside over Alappuzha's desultory beach. These days, hotels and houseboat cruises form the mainstay of the area's economy, with over 400 tourist barges – or *kettu vallam* – plying the nearby backwaters.

Periyar

The **Periyar Wildlife Sanctuary** ❺ (www.periyartigerreserve.org; daily dawn–dusk; charge;), near the market town of **Kumili**, is the most frequented of Kerala's national parks. A former royal hunting reserve, it centres on a reservoir where, from the comfort of a boat deck or bamboo raft, you can sight grazing herds of wild elephant, and even, on rare occasions, one of the handful of tigers that survive in the forests. To protect its fragile populations of fauna from poachers, the Periyar Tiger Reserve has implemented a scheme whereby local forest-dwelling minority people are employed as guides, wardens and hotel staff in the park, thereby reducing illegal hunting. So far, the initiative seems to have been extremely successful, with animal numbers on the increase and local poverty on the wane.

The backwaters are well used as a means of getting around

CENTRAL AND NORTHERN KERALA

Thiruvananthapuram may be the capital and most populous city in Kerala, but **Kochi** (Cochin) ❻ is its economic powerhouse. Dozens of gold emporia and car showrooms lining the glitzy main streets of the modern part of the city on the mainland, Ernakulam, are indicative of the prosperity driven by industrial estates on the outskirts. Few visitors, however, see much of this side of the metropolis, preferring the old-world charm of the former colonial enclave, Fort Cochin, and its neighbouring district, Matancherry, reached by ferry across the harbour.

Fort Cochin and Matancherry

One of the most atmospheric locations in southern India, **Fort Cochin** clusters on a peninsula jutting in to the mouth of the Periyar River, where the Portuguese spice traders gained their first foothold in India in the

---

Kochi

🌐 **Population:** 1.5 million

📞 **Local Dialling Code:** 0484

ℹ️ **Tourist Office:** Government of India Tourism Office: Willingdon Island; tel: 266 8352; www.india-tourism.com

✉️ **Post Office:** GPO, Hospital Road

🏥 **Hospitals:** Medical Trust Hospital; MG Road: tel: 235 8001; www.medicaltrusthospital.com. Ernakulam Medical Centre: NH Bypass, Paalarivattom; tel: 280 7101; www.emccochin.com

✈️ **Airport:** Kochi's Nedumbassery Airport (www.cochinairport.com) is 29km (18 miles) north of the city

🚆 **Trains:** There are two main railway stations, Ernakulam Junction, near the centre, and Ernakulam Town, 2km (1¼ miles) further north

🚌 **Buses:** The KSRTC Central Bus Stand (tel: 237 2033), north of Ernakulam Junction, hosts government-run long-distance services

🚕 **Taxis:** Ashik Taxis: tel: 9288-157 145 or 9656-798 481

early 16th century. Dating from 1506, the stalwart Church of St Francis is a well-preserved survivor from the era of Vasco da Gama, whose body was for a while interred here after he died of fever in a nearby house. Old colonial mansions dotted around the streets of Fort Cochin recall the Portuguese, Dutch and British settlers who made this among the most prosperous ports in Asia. For centuries junks from as far afield as China sailed here to fill their holds with cardamom, cinnamon, cloves and pepper. A quirky vestige of their presence is the much-photographed Chinese fishing nets lining the peninsula's northern shore, operated by a cantilevered system of counterweights.

The district immediately east of Fort Cochin, Matancherry is where the former **Maharaja's Palace** (Sat–Thur 10am–5pm; charge) stands amid a warren of red-tiled warehouses and alleyways. Built by the Portuguese and repaired by the Dutch (who renamed it the 'Dutch Palace'), the building holds some wonderful Keralan-style murals dating from the 17th century, depicting Indian epics in swirling, earthy colours. Tucked away in an alleyway behind it, the little **Pardesi synagogue** (daily 10am–noon and 3–5pm; charge) is used by members of Kochi's diminishing Jewish community. Fewer than a dozen, mostly elderly, Jews remain here, most families having left for Israel. Floored with blue-and-white tiles from Canton, the synagogue holds as its most hallowed

Kerala and Lakshadweep

The Church of St Francis in Fort Cochin

⭐ KATHAKALI

The image of the Kathakali hero, his glossy green face and blood-shot eyes framed by a jewel-encrusted head piece, is emblematic of Kerala. You'll see it everywhere: on matchbox tops, postcard racks and bill-boards. Numerous companies stage tourist-friendly versions of the ritual drama form in visitor enclaves such as Fort Cochin and Kovalam. For the locals, however, Kathakali is foremost a religious ritual, whose traditional context is the temple. And in truth, this remains the most inspirational place to experience Kerala's unique dance drama.

Epic Stories

Amid the heady atmosphere of a Hindu festival, seated cross-legged on the floor of a temple theatre, Kathakali has a magical effect, transporting rapt onlookers to the realm of gods and goddesses. Kathakali plays, as staged in Keralan temple festivals, tend to be all-night affairs starting around 8pm with the lighting of the sacred kalivil-lakku oil lamp. After a musical interlude, the sumptuously costumed dancers are revealed for the first time behind a hand-held quilt screen and the drama begins.

The stories draw mostly on the Hindu epics, the *Ramayana* and *Mahabharata* – sagas recounting the exploits of demons, deities, sages, lovers and their cosmic battles. They're told not in words, but in an arcane language of facial expressions, physical gestures and sign language, backed by sung verses and

The face of the Kathakali hero (on the right) is seen everywhere in Kerala

elaborate drumming. It takes a full night to perform a short play; longer ones last for three or more. The conclusion, however, invariably involves the disembowelling of the baddy and the triumphant dance of the victorious god.

Know Your Hero

Kathakali employs stock characters that are immediately identifiable to Keralan audiences thanks to their distinctive costumes and make-up. Green *(pacca)* characters, who have green-painted faces with scarlet lips and wear vase-shaped, golden crowns surmounted by peacock feathers, are divine heroes such as Krishna, Rama or Vishnu. The heroines ('radiant' or *minukka* characters) are always played by men wearing long-sleeved gowns with scarves draped over hair wound into topknots.

With their elaborate face paints, voluminous skirts, bell belts and heavy jewellery, the actors' costumes take upwards of three hours to put on – a fascinating spectacle which enthusiasts are welcome to watch in the green room.

Training

Costume and make-up skills form part of the Kathakali performer's training, which begins at the age of 7 or 8. It takes at least a decade to master the basic techniques of the form, and many more to become a great actor. Students undergo courses of preparation – eye exercises, yogic stretching and posture practice – before learning the steps and gestures. You can see students at the **Kalamandalam Academy** in Cheruthu-ruthy (www.kalamandalam.org).

Students at the Kalamandalam Academy

Kathakali

The performances are accompanied by accomplished drumming

Looking out over the Western Ghat mountains from Munnar

treasure seven sacred Torah Scrolls capped with gold crowns encrusted by diamonds, rubies and emeralds.

Munnar

As the site of the Western Ghats' most beautiful tea gardens, **Munnar** ❼ fully deserves a couple of days out of anyone's itinerary. The stiff-upper-lipped gentility of the Raj still very much holds sway at the famous **High Raneg Club**, on the south side of town, where you can sip gin and tonic in a bar lined with hunting trophies and the dusty pith-helmets of long-deceased British tea-planters.

An hour's drive out of Munnar is the **Eravikulam National Park** (daily 7am–6pm; charge), the last bastion of the Nilgiri *tahr*, a rare species of mountain goat that survives on the grasslands of the range's uppermost ridges and peaks. The *tahr* was almost wiped out by hunters during the colonial era, but revived after American biologist Clifford Rice attracted herds to his camp using salt licks; dozens of semi-tame *tahr* hang around outside the park gates at Vaguvarai.

Kozhikode and the far north

Kozhikode (Calicut) ❽, the largest city in northern Kerala, was known to the Phoenicians and ancient Greeks, who both traded spices here, but it was the arrival in 1498 of Vasco da Gama and his fleet of caravelas that really put the city on the international map. Although its role as a port has long been usurped by Kochi, the city remains conspicuously prosperous thanks to the money pouring through its banks from the Gulf countries, for which Kozhikode's airport serves as the principal gateway. Sights are thin on the ground, though the **Pazhassi Raja Museum** (Tue–Sun 10am–1pm and 2–4pm; free) and **Krishna Menon Art Gallery and Museum** (same hours; free) both have interesting displays. The only monuments surviving from the time of the Zamorins, the Hindu dynasty that ruled the region from the 12th until the 18th centuries, are a scattering of typically Keralan mosques in the old quarter of Kuttichira, in the southwest of the city.

At Kappad, 16km (10 miles) from Kozhikode, you can visit the place Vasco da Gama made his first landfall – a seminal moment in the history of the subcontinent. Further north, past the French enclave of **Mahé** and the coastal town of **Kannur** (Cannanore), is Tipu Sultan's atmospheric fort overlooking the beach at **Bekal**. A major incentive to venture this far north is the extraordinary masked spirit-possession dances known as *theyyem* held in the surrounding villages.

LAKSHADWEEP

Scattered 200–400km (124–248 miles) west of the Keralan coast, the Lakshadweep Islands are a classic coral atoll, fringed by white, shell-sand beaches and palm groves. Some speculate that the name derives from the estimates of early sailors, who imagined at least 100,000 (one lakh) of these little islets. In fact, there are only 22 (depending on how they are counted), of which just 11 are inhabited – by some 60,600 people.

Foreigners are only permitted to visit one of them, **Bangaram**; a couple of flights per day leave Ernakulam's Nedumbassery airport for the air strip at **Agatti Island**, from where you're transferred by boat or helicopter to Lakshadweep's one and only hotel, CGH chain's **Bangaram Island Resort** *(see p.245)*, situated on a beautiful lagoon. The marine life on the surrounding reefs is impressive. As well as a huge variety of corals, there are over 1,000 species of fish.

Kerala and Lakshadweep

Lakshadweep

Bitra I.
Chetlat I.
Kilttan I.
Perumal I.
Amindivi Islands
Kadmat I.
Amini I.
Bangaram I.
Tinnakara I.
Agatti I.
Pitti I.
Androth I.
Kavaratti
Kavaratti I.
Suneli I.
Cannanore Is
Cheriyam I.
Kalpeni I.
Laccadive Islands
Nine Degree Channel
N
0   50 km
0   50 miles
Minicoy I.
Eight Degree Channel

On an idyllic Lakshadweep beach

ACCOMMODATION

Kerala boasts some of India's most sophisticated tourist accommodation – whether in converted palaces, houseboats, tea planters' bungalows or eco-hideaways deep in the forest – though such luxuries can come at a high price, especially in peak season over Christmas and New Year, when advance bookings are essential everywhere.

Southern Kerala

Chrissie's
Bypass Road, Kumily, Periyar
Tel: 04869-224 155
http://chrissies.in
Four-storey hotel in Kumily village, owned by expats from the UK and Egypt. You get fabulous forest views from the rooms, which are all impeccably clean and comfortable.
$$–$$$

Greenland Lodging
Aristo Road, Thiruvananthapuram
Tel: 0471-232 8114
A decent budget lodge with clean rooms, very convenient for the railway and bus stations. **$**

Karikkathi Beach House
Pulinkudi, 8km (5 miles) south of Kovalam
Tel: 0471-240 0956
www.karikkathibeachhouse.com
A whitewashed, red-tiled cottage nestled under the palm terraces above a secluded cove – this area's most exclusive hideaway.
$$$$$

Palmy Lake Resort
Thathampally, 2km (1¼ miles) north of the boat jetty, Alappuzha
Tel: 0477-223 5938
www.palmyresort.com
Spacious terracotta-tiled chalets scattered around a leafy garden, within walking distance of the lakeside, but well away from the bustle of the town centre.
$$

Surya
Lighthouse Beach, Kovalam
Tel: 0471-248 1012
kovsurya@yahoo.co.in
One of the few genuinely pleasant budget guesthouses packed into the narrow sandy lanes running back from Lighthouse Beach. Quiet, secluded and efficiently run.
$–$$

Varikatt Heritage
Poonen Road, behind the Secretariat, Thiruvananthapuram
Tel: 0471-233 6057
www.varikattheritage.com
The Varikatt is a wonderful old British-era residence, run as an evocative heritage homestay by a retired army colonel. **$$$$**

Villa Jacaranda
Temple Road West, Varkala
Tel: 0470-261 0296
www.villa-jacaranda.biz
Spotless, beautifully styled rooms in a modern guesthouse. The surrounding gardens are shady and tranquil, and the views of sunset over the sea breathtaking.
$$$–$$$$

Central and Northern Kerala

Beach Heritage
Beach Road, Kozhikode
Tel: 0495-236 5363
www.beachheritage.com
Somerset Maugham and Jawaharlal Nehru stayed in this former British club in the 1950s, and little has changed here since.

Brunton Boatyard has retained its Dutch colonial-style architecture

Amazingly good value, given the comfort, location and atmosphere. **$$$**

Brunton Boatyard
Calvetty Road, Fort Cochin
Tel: 0484-221 5461
www.cghearth.com
A luxury hotel in a splendid location, built in the style of Dutch colonial architecture. **$$$$$**

Costa Malabari
10km (6 miles) south of Kannur
Tel: 04897-237 1761
www.costamalabari.com
Simple, but comfortable rooms in an efficiently run guesthouse, screened by cashew groves, close to a string of gorgeous, deserted beaches. 🍴 **$$$**

Delight Tourist Resort
Parade Ground, Fort Cochin
Tel: 0484-221 7658
www.delightfulhomestay.com
A quiet little guesthouse with spotless rooms facing the old parade ground. **$$–$$$**

Harivihar
Bilathikulam, Kozhikode
Tel: 0495-276 5865
www.harivihar.com
Occupying a beautifully converted royal palace, Harivihar ranks among Kerala's top heritage hotels, set amid landscaped gardens dotted with lotus ponds. **$$$$$**

High Range Club
Kanan Devan Hills Road, Munnar
Tel: 04865-230 253
www.highrangeclubmunnar.com
The clock stopped in August 1947 at the High Range Club. You'll need a stiff upper lip and neatly creased trousers to stay here, but the pretence is all part of the fun. Accommodation comes in rooms or cottages. **$$$**

The Old Courtyard
1/371–2 Princess Street, Fort Cochin
Tel: 0484-221 6302
www.oldcourtyard.com
Opening onto an elegant Portuguese courtyard, the eight rooms in this landmark heritage hotel, in the thick of the old fort, preserve their original 17th-century wood floors and antique furniture. **$$$$**

Lakshadweep
Bangaram Island Resort
Book through: CGH Earth (Casino Building, Willingdon Island, Kochi)
Tel: 0484-301 1711
www.cghearth.com
A peaceful luxury resort. The shallow lagoon is fabulously clear and clean, and perfect for swimming. Accommodation is in simple huts set back from the beach. **$$$$$**

RESTAURANTS

Kerala's food reflects the mix of its communities, Hindu, Christian and Muslim. As elsewhere in the south 'meals' predominate, but with the use of fat-grained local rice. In some places you may find tapioca root (*kappa*) replaces rice. Coconut milk and oil are ubiquitous: Keralan fish curries and fried fish are especially good. The Syrian Christians are fond of beef (a strict taboo for Hindus), which can be widely found as 'beef fry' (a dry curry), while the Mapillas Muslims in the north prepare spicy seafood curries. As visitors to Lakshadweep are only permitted as part of a package tour, the only restaurants are at the holiday resorts.

Southern Kerala

Arya Niwas
Aristo Road, near the railway station, Thiruvananthapuram
Keralan *thalis* don't come fresher, more fragrant, or beautifully presented than at this hugely popular banana-leaf 'meals' joint, which has a comfy a/c floor upstairs. **$**

Casa Bianca
96 M.P. Appan Road, Vazhuthacaud, Thiruvananthapuram
This lovely café and restaurant is out of the ordinary for the city. A well-designed interior is the setting for very tasty Italian and Indian food (the pizza is excellent). **$$**

Chakara
Hotel Raheem Residency, Beach Road, Alappuzha
An open-sided restaurant that makes the most of breezes blowing off the beach. Keralan seafood, masala-fried or in coconut-rich gravies, is the house speciality. **$$$–$$$$**

Fusion
North end of Lighthouse Beach, Kovalam
Kovalam's most sophisticated menu, featuring dishes that combine the best of Kerala and Europe. **$–$$$**

Shri Padman
Temple Junction, Varkaka
The rear terrace of this simple local café, which serves basic travellers' grub as well as Keralan vegetarian 'meals', is a great place for crowd-watching. **$**

Waves (aka 'German Bakery')
South End of Lighthouse Beach, Kovalam
Something of a Kovalam institution, the 'German bakery' sells strudel and bread, as well as dishing up a good selection of Thai and European dishes (mainly pasta). **$$–$$$**

Central and Northern Kerala

Arca Nova
Fort House Hotel, 2/6A Calvathy Road, Fort Cochin
Tel: 0484-221 7103
Deliciously spicy Keralan fish steaks, millet-fried or steamed in banana leaves, served at a prime location on a jetty jutting into the harbour. **$$–$$$**

The Old Courtyard Hotel
1/371–2 Princess Street, Fort Cochin
Tel: 0484-221 6302
Enjoy gourmet delicacies, such as the famous house seafood spaghetti, served on candlelit tables against a backdrop of 17th-century Portuguese arches. **$$$**

Paragon
Off Kannur Road, Kozhikode
One of the region's hallmark Muslim dishes is fish *kombathu*, with proper local *pathiri* rice cakes: sample it here. They also serve a range of other Malabari seafood staples (including succulent local mussels). **$–$$$**

ENTERTAINMENT AND SPORTS

The ritual theatre form, Kathakali, is traditionally performed in temples, but a clutch of theatres in Kochi hosts truncated evening shows for the benefit of visiting tourists, preceded by short introductions. Untypically for an Indian state, soccer has traditionally been more popular in Kerala than cricket, although that looks set to change with the advent of the Twenty20 league. In 2010, a consortium of industrial magnates and politicians bid $333 million for a Keralan franchise, based in a brand-new, world-class stadium in Ernakulam.

Kathakali
Kerala Folklore Museum
Bypass Road, southeastern edge of
Ernakulam
http://folkloremuseum.org
One of the best places to catch a Kathakali
performance.

Kerala Kathakali Centre
Bernard Master Lane, near Santa Cruz
Basilica, just off KB Jacob Road, Fort Cochin
Tel: 0484-221 7552
Staged in a large and new theatre, Kathakali
performances here have the added bonus of
translations laid on.

FESTIVALS AND EVENTS

Kerala is perhaps more festival obsessed than any other part of the country, and luckily for visitors, some of the most spectacular events, featuring elephant processions and performances of traditional arts, take place at the height of the winter tourist season.

January–February
Malabar Mahotsavam
Kozhikode
Northern Kerala's premier cultural festival.

Nishangandhi Festival
Thiruvananthapuram
Top-drawer classical music and dance artists from all over the country perform on two open-air stages at the Kanakakannu Palace.

March
Chandanakudam Mahotsavam
Beemapalli, near Thiruvananthapuram
Saint's day at the Beemapalli Dargah Shareef tomb – one of Kerala's main Muslim festivals.

August–September
Nehru Trophy Snake Boat Race
Alappuzha (second Sat in Aug)
The most spectacular of all Kerala's snake boat races.

Onam
State-wide
The region's much-loved harvest festival. Families make *pookalam*, geometric floral decorations, in the courtyards of houses; special Onam songs *(ona paattuu)* are sung; and everyone dons splendid new clothes *(onakkodi)* for the great Onam feast.

Pulikkali
Thrissur
Troupes of men paint their bodies in tiger designs and wiggle around the city's main intersection. Takes place on the fourth day of Onam.

October–November
Arattu
Thiruvananthapuram
The capital's principal deity is processed through the streets, led by the maharaja of Travancore.

PRACTICAL ADVICE

Accommodation

Ranging from flea-infested, windowless lodges to royal palaces hosting heads of state, India's plentiful accommodation reflects the diverse range of travellers on the move through the country at any given time. Only during peak season (late Dec–Jan) and during major festivals, when all hotels in major tourist centres hike their prices dramatically, are you likely to encounter a shortage of beds. However much you're spending, advance reservation – by telephone or online, and using a credit or debit card to make a deposit if requested – is a good idea at any time of year.

If you're arranging accommodation on spec, bear in mind most establishments offer a range of differently priced rooms: check a few of them before deciding, and don't be afraid to haggle over the rate.

Check-out times can vary: 12 noon is the norm, but some places work on a 24-hour-from-check-in basis. As a rule you'll be expected to leave your passport at reception on arrival, and fill out a register and 'C Form'

for the local police, giving contact and visa details.

Bills are settled prior to departure, generally in cash. Credit or debit cards will likely be accepted in upscale hotels, but again it's always a good idea to check beforehand.

HOTELS

When it comes to upscale hotels in India, most regions hold a choice of converted palaces, castles or forts (so-called 'heritage hotels'), and standard five-stars equipped with all the luxuries

The stylish reception area at a Park hotel

you'd expect in Europe or North America. In both cases, bookings are best made via the hotels' own websites, where you'll be offered rates far lower than those generally available to walk-in customers. Tariffs vary wildly in this bracket, starting at around Rs7,000 per night, rising to three or four times more in exclusive boutique places. On top of your bill will be added a government-imposed luxury tax, ranging from 7–13 percent depending on the state, and a more nebulous 'service charge' slapped on by the hotel itself.

Pitched at Indian families and small businessmen, mid-range hotels – basically, any places charging upwards of Rs1,000 per night – usually offer great value for money, with comfy mattresses, clean bed linen, bath towels, en suite bathrooms with hot and cold running water, balconies and TVs as standard. They'll also have basic room service and lifts between floors. Air-conditioning (or 'a/c' as it's called in India), when available, tends in this price bracket to be provided by box units in the walls rather than a central system.

BUDGET ACCOMMODATION

Budget hotels, where you can get a double room for under Rs750, fall roughly into two categories: ultra-basic 'lodges' patronised by mostly Indian travellers of modest means, where access to natural light and running water may be limited; and guesthouses set up primarily for foreign backpackers. The latter tend to be located further from train and bus stations, but are correspondingly more peaceful and pleasant, with rooftop terraces or courtyards to socialise

The delightful Villa Pottipati, near Bengaluru *(see p.215)*

Accommodation

and relax in, and clean, Western-style toilets (as against the smellier 'hole-in-the-floor' variety found in lodges).

Railway stations also have low-priced beds in so-called 'retiring rooms', which might be separate rooms or dormitories – though both tend to be in great demand and rarely available at short notice; they're allocated through the Station Master's office (generally on platform 1).

In pilgrimage destinations, very sparse dormitory accommodation, costing less than Rs100, is also available in *dharamsalas*, with communal washing facilities and toilets. Those in more remote places happily accept foreign guests, but in tourist centres where budget alternatives are to be found *dharamsala* managers will invariably insist backpackers try for a room in one of these first.

In major cities, Ys (www.ywcaindia.org; www.indianymca.org) offer inexpensive hostel accommodation – both in single-sex dormitories and separate rooms – though they tend to be institutional, operating 10pm curfews. Those in the metropolitan cities are also far from cheap, charging comparable rates to midscale hotels.

OTHER ACCOMMODATION

Homestays

A good alternative to mid-range hotel accommodation is paying guest rooms in private houses. Run through local tourist offices, these schemes offer both good-value lodging and an enjoyable way to meet local householders, though you'll obviously have less privacy than in a hotel and may be obliged to respect night curfews.

In south India, and other major tourist regions of the country, you'll also find upscale homestay accommodation, where guests can enjoy top-notch B&B in beautiful locations, such as coffee plantations, tea estates, or in stylish designer homes and beachside villas. Costing as much, or more, than five-star hotels in many cases, they tend to be in smart suburbs or else out in the countryside, and run by sophisticated, upper-class families who enjoy hosting visitors, showing them around the local sights. Most have lavishly illustrated websites with booking facilities.

Camping

Apart from mountain trekkers, no one camps in India – the prevalence of snakes, wild animals, creepy crawlies and budget lodges sees to that. There

Goa's beachside accommodation is often in the form of casual huts

are, however, numerous luxury tent camps dotted around the country, where you can stay on the fringes of wildlife reserves or in remote forest locations in old-style canvas hunting tents – a particularly popular option in Rajasthan and Madhya Pradesh. Fitted with four-poster beds, fans, minibars and attached bathrooms, and lavishly decorated with traditional textiles and handicrafts, they're often as comfortable as high-end hotel rooms, though rarely as large. The biggest concentration of them is in Pushkar, Rajasthan, during the annual camel fair, when the tourist office erects a sprawling canvas township in the desert.

Beach Huts

In the beach resorts of Goa, where government restrictions on building close to the high-tide line are zealously enforced, temporary palm-leaf shacks are a good option. They come in a variety of shapes and forms, from ultra-basic with few comforts to luxury shacks complete with a/c, costing hundreds of dollars per night in peak season.

Transport

GETTING TO INDIA

By Air

The vast majority of visitors arrive in India by air. Mumbai and Delhi airports are the major entry points, although a few international flights from Europe use Kolkata, Chennai and Bengaluru. There are direct, non-stop flights between India and the UK (where many transatlantic passengers can change) on Air India (www.airindia.com), British Airways (www.ba.com), Virgin Atlantic (www.virgin-atlantic.com) and Jet Airways (www.jetairways.com), and one-stop flights on a number of other carriers, including Emirates, Qatar, Gulf, Etihad, KLM, Austrian and Swiss. There are also charter flights in season from UK airports to Goa. These flights are laid on for package tourists, but spare tickets are sometimes sold off to independent travellers. Flying times from the UK to India vary between nine and a half and 11 hours depending on the destination.

India has extensive air connections with other countries in Asia and the Gulf. There are also direct nonstop flights from New York to Delhi and Mumbai on Air India (and also to Delhi on Continental), and from Sydney to Mumbai on Qantas.

The major airports all have left-luggage facilities, porters and licensed taxis, as well as duty-free shops in both the arrival and departure halls and banks (open 24 hours).

International airports include:
Indira Gandhi International (IGI) Airport, Delhi (tel: 011-2566 1080 (international); 011-2566 1000 (domestic); www.newdelhiairport.in) is 20km (12 miles) southwest of New Delhi.

Chhatrapati Shivaji International Airport (BOM), Mumbai (tel: 022-2681 3000 (international); 022-2626 4000 (domestic); www.csia.in) is 29km (18 miles) north of downtown.

Netaji Subhash International Airport (CCU), Kolkata (tel: 033-2232 0501) is 18km (11 miles) north of the city centre.

International Airport (MAA), Chennai (tel: 044-2552 9172; www.chennaiairportguide.com) is 16km (10 miles) southwest of the city.

International Airport (BLR), Bengaluru (tel: 080-6678 2251; www.bengaluruairport.com) is 35km (22 miles) northeast of the city.

Spicejet is a low-cost domestic airline

- **Air India** (tel: 1800-227 722/ mobile users tel: 0124-2877 777; www.airindia.com).
- **Air-India Express** (tel: 022-2831 8888; www.airindiaexpress.in).
- **Go Air** (tel: 1800-222 111/09223-222 111; www.goair.in).
- **Indian Airlines** (tel: 1407 prefixed by the nearest city code (eg in Delhi, call 011-1407) or 1800-180 1407; www.indian-airlines.nic.in).
- **IndiGo** (tel: 1800-180 3838 or 099-1038 3838; http://book.goindigo.in).
- **Jet Airways** (tel: 3989 3333 prefixed with nearest city code (eg in Delhi, call 011-3989 3333)/International flight enquiries, tel: 1800-225 522; www.jetairways.com).
- **JetLite** (formerly Air Sahara) (tel: 3030 2020 (prefixed with nearest city code) or 1800-223 020; www.jetlite.com).
- **Kingfisher Airlines** (tel: 1800-209 3030 or 3900 8888 (prefixed with the nearest city code); www.flykingfisher.com).
- **Paramount Airways** (tel: 044-4343 4444; www.paramountairways.com).
- **Spicejet** (tel: 1800-180 3333/ mobile users tel: 0987-180 3333; www.spicejet.com).

GETTING AROUND INDIA

India's vast railway network has for over a century provided an affordable means for the country's population to travel across the country. The train system is, however, chronically over-loaded, poorly maintained, slow and unreliable. Add to that the distances involved, and it's no surprise that domestic air travel has exploded at the rate it has over the past decade. New flight routes open seemingly every week in India, and since the advent of low-cost airlines challenged the monopoly of the state carrier, Indian Airlines, fares have dropped considerably. For shorter hauls, buses are incredibly cheap, while in the cities you've a bewildering choice of options, ranging from taxis to hand-pulled rickshaws *(see city fact and transport files for details)*.

Domestic Flights

Almost every city is now served by regular flights, and there is fierce competition on popular routes. Fares vary widely. Those on the up-market carriers, like Kingfisher Airlines and Jet Airways, can be relatively expensive, although fares on the more budget-conscious operators can often be a steal.

The domestic airline market is in an almost constant state of turbulence at present, and the two government-owned airlines, the flagship international carrier, Air India, and domestic operator, Indian Airlines, are currently in the laborious process of merging, leading to a certain amount of confusion in terms of services and schedules.

Tickets for all domestic airlines *(see box, left)* can be booked online through their own sites, but for comparing options, you're better off searching through www.cleartrip.com.

Boats

Apart from river ferries there are very few boat services in India. The Andaman Islands are connected to Kolkata, Chennai and Vishakapatnam by boat, as well as to each other. Kerala operates a network of regular passenger ferries

A local boat service

in its backwater districts (www.swtd.gov.in), and tourist services operate between Alappuzha and Kollam (formerly Alleppey and Quilon).

Trains

Rail travel is by far the most enjoyable way to get around the country. There are three basic types of train. The best are the **Super-fast** services: air-conditioned trains on major inter-city routes. These include the excellent **Shatabdi** daytime-only expresses, and **Rajdhani** services, which link Delhi with cities nationwide. The second category is the **Express** or 'mail' inter-city services, which are also fast and comfortable. It's generally best to avoid the third category of train, the painfully slow **passenger** services. There are also special tourist trains (see page 33). For an excellent overview of Indian railway services, check out the authoritative website, www.seat61.com/India.htm.

Fares are generally low, especially if you travel in a non-a/c class, although the price of a long-haul first-class ticket can often be as much as (or even more than) the comparable air fare.

Comprehensive timetable and fare information is available at www.indi anrail.gov.in, or the more user-friendly www.cleartrip.com.

Indian Railways has no fewer than eight different classes, of varying degrees of comfort (see box, p.256), although most trains will only have three or four different types of class.

Obviously, in the hot summer months a/c can be a good option. The drawback with a/c carriages is that they usually have tinted and/or dirty windows, which means you don't get a great view. Sleeper class and second class unreserved, by contrast, just have metal grilles over open windows, which means you'll get a better view.

Carriages have a mix of Western and Indian-style toilets – the latter are usually cleaner and less unpleasant.

Basic bedding (two sheets, a pillow and a blanket) is only provided in first class AC, AC 2-tier and 3-tier; it is also available from the attendant for Rs20 in first class. Reservations are required

Accessibility

For disabled travellers, India isn't the easiest of countries. Don't expect much by way of wheelchair facilities, or access aids – pavements present constant challenges. If you are mobility or visually impaired, travelling with an able-bodied companion has to be the recommended option. Contact a specialist organisation for advice on planning your trip. In Delhi, **Timeless India** (tel: 011-2617 4205; www.timelessexcursions.com) offers 'accessible tours' for wheelchair-bound visitors. See also the Disability India Network website: www.disabilityindia.org.

A standard sleeper-class carriage

Transport

Indian Railway Class Options

- **First class AC (AC1)** Very comfortable compartments with lockable cabins of two or four berths, arranged in tiers.
- **AC 2-tier (AC2)** Two-tier bunks in open-plan carriages arranged in groups of six berths with curtains that pull across to provide privacy.
- **AC 3-tier (AC3)** Like AC 2-tier carriages, but with three-tier bunks. The middle berths fold down when not used for sleeping.
- **AC executive chair** Found only on the most important Shatabdi services. Spacious seating in a/c carriages.
- **AC chair class** The standard class on Shatabdi services. Like executive chair class, but with slightly more cramped seating (six seats across, rather than four) and plainer carriages.
- **First class (non a/c)** This type of compartment is being phased out, and is increasingly rare. They consist of lockable compartments containing two or four berths.
- **Sleeper class** The most common class, with open-plan carriages divided into partitions of six berths with ceiling fans.
- **Second class unreserved** Open-plan carriages of hard seats (no bunks). Can get horribly crowded, although usually OK for shorter daytime journeys.

for all classes other than second class unreserved; reserving well in advance is strongly recommended. Bookings may be made up to 60 days in advance, most conveniently online (via Indian Railways' own site, www.indianrail. gov.in, or the more streamlined www. cleartrip.com). Stations in larger cities such as Delhi and Mumbai have tourist sections with English-speaking staff to reduce the queues for foreigners and non-resident Indians buying tickets, but the waits can still be interminable.

If there are no available places on the train you want, certain services have a tourist quota that may be available. Alternatively, you can try for a **Tatkal** ticket, which guarantees you access to a special 10 percent quota on most trains, though certain conditions apply. Bookable online, they are released at 8am two days before the train departs; you pay a surcharge of Rs75–150, depending on the class of travel.

Cancellations (for which you will need to fill in the same form as for a reservation) will incur a penalty.
(See also Riding the Rails, p.28.)

Buses

Virtually every part of the country is connected to India's extensive and well-developed bus system. Services range from clapped-out old rustbuckets on more rural routes to deluxe, state-of-the-art air-conditioned express coaches on the major highways. Although it's difficult to generalise, buses can often be a bit faster and cheaper than trains, with more frequent services. On the downside, they're generally less comfortable, particularly over long distances, and not quite as safe either.

Buses are either operated by private firms or by the state government. Private services tend to be more comfortable, with padded seats, tinted windows and Bollywood films on tap. On short-haul services you invariably just turn up at the bus stand and buy a ticket on board. For longer routes, however, it's generally necessary to pre-book (at the bus stand if it's a government service or company booking office if it's a private one).

Baggage is usually carried in the boot or squeezed under your seat, although it sometimes ends up on the roof, in which case it's worth locking it with a chain and padlock, and keeping an eye on it during stops en route.

Local city bus services are generally far too cramped, and confusing, to be a viable alternative to auto-rickshaws, although they work out much cheaper.

Cycling

The few cyclists who come to India intending to travel long distances tend to be hard-core mountain bikers who focus on the trans-Himalayan routes, where the traffic is more manageable and pollution negligible.

Cycling is particularly hair-raising in Indian cities, although if you're happy to take your life in your hands you can usually rent an Indian-made bicycle by the hour from street-side cycle hire shops for trips around.

The most sensible approach if you're determined to explore a region of India in the saddle is to book a tour with a cycling holiday company such as Butterfield & Robinson (www.butterfield.com). That way, you'll be guaranteed suitable routes through scenic areas, covering the quietest roads, with a support vehicle to carry your bags and someone to arrange your accommodation and food along the way.

DRIVING

Driving in India is not for the faint-hearted. Roads can be congested and dangerous, and there are many unwritten rules. City roads can often be (or appear to be) totally anarchic, and although things are a lot more peaceful in the countryside, route-finding can often be a problem. In general, it's far better, and quite often even cheaper, to hire a car and driver. If you do decide to drive, you should have an international driving licence (although this might not be insisted on if you have your driving licence from home).

Buses traverse the length and breadth of India

Health and Safety

MEDICAL CARE

No inoculations are legally required to enter India, but it is strongly advised that you get vaccinations against typhoid, hepatitis A, polio and tetanus. You may need to show proof of a yellow fever inoculation if arriving from an infected area. Other diseases against which vaccinations might be considered, particularly for longer trips, include meningitis, rabies and Japanese B encephalitis. There is no vaccination against Dengue fever; the only protection is to avoid being bitten.

Health Tips

Most health troubles that afflict travellers in India can be easily avoided by observing some simple dos and don'ts:

- Drink plenty of fluids at all times
- Never get bitten by mosquitoes; smother any exposed skin in repellent in the evenings and wear long sleeves and trousers
- Get lots of sleep (ear plugs are useful)
- Stay away from food that looks like it's been reheated or left in the open; only eat meat in busy restaurants with a fast turnover
- Don't drink tap water, not even to brush your teeth; stick to the bottled variety (better still, minimise plastic pollution by bringing your own water purification tablets)
- Go easy on alcohol: most Indian beers and liquor are laced with nasty preservatives that can play havoc with your stomach

A personal medical kit covering potential minor ailments is worth putting together (you can do this more cheaply after you arrive in India). Include anti-diarrhoea medication, a broad-spectrum antibiotic, aspirin and paracetamol and clean needles. Take your regular medications, tampons, contraceptives and condoms, as these may be difficult to find in Indian shops, or not of comparable quality.

Also include plasters, antiseptic cream and water purification tablets. All cuts, however minor, should be cleaned and sterilised immediately to prevent infection. Locally available oral rehydration powders (such as Electrolyte) containing salts and dextrose are an ideal additive to water, especially when travelling in the summer months or when suffering from diarrhoea.

Malaria

This mosquito-borne disease is very serious and potentially fatal. There are two common strains in India, both carried by the Anopheles mosquito. Symptoms are similar to acute flu (including some or all of fever, shivering, diarrhoea and muscle pains), and an outbreak may come on as much as a year after visiting a malarial area. If malaria is suspected then medical attention should be sought as soon as possible.

Malaria risk varies in different parts of the country (see the useful malaria map at www.fitfortravel.scot.nhs. uk). Malaria prophylaxis is not always considered necessary (and will never be needed at high altitudes above 2,500m/8,200ft); discuss your needs with your doctor before travel.

The best, and only certain, protection against malaria is not to get bitten. Sleep under a mosquito net impregnated with permethrin, cover up in the evenings and use an effective insect repellent such as DEET. Burning mosquito coils, which are easily obtainable in India, is also a good idea.

Diarrhoea

Traveller's diarrhoea is usually caused by low-level food poisoning and can be avoided with a little care. When you arrive, rest on your first day and only eat simple food such as boiled rice, yoghurt (called 'curd' in India) and banana. An upset stomach is often caused by eating too many rich Indian meat dishes (usually cooked with vast amounts of oil and spices) and failing to rest and let your body acclimatise.

Even the monkeys stick to bottled water

Drink plenty of fluids (although it's best to avoid unboiled or unfiltered tap water). When in doubt, stick to soda, mineral water or aerated drinks of standard brands. Avoid ice as this is often made with unboiled water. All food should be cooked and eaten hot. Don't eat salads and always peel fruit.

With all cases of diarrhoea, it is not a good idea to use imobilising drugs such as loperamide (Imodium) and atropine (Lomotil), unless absolutely necessary – such as for the duration of a bus journey – as they prevent the body ridding itself of infection. The most important thing to do in cases of diarrhoea and/or vomiting is to rehydrate, preferably using oral rehydration salts.

Dysentery and giardia are more serious forms of stomach infection and should be suspected if the diarrhoea lasts for more than two days. Amoebic dysentery and giardia have a slow onset and will not clear up on their own; if you suspect you have either, seek medical help as soon as possible.

Water

Tap water, especially in larger cities, is generally chlorinated and (in theory, at least) safe to drink, although it's best to stick to bottled or filtered water, since the unfamiliar micro-organisms in the mains supply can precipitate mild stomach upsets – or worse if the water has been sitting for some time in a roof tank.

259

Health and Safety

- **Australia High Commission**
  1/50 G Shantipath, Chanakyapuri, Delhi
  Tel: 011-4139 9900
  www.india.embassy.gov.au
- **Canada High Commission**
  7–8 Shantipath, Chanakyapuri, Delhi 110 021
  Tel: 011-4178 2000
  http://india.gc.ca
- **Ireland Embassy**
  230 Jor Bagh, Delhi 110 003
  Tel: 011-2462 6733
  www.irelandinindia.com
- **New Zealand High Commission**
  Sir Edmund Hillary Marg, Chanakyapuri, Delhi 110 021
  Tel: 011-2688 3170
  www.nzembassy.com/india
- **UK High Commission**
  Shantipath, Chanakyapuri, Delhi 110 021
  Tel: 011-2687 2161
  http://ukinindia.fco.gov.uk/en

Altitude Sickness

This can occur above 2,500m (8,200ft). Watch for symptoms of breathlessness, palpitations, headache, insomnia and loss of appetite. With total rest, travellers usually acclimatise within 48 hours. It is important that fluid intake is maintained; at least 4 to 6 litres per day is recommended.

A severe attack, brought on by climbing too high or quickly, is marked by dizziness, nausea, vomiting, severe thirst, blurred vision, weakness or hearing difficulties. The only cure is to descend to a lower altitude at once.

Hospitals

In an emergency you can call an ambulance by dialling 102 or 108 (although depending on how ill you are, you might find it better just to jump in a taxi/rickshaw and make your own way to the nearest hospital). For other forms of assistance following an emergency, contact **East West Rescue** (38 Golf Links, New Delhi; tel: 011-2469 8865; www.eastwestrescue.com). They operate over the whole country and have an extremely good reputation.

Standards of care are comparable with the West in private hospitals, through conditions in government-run hospitals and clinics fall well short of this. Treatment is free in government places, and inexpensive in private hospitals: note that you pay in advance of consulations, tests and treatments. Always obtain comprehensive travel insurance before leaving home.

Sun Exposure

The power of the sun is obvious on the plains and in tropical India, but also be careful in the mountains, where thinner air makes the sun very powerful, even if it feels cooler. Cover up and use a high-factor sunscreen, even if it is cloudy. Overexposure can lead to heat exhaustion, while heatstroke is more serious, and may occur when it is both hot and humid. Babies and elderly people are especially susceptible. The body temperature soars suddenly and the skin feels dry. Take sufferers quickly to a cool room, remove their clothes and cover them with a wet sheet or towels. Call for medical help and fan them constantly until their body temperature drops to 38°C (100°F).

Insect Bites and Stings

Bed bugs can be a problem in cheap hotels; look out for the marks of squashed insects on the walls and floor around the bed. Leeches can also be a problem in wet jungle areas; remove with a lit match or cigarette, or salt.

CRIME

One wouldn't expect to recover a camera left on a park bench anywhere in the world, and India is no exception. However, your valuables are probably less at risk in India than in many parts of the West. Common-sense precautions go a long way: don't leave valuables lying around, and avoid being obvious – a few hundred dollars are a year's earnings to many people. Take particular care to safeguard your passport and credit/ATM cards, particularly when travelling by bus and train. A photocopy of your passport, Indian visa and flight ticket should be kept separately from the originals when travelling. Be wary of confidence tricksters, particularly in Agra, Jaipur and Delhi.

Violence against foreigners is not unknown in India, but it is probably safer to walk through Delhi late at night than many places back home. In parts of the country, such as Goa and the hippy villages of Himachal Pradesh, where drug use among foreigners is common, you're probably more at risk from fellow travellers. Incidents of sexual offences against women occur from time to time, notably in Goa, Delhi and Rajasthan. Lone female travellers are advised to take particular care and basic personal safety precautions.

Travellers are potentially at risk from attacks by terrorists anywhere in

Take care in the hot sun on beaches

the country. There have been numerous high-profile outrages in recent years targeting railway stations, cricket stadia, bars, cafés and other places tourists congregate. Delhi is regarded as a particularly high-risk location at present, so avoid spending time in the tourist ghetto of Paharganj, and shopping centres where large numbers of visitors and expats gather.

Current official advice is to steer clear of Kashmir, even though there has been a marked decrease in violence there over the past few years. Other regions the FCO advises against visiting include Manipur and Tripura in the northeast hills, and rural areas of Jharkland, Chhattisgarh and Orissa.

Police

Indian police have earned a reputation for being incorrigibly corrupt. As a foreigner, any dealings with the police – such as reporting a theft – are likely to involve requests for a small bribe – Rs500 should suffice to oil the wheels. Should you be arrested, contact your consulate at the first opportunity.

Money and Budgeting

CURRENCY

India's currency is the Rupee (Rs), divided into 100 paise. Coins come in units of 5, 10, 25 and 50 paise, and 1, 2 and 5 rupees. Banknotes exist in denominations of Rs5, 10, 20, 50, 100 and 500. It can sometimes be difficult to distinguish between the Rs100 and Rs500 notes, especially in your first few days in India, or under dim street lights.

There exists throughout India a chronic shortage of small notes. Taxi drivers and rickshaw-wallahs in particular will rarely admit to having any, forcing you to part with yours or engage in a bluff of your own. When changing money, therefore, it's a good idea to request part of the sum drawn in small denominations.

Excessive wear and tear on the few small notes that are in circulation has reduced most of them to a dreadful state. Indians are very picky about the condition of money paid to them though, and the tiniest of rips will be grounds enough to refuse a note – trying to palm off spoilt notes on to someone else is a national pastime. Expect grubby, holed and torn Rs5 notes to build up after a time. You can exchange them for new ones at a bank; better still, give them to someone on the street who looks like they might need them more than you.

There is no upper limit on the amount of foreign currency visitors are permitted to bring to India, but you're not allowed to take any rupees out of the country without clearance.

CASH AND CARDS

Foreign currency and traveller's cheques may be exchanged at most banks during working hours (Mon–Fri 10am–2.30pm, Sat 10am–noon). You'll be charged a percentage commission or flat fee for the service, but the main disadvantage with drawing money this way is the often long waits involved for the paperwork to inch its way through the ranks of sleepy clerks and tellers. If you've brought American Express or Thomas Cook traveller's cheques, it's worth going out of your way to change them free of commission at dedicated Amex or Thomas Cook offices.

Credit and Debit Cards

The major plastic payment cards are accepted at most upscale shops, hotels and restaurants in India, but if you're in any doubt check first. Also, it's wise to ensure if the transaction is made using an old-fashioned paper docket rather than chip-and-pin handset that you don't let your card out of your sight.

ATMs (Automatic Teller Machines) are attached to all major banks these days (usually in air-conditioned annexes guarded by armed doormen), and these offer a fast, convenient way to withdraw money. In terms of cost, drawing cash at an ATM may even work out cheaper than traveller's cheques: the exchange rates are usually better and the transaction charges lower (though the percentage of

India remains great value when buying local goods; always carry small notes

commission should be checked with your bank before leaving home).

The main disadvantage with relying on a credit or debit card as your main source of currency is that you'll be in a sticky situation should you lose it, or if it's swallowed by the ATM (Indian banks are obliged to return any withheld cards to their originating branch, even if it's abroad). Always carry some kind of backup, and bring some emergency hard currency or traveller's cheques too, along with the telephone number of your bank at home should you need to contact it urgently.

TIPPING

There's no harm in expressing your appreciation with a small tip, although be aware that many up-market hotels and restaurants automatically add a 10 percent service charge to their bills, so there's no need to tip further (unless you particularly want to). If service isn't included, a tip of around 10 percent is generally a good rule of thumb.

Porters at railway stations expect around Rs20 a bag. Rickshaw and taxi drivers won't expect to be tipped, although of course they'll appreciate it if you do – or just letting them keep the change, assuming it's not too much, does equally well. If you have been a house guest, check with your host whether you may tip the domestic helpers (for instance, the driver or cook) before doing so.

TAX

India does not levy a flat-rate VAT. Instead, numerous separate consumption taxes are charged on things like tariffs in luxury hotels (9–13 percent, state-dependent), liquor and meals in high-end hotels – to name but a few.

BUDGETING FOR YOUR TRIP

Despite rapidly rising prices, India remains considerably cheaper than the UK and US, especially when it comes to goods and services used by ordinary Indians, who typically earn 10 times less than people in more developed parts of the world.

Flights to India from the UK start at around £400, rising to £600 in peak periods, or £1,700–3,000 for first class. From the US you're looking at around $1,000 from New York or $1,400 from the West Coast.

For a budget, backpacker-style holiday you will need to set aside Rs8,000–10,000 (£120–150/US$175–210) per person per week. A standard family holiday for four will cost around Rs30,000 (£400/US$600) per week. A luxury, no-expense-spared break can cost over Rs70,000 (£1,000/US$1,500) per person per week.

Responsible Travel

ECOTOURISM

Many tourism authorities and operators have been quick to jump on the green bandwagon, setting up all manner of 'eco resorts' designed to attract would-be ethical travellers. Just how green many of these are is a matter of conjecture; luxury lodges in rainforests or on remote beaches are inherently polluting just by being there, no matter how scrupulous they are about recycling their waste and water.

Eight Steps to a More Ethical Holiday

- Travel overland rather than by air whenever possible
- Stay longer in one place
- Cycle-rickshaws may be slower than auto-rickshaws and taxis, but they're far greener, and provide livelihoods for some of India's poorest citizens
- Reduce the impact of flying to India by offsetting your carbon emissions; visit www.climatecare.org.
- Purify your own water rather than buy it in plastic bottles
- Dispose of all waste responsibly; outside the metropolitan cities it will probably be burnt after you've left, releasing harmful toxins
- Patronise small-scale, family-run, locally owned businesses rather than large-scale ones whose profits do not benefit the host community
- In coastal resorts, keep your water use to a minimum – dry-season shortages occur when visitors guzzle the annual supply in a few months over the winter

That said, there exist businesses genuinely committed to low-impact tourism. Some gold-standard examples include **Green Hotel** in Mysore (www.greenhotelindia.com), a former royal palace restored as an eco hotel, with all profits funding local charities; **ROSE** in Baijnath, Uttaranchal (www.rosekanda.info), which offers grassroots tourism, providing homestays in a Himalayan village with profits going to local projects; and **Periyar Wildlife Sanctuary** in Kerala (www.periyartigerreserve.org), which employs local tribal people as tourist guides and wildlife wardens. Profits go to conservation work.

VOLUNTEERING

Taking time out of your trip to volunteer for a charity can be a positive way to experience India from the inside. Most of these recommended NGOs welcome volunteers; they all depend on donations to continue their work: **Children Walking Tall**, based in Mapusa, Goa (tel: 09822-124 802; www.childrenwalkingtall.com) is a British-run operation helping slum children in north Goa. **DISHA Foundation Disha Path**, based in Rajasthan (tel: 0141-239 3319; www.dishafoundation.org) is a resource centre for kids with cerebral palsy. Needs donations, sponsors, and volunteers with time or specific skills. **SOS Children's Villages of India** (tel: 011-2435 7299; www.soscvindia.org) has projects across India, helping many children in need.

Family Holidays

TRAVEL WITH CHILDREN

Indians love children and are very tolerant of them; noone will be bothered, for example, by your child throwing a tantrum, or consider it inappropriate for you to be travelling with them, no matter how remote the location.

On the other hand, Indian people generally make little provision for kids when out and about, so don't expect such luxuries as nappy-changing facilities, high chairs or kids' menus in restaurants. If you want a car seat for your children to sit in, you'll have to bring it from home as Indian car-driver rental outfits don't offer them. Buggies and pushchairs are also a rare sight in most of India. The easiest solution is to bring a lightweight fold-up, which can easily be stowed while travelling. Backpack child-carriers are even more adaptable, with the added convenience of keeping your child safe in crowded markets.

CHILDREN'S HEALTH

The potential downside with travelling in India with your children is the inevitable health risk. Little ones, of course, can be more easily affected by the heat, unsafe drinking water and unfamiliar food seasoned with chillies. To avoid the risk of rabies, children should be vaccinated and kept away from stray animals – especially dogs and monkeys.

Make sure you boil all water and milk wherever you are, to kill any potentially harmful bacteria. Powdered milk is widely available, but bring any sterilisation kit you need with you.

Children will be welcomed in India

Family Holidays

ACCOMMODATION

It's more normal for Indians to travel in family groups than not, and every hotel can fix up additional beds for your children for a small additional charge. Nowhere, however, should you expect to find a baby's cot as standard – though some resort hotels in Goa may keep them if they regularly accommodate charter tourists (check with your tour operator). Phil & Teds (wwwphil andteds.com) make lightweight travel cots, weighing as little as 2.5kg/5.5lbs – worth the investment if you intend to cover much distance during your trip.

Unfortunately, rented houses are rare, and in those popular resorts where they do exist are usually either very expensive or else booked up well in advance. Goa is one of the child-friendliest places for a holiday in India, though, with lots of safe beaches and family accommodation to suit all budgets.

History

BEGINNINGS

Neolithic remains have been unearthed in northwest India dating back to around 6500BC, but the first traces of planned, agrarian societies derive from 2500BC, with the Harappan civilisation of the Indus Valley region. Many objects, notably seals, have been found amid the remains of Harappan's astonishingly well-planned towns and cities, bearing elaborate depictions of humans and animals, some with the symbols of an as yet un-deciphered script. In the second millennium BC, however, the Harappan civilisation went into decline and eventually expired – possibly due to flooding and desertification.

Around 1500BC, the so-called Aryan tribes from Central Asia invaded northwest India. Their horses, chariots and semi-nomadic lifestyle gave them considerable advantage in warfare. Although there is virtually no archaeological evidence from this early period, the Aryans composed a series of orally transmitted Sanskrit religious and secular verses, the *Rig Veda*, which give some idea of their highly stratified society. When the indigenous people were subjugated, they became a class of low labourers, the Shudra. Later, another class was added whom even the Shudra despised; these were the 'untouchables'. As the Aryans became more settled, agriculture flourished and the population grew rapidly.

In 326BC, Alexander the Great invaded India. Having crossed the Indus River, his army defeated some Aryans, but became exhausted and was forced to return, opening the way for Magadha, the largest kingdom of the northern plains, to expand into the areas the Macedonians had conquered.

MAURYANS AND GUPTAS

Chandragupta Maurya became king of Magadha around 324BC. He established in the wake of Alexander's departure a vast empire, stretching from Afghanistan southwards all the way to Karnataka, where it is said he passed his final days as a Jain monk. The capital at Pataliputra (now Patna, in Bihar) on the banks of the Ganges was 13km (8 miles) long, and surrounded by a wall with 570 towers. During this period, weights and measures were standardised, coins were minted and wages fixed.

1st-century BC carving of Ashoka Chakravatin

The most famous Mauryan ruler of ancient India was Chandragupta's grandson, Ashoka, who conquered the Kingdom of Kalinga (modern-day Orissa), but later he regretted the bloodshed and converted to Buddhism. He had edicts, written in Brahmi, the first Indian script, carved on pillars throughout the empire, calling for wise government and a moral lifestyle. During his reign, Pataliputra became the world's then-biggest city.

Following the decline of the Mauryans, the second vast empire in Indian history emerged in the 4th century AD. Under the Guptas (AD320 to AD700), Buddhists and Brahmins lived in peaceful co-existence; trade, literature, science and the arts flourished, and a more rigidly hierarchical, feudal, male-dominated society evolved.

THE SOUTH

The people of south India were Dravidians, speaking languages that bore no relationship to those of the north. It is presumed that they predate the arrival of the Aryans. They were fortunate in having produce, such as pearls and pepper, which was in great demand, bringing Romans to their ports, as well as traders from Southeast Asia and China. Although the region lacked the great flood plains of the north, the Dravidians developed sophisticated irrigation systems that boosted agricultural productivity, and with their wealth they developed advanced kingdoms.

The early trade links of southern India brought Christianity in the 1st century (it is believed that St Thomas the Apostle arrived on the Kerala coast in AD52). Buddhism and Jainism also had many adherents until the 7th century, but when the Pallava king transferred his patronage to Shavism, the worship of the Hindu god Shiva, the Hindus gained ground. Arab traders brought Islam to what is now Kerala, and the first mosques were built in the 7th century. There was no conflict with the Hindus or Christians – a peaceful co-existence that was to continue.

THE SULTANATES

In the north, by contrast, the arrival of Islam was extremely violent. A Turkish Islamic dynasty had established itself at Ghazni in Afghanistan in the 10th century, and in 997, Mahmud of Ghanzi started making annual raids into India, his armies looting, killing and sacking Hindu temples without mercy. By the 12th century, after Muhammad of Ghur had taken Lahore and Delhi, Buddhism had almost been extinguished in the land of its birth. A new state was established in 1206 which came to be known as the Delhi Sultanate; it would pass down through five dynasties and last for 320 years.

THE MUGHALS

The eventual collapse of the Delhi Sultanate opened the way for a new force. Babur, the first of the Mughal emperors, defeated the Sultan of Delhi's army at Panipat in 1526. It was during the reign of his grandson Akbar (1556–1605) that the basic institutions and policies of the empire were framed. To cement his rule he took several of the daughters of his former Rajput enemies as wives; unlike previous Muslim rulers, he allowed them to continue to practise Hinduism. Akbar used religion to consolidate his position, realising that any dynasty that wanted to rule India needed support from both Hindus and Muslims.

A keen interest in the arts was characteristic of the Mughal Empire. Monuments left by Shah Jahan, Akbar's grandson, include the Taj Mahal, built in memory of his queen who had died giving birth to their 14th child, and the Red Fort and Jama Masjid in Delhi, which became his capital.

A considerably more austere regime, including the banning of music, was later imposed by Aurangzeb, an ultra-orthodox Muslim who came to the throne after imprisoning his father and killing his brothers. Along with prayer, war with the princedoms of Rajasthan and the troublesome Marathas, led by the warlord Shivaji, was the major obsession of India's last great Mughal ruler in the twilight of his reign.

EUROPEANS

By the time of Aurangzeb's death in 1707, Europeans had become established in India. It was the Portuguese who were the first to begin trading when, in 1498, the explorer Vasco da Gama landed at Calicut, having sailed via the Cape of Good Hope. He arrived in Malabar (Kerala) looking for a mythical Christian empire and spices, which were in great demand in Europe.

Knowing that Goa had an excellent harbour, the Portuguese set about conquering it. Other European countries followed their lead, and in the 17th century, England, France, the Netherlands and Denmark all launched East India Companies, trading mainly textiles from a chain of fortified 'factories' established along the Indian coastline.

The 1857 'Mutiny' had a lasting effect

COMPANY RAJ

Following a century or more of skirmishes between these European states and their Indian allies – both on land and at sea – the seminal contest for power in the subcontinent came down to the struggle between the English and the French. It was in Bengal that the former, led by Sir Robert Clive, made the first successful bid for rule, stepping into the vacuum left after the disintegration of the Mughal Empire

Successful wars against the Marathas and the Sikhs ensued, concluding in treaties that relieved local rulers of all but symbolic power. A huge army, comprised mostly of Indians, facilitated the ongoing expansion, and by 1850 most of the subcontinent had either directly or indirectly fallen under British rule.

Calcutta (modern-day Kolkata) emerged as the capital in India, and the centre of the lucrative opium trade with China. Opium was in the 1830s the world's most valuable trade commodity and most of it was grown on East India Company estates in Rajasthan and Gujarat, with profits used to purchase Chinese tea, which was then sold at further profit back in Britain. Over time, the British were able to find and smuggle tea bushes out of China and cultivate their own in newly opened land in the Himalayan foothills around Darjeeling, Assam and the Nilgiris in the far south. By the 1890s India was exporting more tea than China.

Growing unease at British domination of the subcontinent coalesced in the 1850s into a full-scale Uprising, sparked off by rumours that new cartridges being used by the Company's *sepoys* (native troops) had been coated with fat from cows and pigs, offensive to Hindus and Muslims respectively. On 10 May 1857, soldiers at Meerut, near Delhi, mutinied and headed for the capital. As the bloody battle raged, unrest spread like wildfire across the northern plains. Thousands of lives were lost before the so-called Mutiny was finally quashed and peace re-established on 8 July 1858.

In victory, the British showed no mercy. Roads were lined with gallows, whole villages destroyed and captured Mutineers fired from cannons. The psychological legacy would endure for decades, fuelling deep resentment among both Hindus and the Muslims at British rule, and erasing at a stroke any trust and respect the British may have held for their Indian subjects. In 1876, with the population firmly under the colonial yoke, Queen Victoria was proclaimed Empress of India.

THE INDEPENDENCE MOVEMENT

When World War I broke out in 1914, all factions in India offered their loyalty, including the pro-independence Congress party, whose leaders imagined their support would yield self-government. Victory over Germany, however, did not bring the expected transfer of power. On the contrary: Bengal was partitioned between the predominantly Muslim east and Hindu west – widely seen as a further enforcement of Britain's policy of divide and rule. There were mass protests all over the country, marshalled by the Congress party and its leaders, foremost among them Mohandas Karamchand Gandhi, who advocated non-violent protest to bring about the end of British rule.

The freedom struggle intensified in 1919, after British troops opened fire on a crowd of peaceful demonstrators in Amritsar. Killing 400 and injuring 1,200 or more, the so-called Jallianwala Bagh massacre had far-reaching repercussions, converting millions of former supporters of British rule into committed nationalists.

The Prince of Wales's visit to India in 1921 was greeted with the imprisonment without trial of 20,000 activists. Gandhi embarked on a new crusade in 1930 which captured the imagination of the world. Staged in opposition to Britain's monopoly on the manufacture of salt (which the British taxed), the Mahatma led a movement to make salt from the sea, leading to his arrest, along with that of the entire working committee of Congress.

When World War II broke out in 1939, Congress decided to oppose the war effort, and what it regarded as India's undemocratic involvement in it, by launching the 'Quit India' campaign in 1942. Demonstrations and violence led to 60,000 arrests. Notwithstanding, many Indians supported the British in the war, and the Indian army grew tenfold to 2 million.

FREEDOM AT MIDNIGHT

A Labour government sympathetic to Indian Independence came to power after the war. Talks to devise a constitution were held, but ended in stalemate. Jinnah, the leader of the Muslim League, felt his people were being marginalised and resorted to direct action. Muslim demonstrations in Calcutta degenerated into attacks on Hindus; the Hindus retaliated, and within three days, 5,000 had died, spreading the violence to cities across India.

The Viceroy then made the step of asking the Congress leader, Jawaharlal Nehru, to form an interim government. In February 1947, Britain announced it would hand over power by June 1948, dispatching Lord Mountbatten, a man of great charm who was related to the British royal family, as the Viceroy who would negotiate the transfer.

Thus the end of empire was accelerated beyond most of the participants' wildest expectations – with disastrous consequences. The announcement that Partition would create two independent countries – India and Pakistan – sparked a frantic scramble as millions of Indian Muslims fled to Pakistan, and Hindus and Sikhs travelled in the opposite direction. Around half a million people died in the violence, and 10 million people changed countries.

THE NEHRU DYNASTY

At midnight on 14 August 1947, Nehru, India's first prime minister, proclaimed Indian independence. A majority of the former Princely States acceded peacefully, although some were taken by force. Kashmir prevaricated longer than most, and in the end Nehru deployed the army to forestall the Pathan militiamen who'd entered the state from Pakistan. The region was eventually split in two along the ceasefire line – the roots of a bitter dispute between India and its neighbour which continues to the present day.

Gandhi, meanwhile, was appalled by the attacks on Muslims breaking out across the newly independent country, and staged a hunger strike to bring the atrocities to an end. But Hindu nationalists resented the Mahatma for his liberal views and assassinated him as he walked to his prayer platform in Delhi. The shock brought the nation to its senses, allowing Nehru to act against the extremists and impose order.

Nehru's new India was broadly Socialist, with an economy directed from the centre through a series of five-year plans. Major facilities were installed to manufacture steel, fertilisers and cement, and to build the power stations India needed.

Two years after Nehru's death in 1964, his daughter Indira Gandhi (not related to MK Gandhi) became prime minister. Armed conflict with Pakistan over Kashmir erupted soon after – the first of two major wars with India's neighbours during her premiership. The second, in 1971, resulted in the creation of Bangladesh and a flood of refugees into Calcutta and West Bengal.

Indira's hard-nosed foreign policy was matched by an equally authoritative stance at home. After agrarian and civil unrest emboldened the opposition to call for her government's resignation in 1974, the prime minister declared a State of Emergency, suspending press freedom and civil rights, and imprisoning thousands of perceived opponents. She suffered a landslide defeat at the next elections, but the coalition that followed lasted only two years. By 1980 the iron lady was back in power again.

Indira Gandhi's second term in office was dominated by civil strife in India's most affluent state, the Punjab. In 1984, militant separatists agitating for a Sikh homeland occupied the Golden Temple at Amritsar. Mrs Gandhi ordered in the army and in the ensuing shoot, lasting two days, thousands were killed and terrible damage inflicted on the holy shrine. Eighteen months later two of Indira Gandhi's Sikh bodyguards gunned her down by way of retribution. As news of Indira's death spread, Hindus took to the streets of Delhi, and thousands of Sikhs were massacred.

Her son Rajiv took power. A champion of new technology and modern management, he initiated a programme of radical economic liberalisation, but failed to carry the country with him and lost the 1989 election to V.P. Singh's National Front coalition. In a short but important tenure, Singh introduced legislation to reserve a proportion of government jobs for 'OBCs' – 'Other Backward Classes' – the lower-caste Hindus who had been historically disadvantaged; this had a considerable long-term effect on social mobility.

Rajiv Gandhi was assassinated by a Tamil woman suicide bomber in 1991. Elections then brought Congress back to power under Prime Minister P.V. Narasimha Rao. The Indian stock exchange was opened to foreigners and foreign capital poured in; industrial production and exports grew rapidly.

THE RISE OF THE BJP

In 1992 a group of Hindu zealots destroyed a 16th-century mosque at Ayodhya, Uttar Pradesh, provoking riots. A series of devastating bombs in Mumbai soon after, which killed

The fathers of modern India: Jawaharlal Nehru and Mahatma Gandhi

250 people, was widely interpreted as a Muslim backlash. Reprisals were, in turn, made against Muslims, and the country seemed briefly to be teetering on the brink of all-out civil war.

The BJP (Bharatiya Janata Party), political arm of a resurgent Hindu right-wing, was able to take advantage of the sectarian unrest. In 1998 the BJP did well in elections and its leader, A.B. Vajpayee, became prime minister. The BJP's promotion of Hindu nationalism saw scientific and cultural institutions purged of those who did not follow the pro-Hindu line. Meanwhile, violence against Hindus led to anti-Muslim riots across Gujarat. About 2,000 Muslims were killed and 150,000 fled to refugee camps.

Relations with Pakistan grew more strained through the 1990s. After the Indian government authorised nuclear tests in the Thar Desert, Pakistan detonated its own bomb. In 2001 an attack by terrorists on the Indian parliament, thought to have been backed by Pakistan, brought the two countries perilously close to nuclear war.

THE RETURN OF CONGRESS

By 2004, the upper part of society had never had it so good. The poor, however, had seen very little improvement, and, in that year's elections, unexpectedly voted in Congress and the widow of Rajiv Gandhi, Sonia. Italian-born and Catholic, she would have been unacceptable to many and shrewdly decided to exercise her influence from behind the scenes, nominating ex-Finance Minister, Manmohan Singh, to lead the country. The economy continued to grow strongly.

India's 'Iron Lady': Indira Gandhi

TERRORIST ATTACKS

Relative calm was shattered at the end of 2008 when a series of bombs, placed by Pakistani-backed militants, erupted across northern India. This new wave of violence hit international headlines when jihadi gunmen attacked two luxury hotels, stations, hospitals, a synagogue and innocent bystanders in Mumbai. By the time Indian commandos and police had regained control, 173 had been killed. Security was stepped up across the country.

In April 2009, the opening day of polling in general elections, which resulted in an unexpected triumph for the Congress Party, was marred by further attacks, this time by Maoist rebels in Bihar, Orissa and elsewhere.

Despite repeated droughts and the global economic downturn, India's growth rates continue to break records. Signs of the boom are ubiquitous in the cities. But the gap dividing rich and poor remains a chasm in the countryside, with more than three-quarters of India's 1.2 billion inhabitants subsisting on under £1.30 ($2) per day.

Historical Landmarks

2500–1600BC
Harappan (Indus Valley) Civilisation.

1500BC ONWARDS
Central Asian Aryans migrate to the Indian subcontinent.

563BC
Birth of Siddhartha Gautama, the Buddha.

c.325BC
Chandragupta Maurya founds the Mauryan empire.

c.260BC
King Ashoka converts to Buddhism.

c.AD320
Gupta empire is established.

c.1200
Muslim armies conquer northern India; decline of Buddhism.

1498
Vasco da Gama reaches India.

1526
Babur overthrows Delhi sultanate, establishes Mughal empire.

1642
East India Company opens trading station at Madras (Chennai).

1756
Nawab of Bengal attacks Calcutta; reprisals by Robert Clive consolidate British Empire in India.

1857
Indian Mutiny; India comes under direct British rule.

1885
First meeting of Indian National Congress.

1911
King George V announces that the capital will be transferred to Delhi.

1920–22
Mahatma Gandhi leads Non-Cooperation campaign.

1947
Independence; partition of subcontinent into India and Pakistan.

1948
Assassination of Mahatma Gandhi.

1965
Pakistan invades Kashmir.

1971
Creation of Bangladesh, with Indian support.

1975–77
Indira Gandhi imposes state of emergency.

1984
Indira Gandhi is assassinated following attacks on Golden Temple.

1991
Rajiv Gandhi is assassinated.

1999
War with Pakistan-backed forces around Kargil in Indian Kashmir.

2003
Kashmir cease-fire begins a thawing of relations with Pakistan.

2004
Manmohan Singh elected prime minister; tsunami hits east coast.

2006
In Mumbai, 207 rail commuters die in terrorist bomb blasts.

2008
Gunmen attack the main tourist and business area of Mumbai; 172 dead.

2009
Parliamentary elections held in April–May.

Culture

The term 'culture shock' could have been invented to describe arriving in India, and although widespread westernisation ensures a degree of familiarity for new arrivals these days, even old hands take a deep breath before stepping off the plane in Delhi or Mumbai. Nothing can fully prepare you for that first encounter with the roads outside the airport – the unfamiliar sounds and smells, the density of traffic and apparent absence of rules, the insouciance of drivers weaving at breakneck speeds along the highways, and grinding poverty arranged alongside them.

Once out and about, things that frequently puzzle the uninitiated include the free-for-all nature of Indian 'queues' – don't be surprised to be barged out of the way while attempting to board a train – and the level to which you will be stared and giggled at by strangers. However, when it comes to making yourself understood, rest assured that English is widely spoken in all but the most remote areas, if frequently with a thick accent and turns of phrase that take some getting used to.

INDIAN SOCIETY

With almost 1.2 billion people – around 17 percent of the world's total population – and a bewilderingly diverse range of cultures, languages, castes, sub-castes and belief systems, it is an impossible task to identify a single 'Indian' society. Even so, a few cohering principles may be identified.

Caste

For thousands of years, the overarching form of social organisation in South Asia has been the caste system, a highly stratified hierarchy of social groups defined by their hereditary occupations. Its roots derive from the Aryan colonisers who swept across northern India between 1800BC and 1400BC. The fair-skinned Aryans differentiated between their own three social *varnas* (literally 'colours') – brahmins (priests), kshatriyas (rulers and warriors) and vaishyas (traders and farmers) – and those of the darker-skinned people they subjugated, the shudras, who worked as servants. Below them lay a fifth class of 'outcastes' called panchamas – a term applied to aboriginal groups who through hunting, and polluting occupations such as latrine cleaning, tanning, butchery and corpse disposal, were beyond the social framework.

So deeply ingrained were notions of pollution in traditional Hindu society that members of the higher castes who came within a hundred paces of a

Students at a girls' school; improving literacy is still an issue in rural areas

shudra, or, worse still, an untouchable, would have to endure lengthy purificatory rituals. Today, caste is technically banned under the Indian Constitution, and members of Scheduled and Other Backward Castes (SBCs and OBCs) benefit from various forms of positive discrimination. Even so, no one denies that the old divisions persist, particularly in more rural parts of the country.

Rich and Poor

Caste is often linked to poverty in India, for the simple reason that most of the country's poor are drawn from those at the bottom of the traditional hierarchy. And there are lots of them, however you choose to define poverty. According to World Bank estimates, 42.5 percent of children in India are malnourished, while 456 million people (41.5 percent of the total population) live under the global poverty line. The persistence of such deprivation has to a large extent been masked from an international perspective by the economic boom of the past two or three decades. Since the liberalising reforms of the 1990s, the Indian economy has expanded at a dizzying speed, with current growth rates hovering around 7 percent year on year.

Little of this wealth, however, has trickled down to India's most disadvantaged citizens. Instead, the new prosperity has benefited India's middle class. Best identified by their ability to afford Western-style consumer goods and luxuries, the middle classes' affluence has transformed the complexion of the metropolitan cities, where massive shopping malls, swanky apartment blocks and campuses of air-conditioned

Bustling Kolkata, one of the major cities where wealth and poverty live side by side

offices form huge new suburbs. Thanks largely to the rapid expansion of the IT sector, back-office support and call centres, a workforce of young professionals nowadays commands salaries that would have been beyond the wildest dreams of their parents.

India's big cities are where the widening gulf between rich and poor is most apparent. With little prospect of improvements in living standards, poor landless labourers and their families are deserting the countryside in droves to settle in huge urban shanty towns, the majority of them lacking sewerage disposal and access to clean water.

Closing the gap between the haves and the have nots is the major challenge facing India's politicians today, though one which on present showing seems to have met with little success. All the evidence shows that India does not lack the resources it needs to eradicate poverty, so much as the integrity among its leaders to ensure those resources are equitably distributed.

Culture

RELIGIONS

India is often said to be the most religious place on earth – and with good reason. Four of the world's great faiths originated here (Hinduism, Buddhism, Jainism and Sikhism), with Islam, Christianity and a wealth of other religions very much in evidence.

Hinduism

Followed by over 80 percent of the population, India's dominant religion, Hinduism, is best characterised as an amalgam of diverse beliefs and practices. It has no special founders or prophets, nor any single holy book. Literally thousands of deities are revered – whether in gigantic temples or humble tree shrines. Some Hindus are strict vegetarians; others regularly perform blood sacrifices. In the Himalayas, some ascetics practise extreme forms of self-mortification, while in rural Bengal, itinerant Bauls seek God through Tantric sex and smoking ganja.

The origins of Hinduism may be traced back to the middle of the second millennium BC, when the nomadic Aryan herders invaded northern India from the steppes of Central Asia, bringing with them notions of caste, ritual pollution and reverence for cattle – all features that have endured in Hinduism to this day. The minutiae of the Aryans' religious practices were set down in the *Rig Veda*, a huge compendium of hymns and instructions for rituals, thought to have been transmitted orally for centuries before being set in writing in the first millennium AD. As these Vedic teachings spread southwards, disseminated by brahmin priests, they absorbed many

The Hindu Bull Temple in Bengaluru

of the indigenous religious forms they encountered en route, giving rise to a plethora of deities, and a body of mythological literature which recounted the lives and deeds of these numerous gods.

Of the innumerable gods and goddesses, the most revered are Vishnu, the 'Preserver' (and his avatars Krishna and Rama), and Shiva (aka 'Shankar'), the Destroyer or Transformer, from whose dreadlocks emanate the waters of the River Ganges. The Creator, Brahma, forms the third cornerstone of the Hindu trinity. Alongside Vishnu and Shiva are their respective consorts, Lakshmi (Goddess of Prosperity) and Parvati (the supreme goddess), mother of the elephant-headed Ganesh and lance-wielding Skanda (aka 'Kartikeya', 'Subramanya' or 'Murugan').

Worship of these, and the many lesser deities of Hinduism, takes many forms, but for the majority of Indians, ritual viewing of the god or goddess (*darshan*), and the act of making an offering to them in a temple (*puja*), are the most common. In addition, many features in the natural landscape are held as sacred by Hindus, particularly springs and rivers. Flowing from the Himalayas to the Bay of Bengal, the Ganges is the most holy of all, adored by hundreds of millions. Its waters are believed to be capable of cleansing the soul of a lifetime of accumulated sins.

Among the central precepts of Hinduism is the belief in the cycle of rebirth *(moksha)*. The form an individual will be reincarnated into is determined by the results of deeds performed in previous lifetimes *(karma)*, so it follows that every Hindu should behave as well as possible in this life to ensure a better lot in the next one. Conforming to the restrictions of one's caste *(jati)* will notch up points on the cosmic balance sheet, as will worship of as many deities as possible over time. This explains the popularity of pilgrimage in India. Hindus, even poor villagers, have for centuries travelled far and wide to pray at a shrine or bathe in a river at an auspicious moment.

Islam

Just over 13 percent of Indians are Muslims. Although originally imported by Arab traders in the early 8th century, Islam became a major Indian faith only at the beginning of the 13th century, when the Delhi Sultanate extended its influence eastwards and southwards.

Islamic rule was aggressively imposed at first. Later, however, the message of universal love spread by the Persian poetry of Sufi mystics, or *pirs*, garnered more converts than the sword. Among the *pirs* who settled in India, Mu'inuddin Chishti of Ajmer and Nizamuddin Aulia of Delhi were the most influential. The tombs of these poet-saints are still places of pilgrimage for both Muslims and Hindus, particularly at the time of the saints' *urs* (anniversary of their death).

Sikhism

In the late 15th century, the process fusing Hinduism and Islam was taken a step further by Guru Nanak, founding father of the Sikh faith. A Hindu by birth, Nanak was attracted from his childhood towards the saints and poets of both religions. He saw the essential teachings as being the same and began to preach a message of unity, attracting many followers.

It was the fifth of Nanak's successors, Guru Arjun, who started building the famous Golden Temple at Amritsar, which later became the holiest Sikh shrine. Arjun also systematised the collection of sacred hymns and poems by Nanak and other saints into the holy scripture known as *Granth Sahib* (Book of the Lord).

Ritual ablutions at a mosque in Mumbai

The spread of the Sikh faith alarmed orthodox Muslims, at a time when Mughal rule was becoming stricter under the Emperor Aurangzeb. Guru Arjun was put to death on a charge of sedition in 1606, and his martyrdom convinced his successors that Sikhs must have military training to defend themselves. The 10th Guru, Govind Singh, transformed the pacifist Sikh sect into a martial community, introducing the Five Ks of the Khalsa by which Sikhs are to this day identified: *kes* (uncut hair, bound in the characteristic turban); *kara* (a circular iron bracelet); *kirpan* (dagger); *kargha* (comb); and *kaccha* (special undergarment).

Buddhism

Buddhism derives from the teachings of Siddhartha Gautama, a prince and later spiritual leader born in what is now Lumbini, Nepal, around 563BC. At the age of 29, Siddhartha left his father's palace and took up an itinerant, ascetic life, achieving Enlightenment 20 years later while meditating under a tree in Bodhgaya, Bihar.

The Buddha's teachings emphasise the importance of the 'Eightfold Path' by which the Buddha claimed one could conquer suffering and attain nirvana, the transcendental state of complete emancipation. Hinduism ousted Buddhism as India's primary religion in the medieval era, but pockets of the faith survive in some Himalayan regions, notably Ladakh, which for centuries were under Tibetan rule. Tibetan refugees have further boosted the overall number of Buddhists in recent decades, as has Dr Ambedkar's public conversion in the 1960s, since when millions of Dalits also converted.

Jainism

About the same time as the Buddha was preaching, Vardhamana, better known by his title Mahavira ('great hero'), was establishing another new religion. The focus of the Jains' devotion is the 24 *jinas* – or *Tirthankaras* ('crossing-makers') said to have attained *kaivalya* (perfect wisdom) through different penances. The highest virtue in Jainism is the total

Receiving a Jainist blessing at Saravanabelagola Temple in Karnataka

abjuration of any thought or action that can hurt a living being. Jain monks and nuns carry this non-violence to extreme limits, covering their mouths with a muslin mask to ensure they do not involuntarily inhale insects.

Christianity

South Indian tradition holds that Christianity originally came to India in the 1st century AD with the Apostle St Thomas, who travelled to Kerala via the Romans' maritime spice route. By the end of the first millennium numerous orthodox Christian sects had taken root in the far south of the subcontinent.

When Vasco da Gama arrived in Calicut in 1498 he was surprised to find communities of Syrian-Christians already established in the city. Jesuit missionaries were hot on his heels, evangelising the Malabar and Coromandel coasts in the 16th century. Catholicism retains a high profile in both regions. India's two principal Christian pilgrimage sites are Vailankanni in Tamil Nadu, and Old Goa, where the incorruptible corpse of St Francis Xavier is enshrined.

LITERATURE

Literacy rates average at just under 70 percent in most Indian states, and each region has its own thriving literature. At national level, however, it's English-medium writers who enjoy the largest audiences. Indian English in all its quirkiness is deployed to fabulous effect in Salman Rushdie's Booker-Prize winning novel of 1981, *Midnight's Children*, which introduced

The Reis Magos church in Goa

a worldwide readership to Indian fiction for the first time.

Keralan novelist Arundhati Roy bagged the prize in 1997 for *The God of Small Things*, a haunting tale of cross-caste love set in Kuttanad backwaters. Kiran Desai was the third Indian novelist to win the coveted award in 2008, for *The Inheritance of Loss*, whose backdrop is the political turmoil of the Himalayan foothills. Most recently, Aravind Adiga was awarded the Booker in 2009 for *The White Tiger*, a brilliant evocation of the many and cruel ways in which old rural caste divides infect life in modern-day Delhi.

FILM

India's cinema industry is the largest in the world, churning out on average 1,000 films each year. Most are shot in regional languages such as Tamil, Malayalam, Bhojpuri or Telugu, but the biggest blockbusters come from the studios of north Mumbai, known as 'Bollywood' *(see p.148)*.

With influences as disparate as epic folk theatre, classical American

Traditional music accompanies the Kodungallur Festival in Kerala

MUSIC

As well as being India's number one dream machine, Bollywood is also the source of the nation's popular music, *filmi git*. Scores from current hit films, played day and night everywhere people congregate, quite literally provide the soundtrack to modern life. Most often taking the form of love duets, *filmi* tunes can quickly sound the same to the uneducated ear, though they're infuriatingly catchy.

Although you tend to hear it less than *filmi*, Indian classical music is also extremely popular. Performed mainly in concert halls and five-star hotels, it can roughly be divided into two distinct styles: Hindustani, from the north and west; and Carnatic, from the southern states of Tamil Nadu and Kerala.

DANCE

India has eight officially recognised classical dance styles, drawn from various regions of the country, and from different social and cultural contexts. The most ubiquitous is *bharata natyam*, a form which originated in the great Chola temples of Tamil Nadu, where it was traditionally performed as an offering to the enshrined deity. The Indo-Muslim-influenced *kathak*, by contrast, was developed in the rather more sybaritic atmosphere of the regional courts of Muslim Delhi and Lucknow, where it was an essential accomplishment of the traditional courtesans, or *tawaifs*.

Both of these styles, along with the other popular classic forms, are distinguished by their own resplendent costumes, which lend an opulent atmosphere to recitals.

musicals and MTV pop videos, modern Hindi films have seen a marked shift in both style and content since the golden era of Bollywood in the 1960s and 1970s. Big box office and DVD receipts from the US and UK have sent potential profits skywards – along with the budgets and the fees demanded by big stars. As a consequence, characters and plot lines are more sophisticated and production standards have risen.

The highest grossing Indian film of all time is the 2009 comedy *The 3 Idiots*, a feel-good flick starring Aamir Khan and Kareena Kapoor. Macho action thrillers have also grown in popularity, as have boy-meets-girl rom-coms – the textbook example of the latter being the 2008 classic *Rab Ne Bana Di Jodi* ('A Match Made in Heaven'), in which screen legend Shah Rukh Khan plays a love-struck geek who woos the girl of his dreams by entering a dance competition masquerading as a typical Bollywood-style hero.

SPORT

Cricket is one of the common denominators of life in contemporary India. Every state has its own team. However, it's for international clashes that the strongest passions are reserved, especially those involving arch-rivals Pakistan. Whether dressed in whites or the blue of their One Day International strip, the Indian squad ranks among the top sides in the world. The current crop of players includes such legends as Sachin Tendulkar, the highest-scoring batsman of all time, and the wicket-keeping and batting supremo from Bihar, Mahendra Dhoni.

The incomes of the country's top players rocketed with the advent in 2008 of the controversial Indian Premier League Twenty20 competition (www.iplt20.com), which commands vast audiences.

With so much emphasis in the media on cricket, it's easy to forget that other sports are played in India, notably soccer, which is especially popular in Goa, Kerala and West Bengal. After years in the doldrums, hockey, too, is enjoying something of a comeback – due in no small part to the appearance of astro-turf pitches around the country.

CURRENT AFFAIRS

Since Independence in 1947, the Indian political scene has been dominated by the Indian National Congress (INC). This was the resolutely secular party of Mahatma Gandhi, which Nehru and his dynastic successors, including Indira Gandhi, led. For the past two decades, the main opposition to Congress has come from the right-wing, pro-Hindu Bharatiya Janata Party, or BJP.

It is often said that government in India is stymied by the politics of vested interests. To get elected, politicians have to draw on so-called 'vote banks', drawn from specific regions, religions, castes or other minorities. Promoting the narrow agendas of these groups has thus often taken priority over broader national issues, such as poverty reduction and safeguarding the environment. Meanwhile, corruption scandals are rarely out of the news, with around one-quarter of the country's elected politicians currently embroiled in criminal cases.

Culture

Etiquette

- Remove shoes before entering a temple, mosque or gurdwara (Sikh) or someone's house; wearing socks is usually permissible
- Public displays of affection are frowned upon; even hand-holding between men and women provokes staring in rural areas, although the sight of Indian men holding hands, as a sign of friendship, is common
- Leather goods of any kind should not be taken into temples, as they are regarded as impure
- Modest clothing is essential for both men and women when visiting places of worship, but also advisable generally to avoid giving offence (and in the case of women, to lessen unwanted attention)
- When eating with your fingers, remember to use only the right hand
- Avoid pointing the soles of your feet towards anyone or pointing with your index finger, considered rude; use your extended hand or chin instead

Food and Drink

India's cooking styles are as rich and diverse as its civilisation. The dishes are highly seasoned, but the spices are subtle; it takes some time to get used to the flavours, even if you're familiar with Indian cuisine back home. Don't be afraid to taste local dishes (provided they're served hygienically).

WHERE TO EAT

Most hotels and guest houses in India have somewhere on their premises to eat and drink, whether a simple rooftop terrace or a full-blown restaurant. In off-track destinations where the only places to eat to speak of will be a line of grubby *dhabas* or *chai* stalls, you'll probably opt to eat there. But in major towns and cities at least, dependable independent restaurants are numerous.

Included in the restaurant listings in this book are places ranging from simple *thali* joints, where you eat Rs50 meals with your fingers, to swanky hotel restaurants with valet parking and black-tie service. All of them are outstanding in some way, whether it be location, authenticity of cuisine or the value for money they offer.

MEALS

In large hotels, all the trimmings of British and American breakfasts are usually available: porridge (oatmeal), cereals, eggs and bacon, with tropical, fresh seasonal fruits such as mango, papaya and pineapple, and their juices.

Coffee in north India is usually instant, but do ask for the excellent south Indian filter variety wherever it's available. A number of Starbucks-style

Timings, Tipping and Reservations

As a rule, run-of-the-mill restaurants frequented by Indian workers and tourists open early – by at least 8am – for *puri* and curd (yoghurt) breakfasts in north India, or fresh *idly-wada-chai-coffee* in the south; they then switch to rice plate meals, or *thalis*, at lunch time until 2.30–3pm, when they'll start serving afternoon snacks, such as *masala dosas* and *samosas*. More expensive restaurants open only at lunch times (noon–3pm) and in the evenings (6.30–11pm).

Indians tend to eat late by Western standards, typically sitting down at 9pm – though this doesn't apply to restaurants in the commercial districts, which fill up

as soon as offices close around 6pm. Sunday, when middle-class families often eat out, is the busiest day, and you should definitely book a table if you intend to go to an upscale restaurant then. In fact, it's generally a good idea to reserve ahead for any high-end establishment; phone numbers are given in our listings where this is recommended.

An increasing number of restaurants accept payment by credit or debit card, but you should always check in advance. More workaday places only deal in cash. Bills may or may not include service charges, but a tip of 10–15 percent will always be welcomed by your waiter.

A beautifully presented Keralan meal

coffee chains are also opening up. For safety's sake, the milk (which usually comes from buffalo rather than cows) is boiled, then re-cooled for the cereals.

The typical north Indian breakfast is a pile of hot *chapatis* or *parathas* with spicy fillings and a side portion of *dhal* along with cold set yoghurt. In the south, you'll find favourites such as *dosas* (pancakes made of rice and lentils), *idlis* (steamed rice cakes) and *vadas* (fried doughnuts made of lentils), served with firey bowls of *sambar* broth and coconut *chatni*.

For lunch and dinner, hotels will often provide large buffets, giving you a chance to try several dishes, which people tend to pile up on one plate around a mound of rice. But traditional Indian meals are served on a *thali*, a metal platter, with up to 10 dishes in separate little bowls, so that you can savour the different tastes separately and work out which ones you like. Found at both north and south Indian restaurants, *thalis* are very good value and often change on a daily basis.

You will find it beneficial to follow the Indian custom of drinking something either before or after, but not during, a meal. Drinking does not alleviate a peppery flavour because it will leave your taste buds defenceless against the next hot mouthful. Therefore, it's better to eat some plain rice or one of the soft Indian bananas, or, best of all, yoghurt flavoured with mint.

Indians eat with their fingers, rotating the fingertips around the plate to form the food into a ball with rice or bread. Cutlery may be provided, but a fork is not necessarily any more hygienic than fingers.

WHAT TO EAT

'Curry'

Properly speaking, there is no such thing as a curry. It's a British term invented to refer indiscriminately to India's spicy preparations of fish, meat and vegetables. Hence, in India there is not one 'curry powder' or 'curry sauce', because each dish has its own spices. The combination commonly used in a basic mixture of sautéed onions and garlic is called *masala*, a powdered blend of coriander, cumin, ginger, black pepper, cinnamon, chilli, cardamom, bay leaves, cloves and nutmeg. Saffron adds its own unique colour and fragrance, both to rice and to meat.

Non-Vegetarian

The classical cuisine of the north, Mughlai, derives from the kitchens of the Mughals. With beef taboo for Hindus and pork for Muslims, the meat is generally chicken, lamb or mutton, its classic 'curry' being *rogan*

India is one of the best places for vegetarians

josh. Cubes of meat are prepared in a yoghurt sauce made with chilli, ginger, coriander and garam masala. This dish originated in Kashmir, where they eat lamb in dozens of different ways (if you attend a *wazwan* banquet, there may be as many as 16, 36 or even 52 dishes).

Other dishes include the kebab, balls of lamb minced with almonds and spices; *tabakmas*, mutton ribs with a crispy skin; and *goshtaba*, the most tender lamb from the breast, with every last sinew beaten out of it before it is minced into a fragrant dumpling stewed in yoghurt.

Biryani is a Mughlai speciality, originally exclusively a lamb dish, though chicken, fish and vegetables are now cooked in the same way. This dish is more elaborate than *pulao*, which is a simple mixture of rice and lightly flavoured meat or vegetables. *Biryani* is chicken or lamb cooked in a sauce of ginger, cardamom, cinnamon and cloves, before steaming it with saffron rice and *ghee* (clarified butter). It may be served decorated with almonds, mint and slices of boiled egg.

Chickens tend to be scrawny, but they are tasty in a *makhani* butter sauce as *murg ilaychi*, marinated in yoghurt with cardamom, ginger, peppers and saffron, or *murg do pyaza*, with onions. Tandoori chicken is a popular barbecue in the northwest style, baked in a tandoor clay oven.

Fish and giant prawns, marinated in different sauces, also make very good tandoori dishes. Fresh seafood is widely available, particularly from the kitchens of Goa.

Vegetarian

Favourite vegetable dishes, or *sabzi*, are *aloo gobi* (cauliflower and potato), *bhaingan bharta* (roasted aubergine), *sag panir* (spinach with Indian soft cheese), *bhindi* (okra), *channa* (chickpeas) and *dal* (lentils).

The cuisine of southern India is more vegetarian than that of the north. This is because the region was not subject to the Mughal influence. Whereas the north cooks with the products of its cattle, such as *ghee* for frying, yoghurt for sauces, and milk for desserts, the basis of southern cooking is coconut – its oil is used for frying, and the milk and flesh for sauces. This gives the food a sweeter taste than in other regions.

Rice and Breads

The best rice is the aromatic long-grained basmati, the common or garden variety known as *patna*. Apart from *biryani* and *pulao*, north Indian cuisine does not feature such large quantities of rice as in south Indian cuisine. The Indians in the north prefer to eat their food with a variety of breads, including a floppy, thin *roti* or *chapati*; a slightly thicker *paratha*, sometimes stuffed with vegetables or minced meat; small, deep-fried *puri*; or giant, puffed-up *naan*, baked in a tandoor. Here's a tip: before you tackle the rice dishes of the south, try eating with your fingers in the north by folding a piece of *roti* around each morsel.

Side Dishes and Snacks

Salads don't exist in the Western sense, but *cachumbar* is a refreshing side dish of tomato and onion seasoned with fresh lemon juice or vinegar. The great palate-cooler, eaten both in the north and south, is *raita*, a mixture of cold seasoned yoghurt and either cucumbers, tomatoes or pineapples.

As a sweet condiment, Indians serve not only mango, but mint and coconut, ginger, tomato, dates or even tamarind in a spicy chutney. Some of the flavours in these dishes pack an astonishing double punch of sweet and sharp.

There are some wonderfully tangy Indian snacks. Mumbai's best is the *bhelpuri* sold on Chowpatty Beach *(see p.146)*, a spicy snack made from fried puffed rice, flavoured with tamarind juice, chillies and other spices. *Samosas* are stuffed with meat or vegetables, and *pakora* is a vegetable fritter. *Pani puri* is a small pastry stuffed with spiced tamarind water: put the whole thing in your mouth at once.

Desserts

Ras malai are patties made from cottage cheese and nuts, sweetened with aromatic syrup. *Khir*, rice pudding, invented in India with condensed milk and broken rice, mixed with cardamom and nuts, is far superior to its British counterpart. *Gajar halwa*, a dessert of grated carrots stewed in milk and syrup, is best hot, with raisins and nuts. *Kulfi* is ice cream made with cardamom and pistachio. *Barfi* and *halwa* are sweets made with flour or milk, flavoured with nuts and cardamom.

WHAT TO DRINK

Tea

Tea – or *chai* – is India's national drink and is drunk strong, milky and sweet in tiny cups or glasses. The most cooling drinks are *nimbu pani* (water with fresh lime); fruit juices, especially from the fragrant Kashmiri apple; and *lassi*, a yoghurt-based drink that is refreshing but can take some getting used to.

Alcohol

Attitudes to alcohol vary across India, with Mumbai and Delhi the most liberal. Indian beers (Goa's Kingfisher is one of the best) and wines (produced in the hills outside Bombay and Pune) are certainly drinkable. Among traditional Indian alcoholic drinks are palm toddy in Kerala; *chang*, a barley beer from Ladakh; and *feni* in Goa.

Food and Drink

Cooking street food in Lucknow

PHRASE BOOK

Pronunciation – *p.290* **Phrases** – *p.292* **Menu Reader** – *p.297*

Phrase Book

With 18 official languages, hundreds of others and countless dialects, India can present a linguistic minefield. Luckily for the traveller, English is often understood, and it is usually possible to get by. However, attempts to speak the local language are always appreciated – even in the most touristy parts of the country. The language most widely spoken in the north is Hindi – India's official lingua franca which, largely thanks to the Bollywood cinema industry, is understood just about everywhere. In the south, Tamil has the highest profile. Across the mountains in neighbouring Kerala, Malayalam is the mother tongue.

PRONUNCIATION

This section is designed to familiarise you with the sounds of Hindi using our simplified phonetic transcription. You'll find the pronunciation of the Hindi sounds explained below, together with their 'imitated' equivalents. This system is used throughout the phrase book. When you see a word spelled phonetically, simply read the pronunciation as though it were English, noting any special rules.

Language

Hindi is the official language of India and it is also the most widely spoken vernacular in the forms of different dialects. It is the official language for the states of Bihar, Haryana, Himachal Pradesh, Madhya Pradesh, Rajasthan and Uttar Pradesh. Hindi is also spoken in Surinam, Mauritius and Fiji. Hindi is the native language of about 182 million people, making it the fifth most widely spoken language in the world after Mandarin, English, Spanish and Bengali. In addition, many people speak Hindi as their second language. It is estimated that around 350 million people speak Hindi either as their first or second language.

For many Indians who are educated locally or abroad, English is their first language. English is widely spoken in India and is recognised as the official alternative or associate language to Hindi. It is also the language medium of communication between the central government at New Delhi and states with non-Hindi speaking populations. It is widely used in business, media and scientific research.

There has been a major thrust to promote Hindi as the national language in a bid to gradually phase out English. However, there has always been strong resistance to the imposition of Hindi in certain areas of the country. Hindi has always maintained a strong standing in the north but it is not widely spoken in the south where it bears little relation to the languages spoken there. Evidently, English is the favoured language in the south.

You will notice that in some instances, such as the words 'taxi' and 'passport', the English word is actually used when speaking Hindi. In other instances, two translations are given: a Hindi word and the English word. In these cases it's likely that most Hindi speakers will recognise the English word, but the Hindi word is also provided in case the English is not understood.

Alphabet/Script

Hindi is written in the Devanagari script. Similar to other Indian languages, the alphabets of Devanagari script are grouped based on their pronunciation. The first 11 letters are grouped as vowels. The vowels are organised in the sequence of a short vowel followed by the long counterpart then followed by a string of consonants.

All the vowels are in two versions in the script: full vowel and vowel sign. The vowel signs are much simpler to master than the full vowels. The vowel signs are used when a vowel is followed by a consonant. If a vowel precedes another vowel or if a word begins with a vowel, the full vowel is used.

The pronunciation of the full vowels and vowel signs is no different. The vowel signs are written next to the preceding consonant. The vowel signs can be written before, after, below and above the consonant. They can also appear without the sign at all. 'a' is assumed whenever there is no indication of a vowel sign.

Hindi consonants are divided into five groups depending on the places of articulation. Each group has five letters (sounds) and these sounds, in turn, are divided into three other subgroups – voiced, unvoiced and nasal.

If two or more consonants are adjoined, then the consonants are not written in full. Instead, they are merged together to form a new symbol. Some of these symbols are easy to recognise. However, some are vastly different from the full versions of the consonants.

Hindi utilises punctuation marks in a similar fashion to English. The only exception is the period, which is represented by a vertical line.

Transliteration

As the Devanagari script contains more letters than English, it is sometimes necessary when transliterating Hindi to use two or more English letters to represent one Devanagari letter.

Vowels & Diphthongs			Consonants		
a	अ	run	g	ग	get, gun, mug, give
	आ	father	gh	घ	g + h
i	इ	hit	n	न	sing, wing, bring
	ई	teeth	ch	च	much, such
u	उ	put	chh	छ	ch + h
	ऊ	cool	jh	झ	j + h
e	ए	they	t	त	tree, tea
ai	ऐ	care	d	द	day, do, deed
o	आ	both	dh	ध	d + h (hard)
au	औ	ouch	th	थ	thin, both
ri	ऋ	Krishna	sh	श	she, show, shop
			s	स	seen, sun

English	Hindi	Pronunciation
How much?	कितना?	*kitnaa?*

A simplified pronunciation guide follows each Hindi phrase; read it as if it were English. Among the English phrases, you will find some words included in square brackets; these are the American-English equivalents of British-English expressions. Any of the words or phrases preceded by dashes can be plugged into the sentence above.

General

0	शून्य	*shunya*	100	सौ	*sau*
1	एक	*ek*	500	पाँच सौ	*panch sau*
2	दो	*do*	1,000	एक हजार	*ek hazaar*
3	तीन	*teen*	1,000,000	दस लाख	*dus laakh*
4	चार	*chaar*	Monday	सोमवार	*somwaar*
5	पाँच	*paanch*	Tuesday	मंगलवार	*mangalwaar*
6	छह	*che*	Wednesday	बुधवार	*budhwaar*
7	सात	*saat*	Thursday	गुरुवार	*guruwaar*
8	आठ	*aath*	Friday	शुक्रवार	*shukrwaar*
9	नौ	*nau*	Saturday	शनिवार	*shaniwaar*
10	दस	*dus*	Sunday	रविवार	*raviwaar*

Hello!/Hi!	नमस्ते!	*namaste*
Goodbye.	नमस्ते।	*namaste*
Yes.	हां।	*haan*
No.	नहीं।	*nahin*
Please.	कृपया।	*kripyaa*
Thank you.	धन्यवाद।	*dhanyawaad*
My name is …	मेरा नाम … है	*mera naam … hai*
Where do you come from?	आप कहाँ से आए हैं?	*aap kahan se aaye hain*
I'm from …	मैं … से हूँ।	*main … se hoon*
– Britain	ब्रिटेन	*Britain*
– the United States	अमेरिका	*America*
What do you do?	आप क्या करते हैं?	*aap kya karte hain*
I'm studying …	मैं … पढ़ रहा हूँ।	*main … padh raha hoon*
I work for …	मैं … के लिए काम करता हूँ।	*main … ke liye kaam kartaa hoon*
What does this/that mean?	इसका क्या मतलब है?	*iska kya mutlub hai*
Could you repeat that?	क्या आप दुबारा बोल सकते हैं?	*kya aap dobaara bol sakte hain*
It's because of the weather.	यह मौसम की वजह से है।	*yeh mausam ki wajah se hai*

Arrival and Departure

I'm here on …	मैं यहाँ … पर हूँ। *main yahaan … pur hoon*
– a business trip	कारोबारी यात्रा *karobaari yatraa*
– holiday [vacation]	छुट्टी *chutti*
I'm going to …	मैं … जा रहा हूं *main … jaa raha hoon*

Money and Banking

Where's the nearest …?	सबसे नज़दीक … कहाँ है? *sabse nazdeek … kahan hai*
– bank	बैंक *bank*
– bureau de change	मुद्रा विनिमय कार्यालय *mudra vinimay karyalaay*
– automated teller (ATM)	ऑटोमेटेड टेलर (ए टी एम) *ATM*
I'd like to change some dollars/pounds into Rupees.	मैं कुछ डॉलर / पाउंडस को रुपये में बदलना चाहता हूँ। *main kuch dollar/pounds ko rupaye mein badalnaa chahtaa hoon*

Transportation

1/2/3 ticket(s) to…	… के लिए 1 / 2 / 3 टिकट … *ke liye ek/do/teen ticket*
single [one-way]	एकतरफा *ektarfaa*
return [round-trip]	वापसी *waapsi*
How much …?	कितना …? *kitnaa …*
How do I get to the …Hotel?	मैं … होटल कैसे पहुँचूंगा? *main … hotel kaise pahoonchoonga*
Where can I buy a ticket?	मैं टिकट कहां से खरीद सकता हूँ? *main ticket kahan se khareed saktaa hoon*
Do I have to change trains?	क्या मुझे कोई ट्रेन बदलनी है? *kya mujhe koi train badalnee hai*
Is this the right platform for the train to …?	क्या … जाने के लिए यह सही प्लेटफार्म है? *kya … jaane ke liye yehe sahi platform hai*
Is this the train to …?	क्या यह ट्रेन … जा रही है? *kya yehe train … jaa rahi hai*
I'd like to rent a …	मैं एक … किराए पर लेना चाहूँगा। *main ek … kiraye pur lena chahoonga*
– 3-/10-gear bicycle	3– / 10– गिअर साइकिल *teen-/dus-gear cycle*
– moped/motorbike	मोपेड / मोटरबाईक *moped/motorbike*
Where can I rent a car?	मुझे किराए पर कार कहाँ मिल सकती है? *mujhe kiraye pur car kahan se mil saktee hai*
Where's the next petrol [gas] station?	अगला पेट्रोल पंप कहाँ है? *aglaa petrol pump kahan hai*
I've lost my way.	मैं रास्ता भूल गया हूँ। *main raasta bhool gaya hoon*

Accommodation

I have a reservation.	मेरे पास एक आरक्षण है। *mere paas ek aarakshan hai*
My name is …	मेरा नाम … है। *mera naam … hai*
Do you have a room?	क्या आपके पास कमरे हैं? *kya aapke paas kamre hain*

How much is it …?	यह कितने का है …? *yeh kitne ka hai*
– per night/week	एक रात/सप्ताह *ek raat/saptaah*
Do you have a cheaper room?	क्या आपके पास सस्ते कमरे हैं? *kya aapke paas saste kamre hain*
Can I see the room, please?	क्या मैं कमरा देख सकता हूँ? *kya main kumraa dekh saktaa hoon*
I'd like a room with …	मैं … वाला कमरा चाहता हूँ। *main … waala kamraa chahtaa hoon*
– twin beds	दो बेड *do bed*
– a double bed	एक डबल बेड *ek double bed*
– a bath/shower	एक बाथ/शावर *ek bath/shower*
There are insects in our room.	हमारे कमरे में कीड़े हैं। *hamare kamre mein kirre hain*

Internet and Communications

Can I access the internet here?	क्या मैं यहाँ इंटरनेट का उपयोग कर सकता हूँ? *kya main yahan internet kaa upyog kur saktaa hoon*
What are the charges per hour?	प्रति घंटा शुल्क क्या है? *prate ghuntaa shulk kya hai*
May I use your phone?	क्या मैं आपके फोन का उपयोग कर सकता हूँ? *kya main aapko phone ka upyog kur saktaa hoon*
Hello. This is …	हेलो। मैं … *hello. main…*
I'd like to speak to …	मैं … से बात करना चाहता हूँ। *main … se baat karnaa chahtaa hoon*
Could you repeat that, please?	कृपया इसे दुबारा बोलिए। *kripyaa isse dobaara boliye*
Bye.	अलविदा। *alvidaa*
Are there any messages for me?	क्या मेरे लिए कोई संदेश है? *kya mere liye koi sandesh hai*

Sightseeing

Where's the tourist office?	पर्यटन कार्यालय कहाँ है? *puryaatun kaaryaalaya kahan hai*
What are the main points of interest?	यहाँ मुख्य रुचिकर चीजें क्या है? *yahan mukhye ruchikur cheezen kya hai*
Is there an English-speaking guide?	क्या कोई अंग्रेजी बोलने वाला गाइड है? *kya koi angrejee bolne waala guide hai*
How much does the tour cost?	इस यात्रा का खर्च कितना है? *is yaatraa ka khurch kitnaa hai*
Do you have any information on …?	क्या आपके पास … की कोई सूचना है? *kya aapke paas … ki koi soochna hai*

Shopping

I'd like …	मुझे … चाहिए। *mujhe … chahiye*
How much is that?	यह कितना है? *yeh kitnaa hai*
Can you help me?	क्या आप मेरी सहायता कर सकते हैं? *kya aap meri sahaaytaa kur sakte hain*
I'm just browsing.	मैं सिर्फ ब्राउज कर रहा हूँ। *main sirf browse kur raha hoon*

That's too expensive.	वह बहुत महंगा है। *weh bahut mehengaa hai*
Where do I pay?	मैं कहाँ भुगतान करूँ? *main kahan bhuktaan karoon*
Could I have a receipt, please?	कृपया, मुझे रसीद मिल सकती है? *kripyaa, mujhe raseed mil saktee hai*
Where's the main shopping centre [mall]?	मुख्य बाजार केंद्र कहाँ है? *mukhya bazaar kendra kahan hai?*

Culture and Nightlife

Do you have a programme of events?	क्या आपके पास कार्यक्रमों की सूची है? *kya aapke paas krayakaram ki soochi hai*
What's playing at the cinema [the movies] tonight?	आज रात को कौन–कौन सी फिल्म चल रही है? *aaj raat ko kaun-kaun see film chul rahee hai*
Where can I get tickets?	मैं कहाँ से टिकट प्राप्त कर सकता हूँ? *main kahan se ticket praapat kur saktaa hoon*
What is there to do in the evenings?	शाम को करने के लिए क्या है? *shaam ko karne ke liye kya hai*
Is there a ... in town?	क्या शहर में ... है? *kya shaiher mein ... hai*
– bar/restaurant	बार / रेस्टोरेंट *bar/restaurant*
– discotheque	डिस्कोथेक *discotheque*

Travel with Children

Can you recommend something for the children?	क्या आप बच्चों के लिए कुछ सुझाव दे सकते हैं? *kya aap bachon ke liye kuch sujhaav de sakten hain*
Are there changing facilities here for babies?	क्या यहाँ बच्चों के कपड़े बदलने की जगह है? *kya yahan bachon ke kapde badalne ki jagah hai*
Where are the toilets [restrooms]?	बाथरूम शौचालय किधर है? *shauchaalaya kidhar hai*
Can you recommend a reliable babysitter?	क्या आप एक भरोसेमंद बेबी–सीटर की सलाह दे सकते हैं? *kya aap ek bharosemund baby-sitter kee salaah de sakten hain*

Disabled Travellers

| Do you have facilities for the disabled? | क्या आपके पास बच्चों / विकलांग के लिए व्यवस्था है? *kya aapke paas viklaang ke liye vyavustha hai* |
| Is there access for the disabled? | क्या विकलांग के लिए कोई रास्ता है? *kya viklaang ke liye koi raastaa hai* |

Emergencies

Help!	बचाओ! *bachao*
Go away!	चलो हटो! *chalo hato*
Call the police!	पुलिस को बुलाओ! *police ko bulaao*
Stop thief!	चोर को रोको! *chor ko roko*
Fire!	आग! *aag*
Get a doctor!	डाक्टर को बुलाओ! *doctor ko bulaao*
I'm in pain.	मुझे दर्द हो रहा है। *mujhe dard ho raha hai*
My ... is hurt/injured.	मेरे ... चोटिल / जख्मी है। *mere ... chotil/zakhmee hai*

Phrase Book

– husband/wife	पति / पत्नी *pati/patnee*
– son/daughter	बेटा / बेटी *beta/beti*
– friend	मित्र *mitr*
I'm lost.	मैं खो गया हूँ *main kho gaya hoon*
Can you help me?	क्या आप मेरी सहायता कर सकते हैं? *kya aap meri sahaaytaa kur sakte hain*

Health

I'm ill [sick].	मैं बीमार हूँ! *main bimaar hoon*
I feel faint.	मुझे बेहोशी हो रही है। *mujhe behoshi ho rahi hai*
I feel feverish.	मुझे बुखार जैसा लग रहा है। *mujhe bukhaar jaisa lug raha ha*
I've been vomiting.	मुझे उल्टीयाँ हो रही है। *mujhe ultiyaan ho rahi hai*
Where's the nearest pharmacy?	निकटतम दवाखाना कहाँ है? *nikuttum dawakhaana kahan hai*
What time does the pharmacy open/close?	दवाखाना कितने बजे खुलता / बंद होता है? *dawakhaana kitne baje khultaa/bund hota hai*
Can you make up [fill] this prescription for me?	क्या आप मेरे लिए यह नुस्खा तैयार कर सकते हैं? *kya aap mere liye yeh nuskhaa tayaar kur sakte hain*
How much should I take?	मुझे कितना लेना चाहिए? *mujhe kitnaa lenaa chaahiye*
What would you recommend for …?	… के लिए आप क्या सुझाव देंगे? *… ke liye aap kya sujhaav denge*
– diarrhoea	डायरिया *diarrhea*
– insect bites	कीड़ा का काटना *keera kaa kaatnaa*
I have insurance.	मेरा बीमा है। *mera beema hai*
Can I have a receipt for my insurance?	क्या मैं अपने बीमा हेतु रसीद प्राप्त कर सकता हूँ? *kya main apne beema hetu raseed prapt kur saktaa hoon*

Eating Out

A table for …, please.	कृपया … के लिए टेबल चाहिए। *kripyaa … ke liye table chahiye*
– 1/2/3/4	1/2/3/4 *ek/do/teen/chaar*
Can you recommend some typical local dishes?	क्या आप कुछ विशिष्ट स्थानीय व्यंजन बता सकते हैं? *kya aap kuch vishisht sthaniye vyanjun bata sakte hain*
Where are the toilets [restrooms]?	बाथरूम शौचालय कहाँ है? *shauchaalaya/toilet kahan hai*
The bill, please.	कृपया बिल दीजिए। *kripyaa bill dijiye*
That was a very good meal.	खाना बहुत बढ़िया था। *khanaa bahut badhiya tha*
I'd like a … of red/white wine.	मुझे एक …रेड / व्हाइट वाईन चाहिए। *mujhe ek … red/white wine chahiye*
– glass/carafe/bottle	गिलास / सुराही / बोतल *gilass/suraahi/bottle*
Do you have beer?	क्या आपके पास बीयर है? *kya aapke paas beer hai*

beans	सेम *sem*	mangoes	आम *aam*
beer	बीयर *beer*	meat	मांस *maans*
bread	ब्रेड *bread*	milk	दूध *dhoodh*
butter chicken (boneless chicken simmered in butter and creamy rich tomato sauce)	बटर चिकन *butter chicken*	mineral water	मिनरल पानी *mineral paani*
chicken	चिकन *chicken*	mushroom and peas cooked in a curry sauce	मटर मशरुम *mutter mushroom*
chicken tandoori	तंदूरी चिकन *tandoori chicken*	naan bread (plain bread made of flour)	नान *naan*
chips [fries]	फ्रेंच फ्राईज *french fries*	paneer pakoda (bread slices stuffed with cheese dipped in spicy chickpea flour batter and deep-fried)	पनीर पकोड़ा *paneer pakoda*
coffee	कॉफी *coffee*	paneer uttapam (flat rice bread stuffed with cheese)	पनीर उत्तपम *paneer uttapam*
dog	कुत्ता *kutta*	pork	सुअर का मांस *sooar ka maans*
eggs	अंडे *unde*	rabri (sweet vermicelli mixed with almonds and pistachios)	रबड़ी *rabri*
fish	मछली *muchlee*	rava masala dosa (semolina pancake filled with potato masala)	रवा मसाला डोसा *rava masala dosa*
gulab jamun (a sweet ball made from milk powder, fried in ghee, and soaked in sugar syrup)	गुलाब जामुन *gulab-jamun*	rice	चावल *chawal*
ice cream	आइसक्रीम *ice cream*	rogan josh (mutton cooked with the most intensely hot and fragrant spices)	रोगन जोश *rogan josh*
jalebi (crisp coils of fried batter in syrup)	जलेबी *jalebi*	roti (plain bread)	तंदूरी रोटी *tandoori roti*
kheer (a milky, sweet semi-liquid dessert)	खीर *kheer*	samosa (stuffed triangle-shaped pastries filled with mildly spiced potatoes)	समोसा *samosa*
lamb/mutton	मेमना / भेड़ *memnaa/ bherr*	seafood	समुद्री भोजन *samudree bhojan*
lassi (yogurt-based drink)	लस्सी *lassi*	seekh kebab (minced mutton or chicken cooked in oven)	सीक कबाब *seekh kabab*
lemonade	लेमोनेड *lemonade*	vegetable biryani (flavoured vegetable rice)	वेजीटेबल बिरयानी *vegetable biryani*
lentils sautéed in garlic and fresh tomatoes	दाल मखनी *dal makhni*	vegetable soup	सब्जी का सूप *subjee kaa soup*

Index

Accommodation Index

303

Index

Credits for Berlitz Handbook India

Written by: David Abram
Series Editor: Alexander Knights
Commissioning Editor: Sarah Sweeney
Cartography Editor: Zoë Goodwin
Map Production: APA Cartography Dept.
Production: Linton Donaldson
Picture Manager: Steven Lawrence
Art Editors: Richard Cooke and Ian Spick
Photography: APA/David Abram 5TR, 7TL, 8BL, 13T,
40, 48, 50, 51, 165/T, 166, 168, 169, 171, 172, 175, 209,
210, 212, 248/249, 252, 261, 281, 149B, 155, 156, 158,
186, 189T, 190, 193; Een Ar 83B; AWL Images 109, 110,
111/T, 112; Russ Bowling 76; Prateek Bahadur 119TR; Ignacio
Carpitella 216; Istockphoto 2TL, 6BL/TR, 7MR, 8T, 9BR/TL,
19, 36, 103BL, 123, 124, 125, 126, 127; Daag 23, 196; David
Davies 231; Fraboof 211; Baishampayan Ghose 14T; Charles
Haynes 241; Christian Haugen 119BL; Icultist 243; Ideow 99;
APA/Brita Jaschinski 3TL, 4BL, 6CR, 8BR, 10/11, 12B, 30B,
32TR, 49, 53, 179/T, 181, 182, 183, 184, 203B, 205, 208,
214, 219/T, 221, 222, 225, 235/T, 237, 238, 239, 242, 246,
250, 251, 255, 256, 257, 259, 263, 265, 266/267, 276, 277,
278, 280, 282, 285/T, 286, 288/289; Elley Jones 98; Kiran
Jonnalagadda 114; Jusepics 56; Jorge lascar 74; Hideyuki
Kamon 75, 95; Varun Shiv Kapur 206; Muthahar Khan 233;
Raj Kumar 194, 195; Marek Krzystkiewcz 228; APA/Julian Love
2TR, 4BR/T, 7TR, 9BL, 17, 60/61, 65, 69, 70, 71, 72, 73, 77,
789, 80, 85, 87, 88, 92, 93, 94, 100, 135, 270, 274, 287;
Paul Mannix 34; Ricardo Martins 167; Jane Mejdal 149; Carol
Mitchel 96; Sankarshan Mukhopadhyay 150; Giridhar Appaji
Nagy 224; APA/Abe Nowitz 5TL, 143/T, 147, 151, 153, 161,
279; Photolibrary.com 3TR, 5BL/BR, 6BR/TL, 9ML/TR, 15B,
22B/TL, 38, 42, 43, 47, 52, 54, 58, 90, 91BR, 128/T, 129/T,
130, 131, 133, 134, 146, 148, 154, 188, 189T, 191, 226, 273;
Pablo PD 91TR; B Prabdu 103TR; Punxsutaneyphil 107; Robert
Rybinkar 5BL; The Rohit 121; Royal Rajasthsn on Wheels 33B;
Orval Rochefort 89; Colin Rose 122; Karen Sandhu 176; Jamie
Sandford 200; Mackay Savage 20/21, 105, 106, 113; Dan
Searle 7B; Superstock 242T; Sveta Suvorina 57; Ajay Tallam
31TL; Tips Images 35; Topfoto 271; Sudarshan Vijayaraghavan
203T; Raveesh Vyas 157; VM2827 253; David Wong 115
Cover: Four Corners Images (front); iStockphoto (back)
Printed by: CTPS-China
© 2011 APA Publications GmbH & Co.
Verlag KG (Singapore branch)

Contact Us: We strive to keep our guides as
accurate and up to date as possible, but if
you find anything that has changed, or if you
have any suggestions on ways to improve this
guide, please write to Berlitz Publishing, PO
Box 7910, London SE1 1WE, UK, or email:
berlitz@apaguide.co.uk

Worldwide: APA Publications GmbH & Co.
Verlag KG (Singapore branch), 7030 Ang
Mo Kio Ave 5, 08-65 Northstar @ AMK,
Singapore 569880; tel: (65) 570 1051;
email: apasin@singnet.com.sg
UK and Ireland: GeoCenter International Ltd,
Meridian House, Churchill Way West, Basing-
stoke, Hampshire, RG21 6YR; tel: (44) 01256-
817 987; email: sales@geocenter.co.uk
United States: Ingram Publisher Services,
One Ingram Blvd, PO Box 3006, La Vergne,
TN 37086-1986; email: customer.service@
ingrampublisherservices.com
Australia: Universal Publishers, 1 Waterloo
Road, Macquarie Park, NSW 2113;
tel: (61) 2-9857 3700; email: sales@
universalpublishers.com.au
New Zealand: Hema Maps New Zealand Ltd
(HNZ), Unit 2, 10 Cryers Road, East Tamaki,
Auckland 2013; tel: (64) 9-273 6459; email:
sales.hema@clear.net.nz